Fukuzawa Yukichi in riding costume, Meiji 7 (1874),
about one year before the publication of *An Outline of a Theory of Civilization*

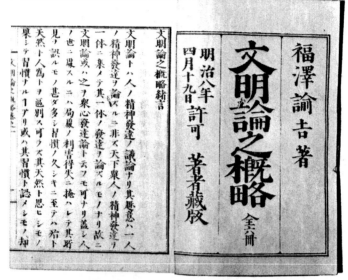

The Preface and the title page of the first edition of
An Outline of a Theory of Civilization (1875)

The first page of what is known as
"A Plan for *An Outline of a Theory of Civilization*" (1874),
a handwritten memorandum for the writing of *An Outline*

An Outline of a Theory of Civilization

Yukichi Fukuzawa

An Outline of a Theory of Civilization

Revised Translation
David A. Dilworth and
G. Cameron Hurst III

Introduction by
Takenori Inoki

COLUMBIA UNIVERSITY PRESS New York

Columbia University Press
Publishers Since 1893
New York   Chichester, West Sussex
Copyright © 2008 Keio University Press
All rights reserved

Library of Congress Cataloging-in-Publication Data
Fukuzawa, Yukichi, 1835-1901.
[Bunmeiron no gairyaku. English]
An outline of a theory of civilization / revised translation, David A. Dilworth and
G. Cameron Hurst, III ; introduction by Inoki Takenori.
p. cm.
Reprint of edition published in 2008 by Keio University Press, Tokyo.
Includes bibliographical references and index.
ISBN 978-0-231-15072-9 (cloth : alk. paper) —
ISBN 978-0-231-15073-6 (pbk. : alk. paper)
1. Japan—Civilization. 2. Civilization—Philosophy. 3. East and West. I. Title.

DS821.F87413 2009
901—dc22

2009017885

Columbia University Press books are printed on permanent and durable acid-free paper.
This book is printed on paper with recycled content.
Printed in the United States of America

c 10 9 8 7 6 5 4 3 2 1
p 10 9 8 7 6 5 4 3

References to Internet Web sites (URLs) were accurate at the time of writing. Neither
the author nor Columbia University Press is responsible for URLs that may have
expired or changed since the manuscript was prepared.

CONTENTS

TRANSLATORS' NEW FOREWORD AND ACKNOWLEDGMENTS

FUKUZAWA Yukichi (1835–1901) arose from low samurai origins in the last decades of the Tokugawa period to become one of the representative intellectuals of modern Japan. He stood among the vanguard of a long list of brilliant figures who contributed to the dynamic modernization of Japan in the Meiji period. His *Seiyō jijō* (Conditions in the West, 1866) and *Gakumon no susume* (An Encouragement of Learning, 1872–76) were early best-sellers which exerted a considerable degree of influence on society in their day. *Bunmeiron no gairyaku* (An Outline of a Theory of Civilization, 1875) was his most sustained philosophical effort during a long career of activity as a leading educator (as founder of Keio University, the first private university in modern Japan), engaged speaker and thinker, and controversial journalist. *Bunmeiron* especially reflects the progressive edge of ideas generated by the *bunmei kaika* ("civilization and enlightenment") phase of intellectual modernization of the 1870s. Today it looms as the peerless and indeed monumental work of its times.

The present publication issued by Keio University Press is a carefully revised update of an original co-translation we initially endeavored in Kyoto during the spring of 1969. The story of this accomplishment brings back the fondest memories of collaboration. While we were engaged in different research paths not related to the Meiji era, our residences (within biking distance in the Ginkaku-ji and Jōdo-ji areas of Kyoto) afforded the opportunity of alternating weekly visitations in which we took up the daunting task of rendering Fukuzawa's *Bunmeiron no gairyaku* into readable English. At the time we did not have a clear idea of the full stature of this classic of Japanese intellectual history, though we were soon impressed by its intellectual acumen, sweeping world-historical scope, and timely reflection on the changing times of the early Meiji period.

Without pretension, we used the 1962 Iwanami-bunko paperback edition, the cheapest and most available on the market. Gradually Fukuzawa's often outrageous rhetorical flourishes and pungent genius provided its own cheering encouragement of learning. We came to relish Fukuzawa's late Bakumatsu and early Meiji period Japanese-style, while also finding it a treasure trove of an insider's view of pre-Meiji Japanese culture. To a gratifying degree, we came to appreciate how Fukuzawa wrote in a first-person authorial voice—he is ever so present in his own pages. We cheered as he skulled the curmudgeons and shamed the credulous. We cherished his homey metaphors. All the while we felt the powerful undertow of his serious discourse on the necessary transformation of the feudal-mindedness of the past into nation-mindedness in the present. And as translators we experienced first-hand the economical organicity of *Bunmeiron* which, like the few light ribs of a bird's feather, was built to sustain arduous flights.

Gradually the project became a labor of love. In retrospect, we realize that it nourished and provided lasting outlook on our own lives and scholarly careers.

In mid-summer of 1969 we brought back a nearly completed rough draft of this original "Kyoto" translation to the United States. Our labor of love now consisted of stacks of crinkly typing paper. (These were the good old days before the word-processor.) Miss Darcy Murray, an undergraduate at Manhattanville College, contributed to the translation of the tenth chapter during the 1970–71 academic year. Sophia University Press (at the time a wing of *Monumenta Nipponica*) was then kind enough to accept the shipment of the entire manuscript.

After all these years we still fondly remember the warm help we received from Edmund R. Skrzypczak, then Editor of *Monumenta*

Nipponica and Sophia University Press, who, with his staff member, Mr. Sawada Tetsuya, during the spring and summer of 1972 contributed his considerable expertise toward the publication of our translation of *Bunmeiron*. And we remain grateful to Mr. Milton Rosenthal, Division of Cultural Development, UNESCO, Paris, who endorsed our work at the time of the Sophia University publication.

The present "Tokyo" version of almost forty years later is a carefully revised redaction of this original translation, giving it in effect a brand new life. As our own springs and autumns have piled up, we are now in a better position to recognize the classic status of Fukuzawa's *Bunmeiron*, a status which includes its essential boldness in converting Western social contract theory into a dissertation on Japan's national defense, its (in world-comparative terms) far-ranging historical learning, and its forthright re-articulation of the Japanese cultural symbolic to a needful Meiji readership. Fukuzawa in effect was engaged in writing the script for the modernization of Japan after two and a half centuries of national seclusion under the Tokugawa military regime. Though reflective of centuries of Japanese intellectual traditions—which he did not fully credit—*Bunmeiron* contains a rare authenticity. It breathes the spirit of his own motto of *dokuritsu jison*, "independence and self-respect." Its central teaching of raising the intellectual and moral levels of the Japanese people comes across as spot-on, absolutely cogent, and prophetic.

Probably there are few works of Japanese intellectual history as readable as *Bunmeiron* to gain access into the intense and sophisticated intelligence of the Japanese people. *Bunmeiron* continues to shine forth today as an exemplary articulation of such essential aspects of the national character. Moreover, it does so in its own performative language. Be that as it may, the authenticity and cogency of Fukuzawa's argumentation affect us as having a ring of truth in a universal and perennial frame of reference. Parallel themes of independence and self-respect, of grass roots intellectual and moral elevation of the individual and national spirit, and of free and unsponsored initiative in the private domain, had already gained currency in nineteenth-century North America through the writings of Fukuzawa's elder but near contemporary, Ralph Waldo Emerson (1803–82). Many of Fukuzawa's articulations bear comparison with the best of the contemporary American transcendentalists, Emerson, Walt Whitman, et al., who similarly rang the changes on a universally appealing individualistic, cultural, and political ethos of self-reliance.

Fully to render Fukuzawa's multifaceted intellectual accomplishment in its own context, our original "Kyoto" translation needed to undergo a process of revision, chiefly to substantiate his range of precise historical information through an additional register of footnotes. To our great good-luck, the 150th Anniversary of Fukuzawa's founding of Keio-gijuku brought forward a "dream team" editorial staff at Keio University Press to support this supplementary work. Keio-gijuku-daigaku-shuppankai had already published a definitive edition of *Bunmeiron* in its *Fukuzawa Yukichi chosakushū,* volume four, 2002 (second edition, 2004).

The process of thorough revision of our English translation of *Bunmeiron* began in the second half of 2007 under the ever so gracious leadership of Mr. Sakagami Hiroshi, President of Keio University Press. Mr. Sakagami appointed an impressive editorial staff consisting of Ms. Nagano Fumika, Ms. Omuro Sae, Mr. Handa Takeru, and Ms. Katahara Ryoko, all of whom brought outstanding technical expertise to the work. Ms. Nagano Fumika, who is a Part-time Lecturer, Faculty of Letters, Keio University, turned out to be the "muse" of our new endeavors. Her versatility in English was an indispensable asset in the meticulous cross-checking of the original translation and in providing precise nuances to Fukuzawa's already charming style. Ms. Omuro Sae, Mr. Handa Takeru, and Ms. Katahara Ryoko contributed astute scholarly as well as technical backup. In addition, Mr. Sakagami composed a larger committee that involved the ongoing participation of Professor Emeritus Nishikawa Shunsaku, an outstanding Fukuzawa scholar, and Professor Helen Ballhatchet, both of Keio University. Professors Nishikawa and Ballhatchet trained their sharp scholarly eyes on both the big issues of intellectual interpretation and minute details of re-translation. We would also like to express our gratitude to Professor Lin Shaoyang of the University of Tokyo for supervising the Pin-yin words we employ in this work.

The process of re-translation began with the visit to New York City by Professor Sakamoto Tatsuya, Executive Director of Keio-gijuku, and Ms. Morizawa Juli, Manager, International Communication and Public Relations Office of the President and 150th Anniversary Commemorative Project Office, of Keio University in the spring of 2007. We had the honor of renewed conversation with and encouragement from each of them at Keio University in the winter of 2008.

As we look back now, Fukuzawa's *Bunmeiron* has been a blessing in our lives, a happy discovery and memory of the Kyoto days of 1969 and now, in its re-publication in a new life by the brilliant staff of Keio University Press, a source of humble pride for making re-available to the wide world this work of Fukuzawa's and Japan's timely genius.

D.A.D.
G.C.H.

INTRODUCTION

Fukuzawa Yukichi (1835–1901) is one of the finest intellectuals and social thinkers to have emerged from modern Japan. A primary feature of his thought is its concrete, practical nature; it issues less from working through conceptual or abstract arguments than from an acute sense of crisis in the problems that his contemporary Japan was actually facing. In this context, he was like Ōkubo Toshimichi, Saigō Takamori, and Kido Takayoshi, all of whom made a significant impact on the politics of the period. Considered from a wider perspective of time, however, he was also a political theorist whose influence on Japanese society eventually exceeded that of his contemporaries. His career is an historical example of the power of thought actually being superior to political and military power.

Fukuzawa was in his mid-thirties when the Meiji Restoration dramatically transformed Japan's political system. He was a harsh critic of the Tokugawa feudal system of lineage, and deeply understood Western Learning, Chinese Learning, and Japanese history. He firmly believed that the future direction of the new Japan would be determined by how the Japanese understood Western civilization, and the means by which they maintained balance while adopting from it. What paths of development had Western civilization been following? By comparison, what characteristics or points of conflict did Japanese history and civilization present? Why was the adoption of Western civilization so vital to the preservation of Japan's independence? Fukuzawa systematically lays out that vision and methodology with limpid prose in *An Outline of a Theory of Civilization* (1875).

I would like to preface my introduction to the contents and features of this work with a simple overview of Fukuzawa Yukichi's life. In Chapter Ten, "A Discussion of Our National Independence" of *An Outline* he writes: "I was born into a family of minor retainers in the service of a weak *fudai* daimyo during the time of the Tokugawa shogunate" (p. 243). His father, Hyakusuke, was a low-ranking samurai of the Nakatsu domain in Buzen (modern-day Ōita prefecture). Although Fukuzawa was born in Osaka, where his father had been ordered to serve as an overseer of the treasury, he grew up in Nakatsu. For a low-ranking samurai, the restrictions surrounding one's lineage presented obstacles so great that regardless of intellectual ability, personal advancement was little more than a quixotic dream. Becoming a low-ranking samurai from outside the samurai class was not exceptionally difficult, but becoming a high-ranking samurai from the lower ranks was well near impossible.

Fukuzawa's father, who possessed a decent library and enthusiasm for learning, died when Fukuzawa was only a year and a half old. In the early spring of 1854, at the age of 19, Fukuzawa left his hometown of Nakatsu for Nagasaki, where he pursued Dutch Learning. One year later, he entered the school of Ogata Kōan, a famous physician and scholar of Dutch Learning in Osaka. Fukuzawa's abilities were already widely known around the domain and in 1858 he was summoned to the administrative capital of Edo to open a school for Dutch Learning.

Fukuzawa traveled overseas three times before the Meiji Restoration. He first went to America (San Francisco, Washington, D.C., and New York) in 1860 aboard the *Kanrinmaru*, a boat that went in advance of a government delegation that was to exchange the ratification documents for the U.S.-Japan Treaty of Amity and Commerce. He traveled in Europe between 1861 and 1862, passing through Hong Kong, India, and the Suez Canal on his way. His purpose was to negotiate a Sakhalin border treaty with Russia and to visit six

European countries to postpone the opening of the Japanese cities and ports (Edo, Osaka, Niigata, and Hyōgo). And in 1867, he traveled again to the U.S. in the retinue of a delegation sent by the Bakufu to receive delivery of a warship.

These experiences not only exposed him to Western society and ways of life, but also to the vitality and superior development of Western civilization. The trips also enabled him to perceive directly from his own observations, and not just written material, a dangerous scenario in which Japan might share the miserable conditions of those Asian countries which had become colonies for the West. He saw the fate that awaited any country that lost its independence, and this knowledge eventually provided a basis for his thought.

Fukuzawa could see that Tokugawa rule was already weakening and, after withdrawing from the Bakufu, began to pour his energies into cultivating bright minds at his private school, which he formally named Keio-gijuku (the predecessor to Keio University). He had decided that such an endeavor was the greatest contribution he could make toward strengthening Japan at the time. Even when called on to serve in the Meiji government thereafter, he adamantly refused. Instead, from an entirely civilian standpoint, he addressed the formation of a nation-state based on such ideas as individual independence, freedom, and equality. *An Outline of a Theory of Civilization*, together with *An Encouragement of Learning* (1872–76), which was penned around the same time, demonstrate Fukuzawa's praise of freedom and equality, and his belief in the necessity of cultivating knowledge and virtue for the advancement of civilization. They are classics that give a clear-cut indication of the path Japan should take while maintaining its independence. Fukuzawa's view of history, society, and humanity is on display in these texts, laced with his particular brand of humor and wit.

What, then, was Fukuzawa's motive in writing *An Outline of a Theory of Civilization*? Looking back in a mode of self-reflection in a later work of 1897 called *Zenshū shogen* (Preface to the Collected Works of Fukuzawa), Fukuzawa writes: "My publications up to this time had been aimed at importing Western things and ideas, and also at expulsion of the old and evil practices in Japan. In other words, they were a sort of piecemeal introduction of civilization."[†] Meanwhile, he was producing theoretical works about much of Western civilization, in an attempt to "appeal to the Confucian scholars and win their approval."[‡] Japan had already weathered the turbulence from the sudden overhaul of its social and governmental institutions following the Restoration, and entered finally into a period in which the leaders had to reassess their direction. It was an age, moreover, that saw the dispatch of talented youth overseas to gather knowledge and information. Fukuzawa wrote *An Outline* for intellectuals who would influence the politics and economy of the new Japan, not simply for scholars of National Learning, scholars of Confucian Learning, or even scholars of Western Learning who had been influenced by Christianity.

This work consists of ten chapters. In the Preface he says: "a theory of civilization concerns the development of the human spirit," but he is not talking about the spirit of a single human being (p. 1). Rather, he is referring to "the spiritual development of the people of the nation as a whole." This is an important distinction in the social sciences. In Chapter Four, "The Knowledge and Virtue of the People of a Country," he explicates the concept of the "spirit." As an illustration, he notes that there is little fluctuation in annual rainfall, cases of crime, and the numbers of suicide victims, over an extended period. Here, he artfully explains the meaning of "total quantity," showing in essence that nobody can predict the actions or thoughts of an individual on a micro scale, though the aggregate numbers on a macro scale are, as a rule, stable. The corollary is that more general movements and amounts are meaningful and can provide material for argument and speculation.

Taken as a whole, "the spirit of a nation" is a barometer that indicates the degree to which the spirit of an entire nation's people has developed. In illustrating how this "spirit" may establish the overall power and tendencies of a nation, Fukuzawa offers a notion that is easy to grasp: "the outcome of a war does not depend on generals or weaponry, but entirely on the spirit of a people" (p. 76). This is a clear-cut example of his belief that, essentially, the advancement of

---

[†] *The Autobiography of Fukuzawa Yukichi with Preface to the Collected Works of Fukuzawa*, trans. Eiichi Kiyooka (Tokyo: Hokuseido Press, 1981), appendix 88.
[‡] Ibid., 89.

civilization depends neither on the existence of a few elite individuals nor on the technology of its machines, but rather in the end on the degree to which the people's spirit has developed. Fukuzawa suggests that the Japanese are able to engage in objective discourse concerning civilization in this sense. The reason is that they can critically observe and compare the course of Western civilization, not from within its existing framework, but from outside.

Another point worth noting is Fukuzawa's establishment of "a basis of argumentation," which involves seeing the world in a relative (sometimes pluralistic) way. Whether something is heavy or light, long or short, good or bad, right or wrong is relative and only determined through comparison. Moreover, "When investigating things it is necessary to clear away the non-essentials and get back to their source" (p. 7). Only after establishing such a basis can controversial issues be argued with clarity. In such arguments it will not be surprising if no one has the same opinion. The interaction of people—society, in other words—enables an exchange of differing opinions that deepens mutual understanding and leads to a more sophisticated resolution of problems. As Fukuzawa clarifies, "What I mean is that, if there is any opportunity for two people to come together—whether it be in business or in academic circles, in a drinking bout or in a legal dispute, in everyday quarrels or even in wars—and to express frankly in word and deed what is in their hearts, then the feelings of both parties will be soothed, and each will, in effect, open both eyes and be able to see the other fellow's merits" (pp. 12–13).

If the advancement of civilization is relative, then where does Japan stand? Fukuzawa divides civilization's development into three phases, "the primitive stage," "the semi-developed stage," and "civilization," calling them the "ages of civilization" (p. 18). He places Japan in the middle stage, "semi-developed." Of significance here are the provisions for his conception of civilization. Fukuzawa cautions that there are two sides to civilization: "We can distinguish in civilization between its visible exterior and its inner spirit. It is easy enough to adopt the former, but difficult to pursue the latter" (p. 21). He then asks, "But what, then, is the spirit of civilization?" He answers for himself, "It is a people's spiritual makeup" (p. 22). Enlightened people understand the laws of nature and conduct all their activities, private and public, with positive initiative: "Their spirits enjoy free play and are not credulous (*wakudeki*) of old customs" (p. 18). He adds: "They neither yearn for the old nor become complacent about the present. Not resting with small gains, they plan great accomplishments for the future" (p. 19).

Maruyama Masao, late member of Japan Academy, points out that Fukuzawa's key concept of *wakudeki* is related to "credulity" and "superstition," two words used in the *History of Civilization in England* (1857–61) by the historian Thomas Buckle (1821–62), whom Fukuzawa read meticulously.[†] Maruyama cites Morohashi Tetsuji's *Dai kanwa jiten* (Great Chinese-Japanese Dictionary) to show that in old China the term *wakudeki* in reference to men primarily meant "losing one's bearings in alcoholic and sexual debauchery, addiction to those desires." However, in *Yume no shiro* (Instead of Dreams, 1820) by Japanese merchant-scholar Yamagata Bantō (1748–1821), the term is used to mean, "caught up in heretical doctrine," or "bewildered by groundless speculations." In other words, its meaning was akin to "superstition." For Fukuzawa, *wakudeki* meant a spiritual stagnation synonymous with *meishin*, a term also rendered as "superstition." It refers to an attitude in which one forgets the customary function of an object and cherishes it to such a degree that, absent of all context, one becomes blindly attached to the object itself. Fukuzawa earnestly explained that this mindset impeded the progress of civilization. During lawless times of war, for example, warriors possessed a pair of swords because they offered physical protection. But not disarming in times of peace and instead esteeming those swords to an abnormal degree while continuing to wear them long after forgetting how to actually use them is, Fukuzawa laughs, a typical example of credulity.

Of further note, in *An Outline of a Theory of Civilization*, Fukuzawa uses the word *wakudeki* in his criticism of national polity theory. Specious claims that modernization would change Japanese polity were circulating at the same time. If such arguments were to prevail, however, progress would be stamped out. Responding to xenophobic

---

[†] "Fukuzawa ni okeru 'wakudeki' to iu kotoba" (The word *wakudeki* in Fukuzawa's works), *Maruyama Masao techō* 44 (2008): 1–37.

thinking, Fukuzawa drew distinctions between "national polity," "political legitimation," and "blood lineage." Preserving national polity meant preserving independence. Among Asian countries, China and India had lost their national polity, but Japan's national polity had not once changed. Certainly, political legitimation had changed when Japan's political power shifted from the imperial court to the shogunate. But compared to national polity, national legitimation and lineage were secondary in importance at best. Fukuzawa believed that it was necessary, in fact, to introduce Western civilization in order to preserve national polity. In a letter written in the fall of 1874, Fukuzawa said: "My sole aim, then, is the preservation of our national independence." The claim that "introducing Western civilization would endanger national polity" was therefore a gross example of confused priorities. The "discourse of national polity," with its stress on an unbroken line of emperors, was in fact a typical example of *wakudeki*, and was, as Fukuzawa argued, a danger to the preservation of Japan's true national polity.

Fukuzawa's thought, however, differed dramatically from any simple view of history as a progression that emphasized improvements in the economic conditions of human life. He makes this point clear in Chapter Three, "The Essence of Civilization," where he refines his concept of civilization. He says that "'civilization' means not only comfort in daily necessities but also the refining of knowledge and the cultivation of virtue so as to elevate human life to a higher plane" (p. 45). In other words, if civilization were defined as progress in comfort and dignity, then the mechanism that would provide such comfort and dignity would be knowledge and virtue. Civilization, then, is the progress of man's knowledge and virtue. Accordingly, shifting from a monarchy to a democracy does not necessarily amount to progress in civilization. Fukuzawa asks rhetorically: "it seems that in civilized countries monarchs are not allowed. Is this correct?" He then sweeps the notion aside: "this is looking at the world with one eye closed" (p. 49). Since there are bad republics even as there are good monarchies, Fukuzawa cautions that "We have to consider the realities of government rather than judge by their names only" (p. 51). It is here that Fukuzawa's pragmatism emerges in full clarity.

Assuming that civilization is regulated by the progress of knowledge and virtue, how should we measure the knowledge and virtue not of individuals, but of an entire nation? He notes in Chapters Four and Five that since there are fools in the West and also people of superior knowledge and virtue in Asia, the issue lies with the total knowledge and virtue of a country, the distribution of that knowledge and virtue and its fluctuations. Fukuzawa's explanation for measuring this totality of knowledge and virtue is also a point of great interest since it demonstrates his keen understanding of statistics.

In his treatment of causality, the distinction between "proximate cause" and "remote cause" is extremely scientific. He demonstrates these concepts with a clever example. If someone, while drunk, has fallen off a horse and sustained partial paralysis, what kind of treatment is called for? An incompetent doctor who merely perceived the "proximate cause," namely, falling off the horse, would simply put a cast around his back. Actually, a poor diet from years of drinking had weakened his spinal cord, and the paralysis came from being thrown from the horse. Proper clinical medicine would advise dealing with the "remote causes" of drinking and weakening the spinal cord (p. 67). Fukuzawa berated those who could not grasp remote causes and simply let credulity guide them in what appealed immediately to their senses: "venturing grand schemes as the spirit moves them, they merely grope in the dark, tapping their canes in pitch-blackness" (p. 68). In this context, Fukuzawa again emphasizes that the dynamics of a time are an important factor in determining the outcome of events. Whether the actions of certain historical figures are viewed as a success or failure depends on the dynamics of the time, and as examples he offers Confucius, Mencius, Emperor Go-Daigo and Kusunoki Masashige. The spirit of the people of those eras—or, expressed differently, the very "level of knowledge and virtue distributed among the people of the age"—is both a remote cause and a measure of that civilization (p. 69).

Fukuzawa called this general state of knowledge and virtue "public opinion." Public opinion depends on individuals of superior intellect, not on gross numbers or financial power. There are individuals who possess the intellectual power of a hundred, even a thousand, people. Feudal despotism bottles up this kind of intellectual power and society stagnates. Even during the Meiji Restoration, "It was a battle between intellectual power and despotism. The cause behind the whole struggle was the intellectual forces at work in the country at large. This was the remote cause" (p. 88). Again, sheer numbers are not the issue; this intellectual power must be disseminated by a limited number of exceptional individuals through freedom of the press and freedom of speech. Fukuzawa essentially believed that the people had to be led by those with great wisdom. Even in this context, however, we can see that Fukuzawa does not praise democracy unconditionally. Rather, he gives careful consideration to the conditions by which it functions. In particular, we must note that at the time Fukuzawa was writing *An Outline*, he believed that it was not possible to place complete reliance on public opinion in Japan, and that he was not arguing for the immediate introduction of a democratic form of government.

A further point of significance is Fukuzawa's belief that individuals, even if exceptionally talented, have no power without unity. Sodium and hydrochloric acid are hazardous substances, but if you mix the two together, they become ordinary salt that can be used in the kitchen. Lime and ammonium chloride are not hazardous in isolation, but when mixed they pack enough power to knock a man down (p. 92). Fukuzawa displayed ample humor when it came to providing easy-to-understand examples such as these. He also provided economic analogies: if individuals kept money stashed away at home, it would achieve nothing, but if they deposited it in a bank, it could amount to quite a large fund for industrial investment. In just the same way, the opinion of a single individual might not be worthy of attention, but once brought together, the individual opinions of all the people acquire sophistication and significance.

Fukuzawa also discusses the nature of intellect and morality as foundations for civilization, their differences and the characteristics of their functions. In Chapter Six, "The Distinction between Knowledge and Virtue," and Chapter Seven, "The Proper Times and Places for Knowledge and Virtue," Fukuzawa writes that morals, as a kind of behavior of the heart, have an internal function. Knowledge is a function for thinking about things, explaining them, and understanding them. Here, Fukuzawa creates another distinction, this time between "public" and "private." With virtue and knowledge, public and private, he has a pair of binaries. But what exactly is he trying to demonstrate with these four components? "Private virtue" is a function corresponding to values such as fidelity, purity, modesty, integrity; "public virtue" to a sense of shame, justice, fairness, courage; private intellect to thoroughly investigating the logic of things. "Public knowledge" corresponds to a function for dividing human affairs according to their relative importance, then determining priorities based on circumstances. Of supreme importance to Fukuzawa was "public knowledge," which he called "the wisdom of great knowledge."

Fukuzawa points out that among these values in Japan the meaning of virtue has been interpreted in a limited way, and that there is a strong trend of overvaluing private virtue. The function of wisdom is subsumed under knowledge, while virtue is mainly used to denote nothing more than a passive kind of private virtue. Private virtue is, like the senses, something that people cannot do without, but someone who only possesses private virtue will not manage his official duties reliably or effectively. The function of wisdom or public knowledge that considers the relative merits of the world around us exerts a wide influence on society, but Japan lacks this wisdom rather than morality. Concerning the latter, the influence of Shintoism, Confucianism, and Buddhism is enormous in Japan. There has not been any large difference in what they have advocated. Furthermore, "the moral teachings of both East and West are really evenly matched" (p. 128). Unlike knowledge, one could perhaps even say that morality as an ideal has neither changed nor progressed since the beginning of time. While citing numerous examples, Fukuzawa asserts that knowledge was more important than virtue, public virtue more important than private virtue, and public knowledge more important than private knowledge in a civilized society.

It is clear from *An Outline of a Theory of Civilization* that Fukuzawa drew particular influence from the writings of Buckle and François Guizot (1787–1874) in his understanding of the differences between Western and Japanese historical development. Guizot's *General History of Civilization in Europe* (1828) certainly provides some of the foundation for Chapter Eight on "The Origins of Western Civilization." Fukuzawa, however, makes free use of Guizot's arguments and focuses on the notion that the origins of Western civilization derive from the "pluralism of authority." His arguments are concise. In the West, several kinds of authority have stood shoulder to shoulder: religious authority to explain spiritual issues where sense and reason can provide no answer; popular authority (democracy), which is found in free cities; or the authority bound under a monarchy, as in the power of nobles. Furthermore, there is continuity between the barbarism of the Germanic tribes and the spirit of freedom and independence. He draws attention to the historical process by which these different mindsets and authorities coalesced into a united government.

What does this tell us about Japan? He notes that Japan's authority is more centralized vis-à-vis the pluralist West, resulting in an "imbalance of power." In Chapter Nine, "The Origins of Japanese Civilization," Fukuzawa writes that this imbalance of power exists in all aspects of personal relationships and social relations among the Japanese. The imbalance of power wielded by men in gender relations, by parents in filial relations, and by older brothers in fraternal relations extends to teachers and students, masters and servants, the rich and the poor, novices and veterans, main households and branches. In considering these references to the imbalance of power, however, we should note that Fukuzawa did not simply recycle all of Buckle's theories. He omits the climate-geography causation theory, which Buckle explains in Chapter Two of his work: "Man is affected by four classes of physical agents, namely, climate, food, soil and the general aspect of nature." Fukuzawa instead crafts an argument appropriate to Japan's condition.

Another important point is that this imbalance of power divided society into two parts, creating a conscious distinction between "the ruler and the ruled" among all Japanese. This gave rise to a situation that dampened a spirit of independence; "the ruled were simply the slaves of the rulers" (p. 180). The whole of religion, scholarship, commerce and industry consequently became ensnared in the government. People, meanwhile, did not try to dissolve the barriers between the classes, but they did praise those who were able to free themselves from the restraints of class and rise in society. The warlord Toyotomi Hideyoshi, who rose from a peasant-warrior to become Japan's de facto ruler, is a typical example. But from Fukuzawa's perspective, he was nothing more than a selfish man who abandoned the members of his original class.

It is here that Fukuzawa's observation about the public and the private becomes clear. More specifically, in Japan the "public" is government and signifies the ruling class. Japanese history shows a shift in political authority from the imperial court to the warrior class, and the people themselves make no appearance on the stage. Fukuzawa notes that in their writings, the distinguished historians Arai Hakuseki and Rai San'yō focused on the ruling class. Fukuzawa writes: "in Japan there is a government, but no **nation**" (p. 187). Very few ever tried to break free from their class. Even religion devoted itself to entering the government and becoming part of that authority. It is for that reason that Japan has had no religious wars. Scholarship endeavored to become a scholarship that served the rulers, and religion supported despotism. Fukuzawa says that this kind of imbalance of power has obstructed the progress of civilization in Japan.

What did Fukuzawa think was the task facing Japan at the time? He compares Japan and the West, and admits that the intellectual vitality of Western people, the will to self-government, and the desire for social order were far greater than in Japan. Certainly, the feudal system based on lineage had ended, and the ideas of obligation, pedigree, moral duty, and discrimination that permeated Japanese thought had largely disappeared. The human spirit had reclaimed its vitality, but there were no grounds for unbridled optimism. Fukuzawa paints the situation: "The goal of both scholar and civil servant is money alone. It is said that as long as one has money he need not work hard, and that money knows no enemy on the face of the earth; it is money which sets the prices on human conduct" (p. 229). This does not exactly create peace of mind and Fukuzawa conveys a sense of impending crisis. A theory of national polity that ignores reality and is based on illusions can neither stabilize public sentiment nor elevate conduct merely by announcing the restoration of imperial rule. Christianity, in so far as it relates to private virtue, is not a fallacy, per se, but it is clear from the history of religious wars in the West that the independence of a nation cannot be achieved by transferring its teachings to politics.

In Chapter Ten, Fukuzawa uses this perspective on the status quo to propose that the world is in an age where the fate of a nation is determined by the degree of its success in foreign relations. Fukuzawa believes that there are only two elements to these relations. He says: "in times of peace, exchange goods and compete with one another for profit; in times of war, take up arms and kill each other" (p. 234). He continues: "War is the art of extending the rights of independent governments, and trade is a sign that one country radiates its light to others" (p. 235). Foreign relations, which not only stimulate great economic profit but also exert influence on the moral conduct of citizens, become more refined when two countries are conscious of being equals. Fukuzawa jokes that, in spite of this, when you see Japanese in contact with foreigners, "They act like a young bride before her old mother-in-law" (p. 241).

So why are the Japanese unable to demand equal treatment in their contact with foreign countries? The ones demanding equal treatment were in positions of power under the previous regime. They are consequently unable fully to appreciate the importance of equality, and lack a feeling of urgency toward foreign relations because of their limited experience in diplomacy. In order to improve their general character, each Japanese citizen must first wake up to this problem, face up to the choices Japan must make, and possess a spirit of independence and self-reliance. Fukuzawa asserts that this is not a problem that can be resolved by merely assimilating the surface of Western civilization.

Fukuzawa also warns that it is folly to try to supplement this lack of equality and independent spirit with an overdependence on military might, as the anti-foreign factions argue. So what can Japan do? He sums up by saying: "namely, to establish our goal and advance toward civilization. What is that goal? It is to be clear about the distinction between domestic and foreign, and thereby to preserve the independence of our country" (p. 254). For modern Japan to become a full member of the international community where it will further thrive, it must first become a nation-state based on citizens who possess self-respect and a spirit of independence.

Fukuzawa poses questions that readers will no doubt recognize are relevant today. His words still send a powerful message and warning not only to developing countries, but also to citizens of developed countries who live in liberal democracies, Japan included. I would finally like to highlight two or three concrete points from this text that demonstrate this notion.

One is his strong emphasis on the spirit of civilization. Fukuzawa's intellect, humor, and confrontational approach have sometimes led people wrongfully to accuse him of being anything from "a money worshipper" to "a supporter of foreign aggression" to "someone infatuated by the West." But in reading this text, one point becomes clear: Fukuzawa's primary belief is that it is the spirit, not the form, which is important to a civilization that can refine the mind and provide a sense of comfort. Fukuzawa stresses that even in a society and civilization imbued with this spirit, knowledge is more important than virtue, public virtue is more important than private virtue, and public knowledge is more important than private knowledge. Neither can readers fail to notice the moderate ideology drawn from these pages. It is clear that his basic message, "balance is paramount," applies to both authority and religion alike. Respect for both plurality and a spontaneous independent spirit is preferred to an imbalance of power and credulity. Whatever the religion or political system, there are strong points and weak points.

We still have much to learn from the critical perspectives of a person like Fukuzawa, who was able to transcend *wakudeki*. Fukuzawa's warning about Japan's chronic ineptitude in foreign affairs is even more relevant. He says: "to fight for one's own advantage is really to fight for principles. It is high time for our country to fight with the foreigners for its own advantage and for principles" (p. 96). Even now, 130 years after the writing of this text, foreign affairs remains one of Japan's highest priorities. The Japanese, however, have yet to answer all of the questions that Fukuzawa posed.

Inoki Takenori, *Director-General*
International Research Center for Japanese Studies
[Translated by Ry Beville]

A NOTE ON THE TEXT

This English translation of Fukuzawa Yukichi's *Bunmeiron no gairyaku* (An Outline of a Theory of Civilization) has been revised and reset from the first edition published by *Monumenta Nipponica* and Sophia University Press in 1973. In this new edition, Fukuzawa's original notes to the text are indicated with asterisks. Additional notes are indicated by daggers and given in square brackets. English words employed by Fukuzawa in the original Japanese text are shown by the use of bold face.

All Japanese names appearing in the text are written in the Japanese order, i.e. with family name followed by first name. All Japanese words are romanized according to the modified Hepburn system. Macrons have been included to indicate long syllables but have been eliminated from fully anglicized words, such as "Tokyo" or "Kyoto." With the exception of Confucius (Kong Fuzi) and Mencius (Mengzi), all Chinese names are rendered according to the Pin-yin system. The original Chinese and Japanese versions of names are given in the index.

PREFACE

A theory of civilization concerns the development of the human spirit. Its import does not lie in discussing the spiritual development of the individual, but the spiritual development of the people of the nation as a whole. Therefore a theory of civilization may perhaps be termed a theory of the development of the human mind. Now, in men's social dealings many err in their views because their interests are limited to immediate profits or advantages. And once customs are long ingrained, it becomes almost impossible to distinguish what is natural from what has been man's doing. In many instances what was thought to have been natural was actually the result of custom, and vice versa. A theory of civilization is thus difficult because it purports to discover regularity in the midst of confusion.

Modern European culture has developed for over a thousand years since the fall of Rome, and its origins are even more ancient. But 2,500 years have also gone by since the founding of the Japanese nation.[†] In that time our own civilization has advanced to its present level of development; but the direction of Japan's progress perforce has been different from that of Western civilization. Since the arrival of the Americans during the Kaei era [in 1853], our country has concluded commercial treaties with several nations of the West. Only since then have the Japanese begun to know that the West really exists and to realize the enormous differences between the civilizations of the East and the West. People have been given a sudden jolt; public sentiment has been thrown into confusion. True, we have often been shaken by

---

† [Fukuzawa's reference is to Kōki (an Imperial Year), a Japanese epoch used before World War II; the first year of Kōki was 660 B.C. when Emperor Jinmu was enthroned as the first emperor of Japan, according to the *Nihon shoki* (Chronicles of Japan, also known as the *Nihongi*, completed in 720).]

1

the changing fortunes of history in our two and a half millennia. But as a force which has shaken the very depths of men's minds, the recent relations with foreigners have been the most powerful single set of events since Confucianism and Buddhism were introduced from China in the distant past.[†] Furthermore, Buddhist and Confucian teachings transmitted Asian ideas and practices. They were different only in degree from Japanese institutions, so they may have been novel, but they were not so very strange to our ancestors. The same cannot be said of relations with foreigners in recent history. We have suddenly been thrust into close contact with countries whose indigenous civilizations differ in terms of geographical location and cultural elements, in the evolution of those cultural elements, and in the degree of their evolution. They are not only novel and exotic for us Japanese; everything we see and hear about those cultures is strange and mysterious. If I may use a simile, a blazing brand has suddenly been thrust into ice-cold water. Not only are ripples and swells ruffling the surface of men's minds, but a massive upheaval is being stirred up at the very depths of their souls.

The first expression of this disturbance in men's minds came with the Meiji Restoration a few years ago, and then later with the abolition of the feudal *han*[‡] and the creation of centralized prefectures (*haihan chiken*). This is the extent of the changes so far, but there cannot be any stopping with just these measures. There may no longer be signs of the military insurrections which broke out several years ago, but the violent upheavals in men's minds continue to increase daily. For these upheavals have become spurs prodding the people of the nation forward. They have caused dissatisfaction with our civilization and aroused enthusiasm for Western civilization. As a result, men's sights are now being reset on the goal of elevating Japanese civilization to parity with the West, or even of surpassing it. Since Western civilization is even now in a process of transition and progress day by day, month by month, we Japanese must keep pace with it without abating our efforts.

---

† [Buddhism and Confucianism were first introduced in Japan in the sixth century (538 or 552) from Baekje, a kingdom located in southwest Korea.]

‡ [A *han* was the domain of a daimyo, a local lord in the Japanese feudal system.]

The arrival of the Americans in the Kaei era has, as it were, kindled a fire in our people's hearts. Now that it is ablaze, it can never be extinguished.

Such has, indeed, been the jolt to men's minds. The resultant complications and confusion in Japanese society almost defy imagination. At a time like this, to try to articulate a coherent theory of civilization is perhaps an overly ambitious task for a scholar. True, Western scholars are daily expounding new theories which never cease to amaze men by the novelty of the ideas contained therein. But they are dutifully engaged in refining and passing on a spiritual heritage which goes back thousands of years in the West; even though their theories sound new and strange, they all derive from the same source. Consequently they are not really new creations. The situation is entirely different for us in present-day Japan. Contemporary Japanese culture is undergoing a transformation in essence, like the transformation of fire into water, like the transition from non-being to being. The suddenness of the change defies description in terms of either reformation or creation. Even to discuss it is extremely difficult.

I trust that we present-day scholars will measure up to this challenge. But let me point out that in addition we have an accidental opportunity for greatness thrust upon us. Since the opening of the ports Japanese scholars have been assiduous in mastering Western Learning. Though the results have been sketchy and limited so far, we have been able to get some idea of Western civilization. Yet just twenty years ago we scholars were steeped in a purely Japanese civilization; there is little danger of our falling into vague inferences when discussing the past. We also have the advantage of being able directly to contrast our own personal pre-Meiji experience with Western civilization. Here we have an advantage over our Western counterparts, who, locked within an already matured civilization, have to make conjectures about conditions in other countries, while we can attest to the changes of history through the more reliable witness of personal experience. This actual experience of pre-Meiji Japan is the accidental windfall we scholars of the present day enjoy. Since this kind of living memory of our generation will never be repeated again, we have an especially important opportunity to make our mark. Consider how all of today's scholars of Western Learning were, but a few years back, students of Chinese Classics, or of Shinto or Buddhism. We were all either from feudal samurai families or were feudal subjects. We have lived two lives, as it were; we unite in ourselves two completely different patterns of experience.

What kind of insights shall we not be able to offer when we compare and contrast what we experienced in our earlier days with what we experience of Western civilization? What we have to say is sure to be trustworthy. For this reason, despite my personal inadequacies, I have endeavored in this humble work to put to use my own limited knowledge of Western Learning. I have generally paraphrased rather than directly translated Western sources in order to apply their content to the Japanese context. For my whole purpose has been to take advantage of the present historically unique opportunity to bequeath my personal impressions to later generations.

My observations are roughly sketched, and there may be many errors in perspective, for which I of course apologize. My only wish is that later scholars will undertake wider studies, reading more Western books than I have been able to, and studying the Japanese situation in greater detail, that they may be able increasingly to broaden their perspectives and to refine the problem such that they can truly write a complete theory of civilization. If they do, the whole landscape of Japan will be renewed. I too, not being old, hope to essay this larger study myself some day. Indeed, my sole joy will be to continue my research in the days to come, in the hope of contributing my share to this larger effort of understanding.

When quoting Western works and directly translating source materials, I have cited authors and editions used. But when I state the main ideas of an author or paraphrase the gist of the contents of another's work, I have not felt it necessary to record each and every item. These sources have become like food already digested within me. The food has been assimilated into my own body. If there are any clever ideas contained in this work, then, the reader can presume they are not my own, but ideas which I have taken and assimilated from others.

In the writing of this book, I have often consulted colleagues and benefited from their valuable suggestions. Also, I have often profited from their comments on things they had read. Among them, I owe a particular debt of gratitude to Obata Tokujirō,[†] whom I have troubled to read and correct my work in its entirety. There are many passages in which he has polished my ideas.

25 March 1875   Fukuzawa Yukichi

---

† [Obata Tokujirō (1842–1905) was a prominent disciple of Fukuzawa and later President of Keio-gijuku.]

Chapter ONE

ESTABLISHING A BASIS OF ARGUMENTATION

LIGHT and heavy, long and short, good and bad, right and wrong are all relative terms. If there were no light, there could be no heavy; if there were no good, there could be no bad. Thus, light is light relative to heavy, and good is good relative to bad. If there were not such relativity between one and the other, we could not debate over light and heavy or good and bad. The criterion in terms of which something is judged relatively heavy or good may be called the basis of argumentation. An old proverb says that "The belly must be saved at the cost of the back." Another asserts, "Sacrifice the small for the large." Thus, in the case of the human body one must protect the stomach even at the expense of receiving a wound on the back, because the stomach is more vital than the back. And in dealing with animals, the crane is of greater value than the loach, so the loach is used as food for the crane. In the change from the feudal order, in which the daimyo and samurai lived in idleness, to the system we now have, it may have seemed unnecessary to dispossess those with property and force on them the hardships of the propertyless. But if you think of the Japanese nation and the individual *han* in relative terms, then the nation is important, the *han* unimportant. Abolishing the *han* is the same as putting a greater premium on the stomach than on the back, and taking away the stipends of the daimyo and the samurai is like killing the loach to feed the crane.

When investigating things it is necessary to clear away the non-essentials and get back to their source. By doing this, details can be subsumed under general principles and thereby the basis of argumentation can be even more ascertained. Newton, in discovering the law of gravity, first established the principle of inertia (the first law of motion), namely: if something begins to move, it will continue to move without stopping, and if it is stopped, it will remain still and not move until acted upon by an external force. Once he clearly established this law, the principles of motion of all things in the universe must conform to it. Such a "law" can be called a basis of truth. If there were no such law, in debating the principles of motion the opinions on the subject would be of endless diversity. There would be one principle for the motion of ships, another principle for vehicles. The number of items brought into the discussion would merely keep on increasing, and there would be no single fundamental law upon which they all would rest; without some one ultimate principle, nothing could be established with any certitude.

Therefore one cannot discuss the right and wrong, the merits and demerits of an issue without first establishing a basis of argumentation. A castle wall will be of advantage to the man who guards the castle, but a hindrance to one who attacks. The enemy's gain is the ally's loss; the convenience of one who is leaving is an inconvenience for one who is coming. Thus, in discussing the merits and demerits of such issues you must first establish the point of view from which you are going to argue; whether as the protector or the defender, the enemy or the ally—whichever it is to be, you must first establish the basis from which you will argue.

At all times of human history there have been numerous mutually conflicting views; when you go to their basic positions you will discover they are radically opposed, and this explains the friction between their sets of final conclusions. For example, Shinto and Buddhist positions are always at odds, yet if you listen to what each proclaims, both of them will sound plausible. But when you go to the basic positions of the two, you see that their points of departure are different—Shinto stressing good and ill fortune in the present, and Buddhism preaching the rewards and punishments of the future—and this is why both positions eventually differ. There is disagreement on many points between the Japanese scholars of Chinese Learning and Confucianism, and of those of the Japanese Learning school. Ultimately the fundamental issue that divides them is that the former accept the overthrow of evil rulers by Tang and Wu as correct, and the latter stress the unbroken lineage of the Japanese emperor. This is the only thing that bothers our scholars of Chinese Learning and Confucianism. All the while debating over fringe issues without ever getting down to the essentials, the Shintoists, Confucianists, and Buddhists never pass a day without their disputes. Their debates are as interminable as those arguments over the superiority of the bow and arrow versus the sword and the spear. To reconcile the two sides, there is but one method: point out a new theory more advanced than the ones now held, and people can judge for themselves the relative advantages and defects of the old and the new. Thus, the argument between the proponents of bow and arrow and those of sword and spear was quite heated at one time, but since the introduction of the gun no one argues the point anymore.*

When two men's original premises differ, there may be certain superficial similarities in what they have to say, but as one pushes them back to fundamentals one comes to a point where they part company. The two seem to agree in their discussions of the merits and demerits of various topics, but as we probe further into their logical grounds, their views go in opposite directions. For example, the obdurate samurai all invariably hate foreigners. Men of a scholarly nature, or at least of some knowledge, may also dislike foreigners because of their conduct. In so far as the latter are displeased with foreigners you can say their opinion agrees with that of the obdurate samurai; but when the source of their displeasure is examined you will find there is a disparity. One group looks on the foreigner as of a different species and hates him regardless of his merits or demerits. The other, somewhat more broad-minded,

---

* Listen to Shinto priests and they will tell you that, since there are burial ceremonies in Shinto, they too preach a doctrine of future life. Buddhist priests will tell you that, since they have offerings and prayers in such sects as the Hokke [branch of Japanese Buddhism founded by Nichiren (1222–82), who emphasized the teachings of the Lotus Sutra (*Hokkekyō*)], they too value present good and ill fortune. It is a highly complicated argument. But these things are due to the commingling of Shinto and Buddhism since ancient times. Buddhists try to mimic Shinto priests, and the Shintoists try to take over monkish offices. But when one discusses the general thesis of the two teachings, it is clear from observing their customs of a thousand years that one stresses the future and the other the present. Nowadays it is not worth listening to their long-winded arguments.

does not have a sweeping hatred or dislike for foreigners, but he realizes that some harmful effects can follow from dealings with them and feels indignant at the unfair treatment dealt out by so-called "civilized" foreigners. The two groups resemble each other in that they hate certain foreigners, but, since the source of their hatred is different, their ways of dealing with foreigners differ. In short, the arguments of those who advocated expelling the foreigners (jōi-ka) and those who advocated opening the country (kaikoku-ka) can appear to be similar, but somewhere along the line they divide because of their fundamental premises. Even when human beings are engaged in pleasurable activities, though all may share the same experiences, many nevertheless differ in their likes and dislikes. From a single, superficial observation of what a person does one must not make hasty judgments about his inner disposition.

Often, when people discuss the pros and cons of a thing, they start by bringing up the two opposite extremes of the argument; both parties are at odds right from the very beginning and are unable to draw closer from that point on. Let me give an example. Nowadays if a person mentions the new theory of equal popular rights, someone of the old school immediately sees it as an argument for a democratic form of government. He asks what will become of Japan's national polity if Japan were now to become a democratic government, expresses fears about the immeasurable harm that will ensue, seems so upset you would think he envisions the country's immediate plunge into political anarchy. From the beginning of the discussion he imagines some far-off future and vehemently opposes the other's argument, without ever investigating what equal rights means or asking what it is all about. On the other hand, the proponent of this new theory right from the beginning considers the defender of the old school as his enemy and attacks the old theory just as irrationally. The argument finally turns into a battle of mutual enemies; a meeting of minds never takes place. It is because they each start from one extreme that such conflict arises.

Let me give a parallel closer at hand. There were two men, one a tippler, the other a teetotaler. The tippler hated rice-cake, the teetotaler hated sake. Both expounded on the harmfulness of what they disliked and advocated its abolition. To counter the tippler's argument, the teetotaler said that if rice-cake were judged harmful, it would mean abolishing a national custom of several hundred years' standing in our country; on the first day of the New Year Japanese would have to eat boiled rice with tea. All rice-cake makers would be put out of business, and the growing of rice for rice-cake would have to be prohibited everywhere in the country. He concluded that this should not be done. The tippler, in refutation of the teetotaler, said that if sake were considered harmful, all the sake shops in the land would immediately have to be demolished, and anyone who became intoxicated would have to be given a stiff penalty. In all medicines one would have to substitute sake porridge for the distilled kind, and water cups would have to replace sake cups in the wedding ceremony. He felt that this should not be done. In this manner, when the two extremes of differing views confront each other, they necessarily clash; agreement is impossible. This eventually leads to disharmony between men and produces great harm in society. Japanese history is full of such examples. When such disharmony arises between scholars and gentlemen, the battle is conducted with tongue and pen; a theory is propounded, a book is written, people are persuaded by so-called abstract theory. But the uneducated and illiterate are unable to resort to the tongue and pen, and many, dependent on physical force, are apt to turn to such methods as assassination.

When two people argue, they attack only each other's weak spots and make it impossible for either party to show his true self. These weak spots are the bad aspects which always accompany a person's good points. For example, countryfolk are honest, but pig-headed, while townsmen are clever, but insincere. Honesty and cleverness are virtues in men, while pig-headedness and insincerity are their attendant evil aspects. When you hear arguments between countryfolk and townsmen, you find that many of their disputes stem from this difference. The countryman sees the townsman and calls him an insincere smart aleck, while the townsman ridicules the countryman and calls him a stubborn lout. Both parties are closing one eye to the other's good points and seeing only his bad side. If both sides could be made to open both eyes, with one eye observing the other fellow's virtues and with the other seeing his faults, perhaps the virtues and faults would cancel each other out and their dispute could be reconciled. The virtues might completely make up for the faults and the quarrel subsides. Also, by seeing each other in a friendly light, in the end the two might both profit from each other.

Scholars are no different. For example, the schools of thought in our country at the present time can be divided into two groups, the conservatives and the reformers. The reformers are quite keen in their judgment and open to progressive ideas, while the conservatives are caution-minded and desirous of holding on to the old. The latter exhibit the defect of stubbornness, while the fault of the former is a tendency toward rashness. Yet there is no law necessarily linking sober-mindedness with stubbornness, or keenness of mind with rashness. After all, there are those who drink sake without becoming drunk and those who eat rice-cake without getting sick. Sake and rice-cake do not invariably lead to intoxication or upset stomachs. Whether they do or not depends entirely on how a person regulates his use of them. Consequently, conservatives do not have to hate reformers, and reformers do not have to scorn conservatives. You have four things involved here: sober-mindedness, stubbornness, keenness of mind, and rashness. Put sober-mindedness and rashness, or keenness of mind and stubbornness, together, and they will always clash and be mutually inimical. But put sober-mindedness and keenness of mind together, and they will always get along well with each other. Only when you get such compatibility will the true selves of both parties be manifested and their antipathies gradually disappear.

During the Tokugawa's reign there was constant friction between those retainers of a daimyo who lived in the *han* quarters in Edo and those who stayed in the *han* territory—they were practically like two enemy forces within the same *han*. This was another example of true selves not being revealed.

Such evils will naturally be eliminated as man's knowledge progresses, but the most effective way to eliminate them is through constant intercourse in society. What I mean is that, if there is any opportunity for two people to come together—whether it be in business or in academic circles, in a drinking bout or in a legal dispute, in everyday quarrels or even in wars—and to express frankly in word and deed what is in their hearts, then the feelings of both parties will be soothed, and each will, in effect, open both eyes and be able to see the other fellow's merits. The reason intellectuals today are advocating the creation of popular assemblies, speech clubs, a better road system, freedom of the press, and the like is that these are of particular importance as aids to intercourse between men.

In all discussions people will have diverse opinions. If opinions are of a high level, the discussion will be at a high level. If the opinions are shallow, the discussion will also be shallow. When a person is shallow he tries to refute the other side before both sides have come to the heart of the matter—this results in the two viewpoints going in opposite directions. For example, if today there were to be a discussion of the pros and cons of dealing with foreigners, both A and B might be in favor of opening the country, and their ideas might appear to be in agreement. But as A begins to explain his ideas in detail and starts getting more and more abstruse, B will begin to take offense and, before you know it, the two will be at odds. B, a common man, is probably only repeating commonly heard views. Since his ideas are quite shallow, he is unable to fathom the main point of the discussion; suddenly hearing a more abstruse statement, he loses his bearings completely. Things like this happen often. The situation can be likened to that of a person with a weak stomach who, when he takes some nourishing food, cannot digest it and instead gets sicker. One must not jump to a hasty conclusion from this simile; it might seem that advanced discussion brings only harm and no good whatsoever, but this is not true. Without advanced discussion, there would be no bringing those who are backward to a more advanced stage. Prohibit nourishing food because a patient has a weak stomach, and the patient will eventually die.

Throughout history, the above type of misunderstanding between people has produced many regrettable situations. Consider the people of a particular era: in any country at any time there are very few who are either extremely stupid or extremely intelligent. The majority fall between these two extremes; shifting with the times, with neither blame nor merit, they spend their whole lives blindly following the crowd. Such people constitute the so-called "common man." They are the source of so-called "public opinion." Neither reflecting upon the past nor looking ahead to the future, they simply react to their immediate circumstances—as if their heads were locked in a fixed position. Today there are many such people—and their voices are loud. They would limit discussion in the country to their ideas and brand anything that departs even slightly from their scheme of things as unorthodox. What kind of minds do they have, these people who squeeze everything into their own frame of reference and try to force all discussion to follow a straight line? If they were allowed to have things their way, what possible use to the nation would such "intellectuals" be? On whom would we be able to rely for looking into the future and opening the door to civilization? Such is their gross misunderstanding.

Consider if you will how, since ancient times, progressive steps in civilization were always unorthodox at the time they were first proposed. When Adam Smith first expounded his economic theory, did not everyone condemn it as heresy? Was not Galileo punished as a heretic when he articulated his theory of the earth's rotation? Yet with the passage of time the mass of "common men," guided by the intellectuals, were, before they knew it, drawn over to the side of these "heresies"; as a result, at our present stage of civilization even school children entertain no doubts about the theories of modern economics and the earth's revolution. Doubt these theories? We have reached a point where anyone who questioned them would be regarded as a fool and counted out of society! To take a more proximate example: just ten years ago our solidly entrenched feudal system, in which 300 daimyo each governed independently and held the power of life and death over his subjects by reason of a clear distinction between lord and vassal, high and low, was thought to be a thing that would endure forever. Yet in an instant it crumbled and was replaced by the present imperial system. Today no one considers this new system strange, but if ten years ago a warrior within a *han* had proposed such measures as the abolition of the *han* and the establishment of prefectures, do you think for an instant the *han* would have debated the matter? Why, the man's very life would have been in immediate jeopardy!

Thus the unorthodox theories of the past become the commonly accepted ideas of the present; yesterday's eccentric notions become today's common knowledge. Therefore the unorthodox views of today will most certainly become the common ideas and theories of the future. Without fear of public opinion or charges of heresy, scholars should boldly espouse what they believe. Even when another's thesis does not square with your own, try to understand his intention and accept those points which can be accepted. Let those points which do not merit acceptance run their course, and wait for the day when both positions can be reconciled, the day when the basis of argumentation will be the same. Do not try to pressure others into your own way of thinking, nor try to induce conformity in every discussion, everywhere.

In conclusion, in order to discuss the merits and demerits of a matter, one must first consider whatever bears on its merits and demerits and then settle which are heavy, which light, which good, which bad. Discussing the merits and demerits of a matter is simple, but it is quite difficult to establish what is heavy, light, good, or bad. One cannot argue the good of the nation from the advantage of one individual. One must not discuss what is convenient for the coming year and err in plans for a hundred years ahead. One must listen to all theories, old and new; obtain extensive knowledge about conditions in the world; judge, without prejudice or personal feeling, where the highest good lies. Breaking through a thousand obstacles and remaining unfettered by the bonds of public opinion, one must occupy a lofty vantage point, from which to look back upon the past and to cast a sharp eye to the future.

Now, while it has not been my intention to pre-determine a basis of argumentation, to point out how to arrive at it, and then to force everyone to agree with my view, I do wish to ask one question of every man in this land. It is simply this: Are we at this time to go forward, or are we to turn back; to go forward and acquire civilization, or to turn back to a stage of primitivity? If you are of a mind to go forward, then perhaps my discussion ought to be read. Still, it is not my purpose to explain how actually to attain civilization. That I leave to the devices of my readers.

WESTERN CIVILIZATION AS OUR GOAL

I N the preceding chapter I argued that such designations as light and good and bad are relative. Now, the concept "civilization and enlightenment" (*bunmei kaika*) is also a relative one. When we are talking about civilization in the world today, the nations of Europe and the United States of America are the most highly civilized, while the Asian countries, such as Turkey, China, and Japan, may be called semi-developed countries, and Africa and Australia are to be counted as still primitive lands. These designations are common currency all over the world. While the citizens of the nations of the West are the only ones to boast of civilization, the citizens of the semi-developed and primitive lands submit to being designated as such. They rest content with being branded semi-developed or primitive, and there is not one who would take pride in his own country or consider it on a par with nations of the West. This attitude is bad enough. Not only this: The more those with some intelligence become aware of this situation, the more convinced they become of the situation of their own countries; the more convinced they become of the situation of their own countries, the more they awaken to the distance separating them from the nations of the West. They groan, they grieve; some are for learning from the West and imitating it, others are for going it alone and opposing the West. The overriding anxiety of Asian intellectuals today is this one problem to the exclusion of all others.* At any rate, the designations "civilized," "semi-developed," and "primitive" have been universally accepted by people all over the globe. Why does everybody accept them? Clearly, because the facts are demonstrable and irrefutable. I shall explain this point further below. For there are stages through which mankind must pass. These may be termed the ages of civilization.

First, there is the stage in which neither dwellings nor supplies of food are stable. Men form communal groups as temporary convenience demands; when that convenience ceases, they pull up stakes and scatter to the four winds. Or even if they settle in a certain region and engage in farming and fishing, they may have enough food and clothing, but they do not yet know how to make tools. And though they are not without writing, they produce no book learning. At this stage man is still unable to be master of his own situation; he cowers before the forces of nature and is dependent on the favors of others, or on the chance vagaries of nature. This is called the stage of primitive man. It is still far from civilization.

Secondly, there is the stage of civilization wherein daily necessities are not lacking, since agriculture has been started on a large scale. Men build houses, form communities, and create the outward semblance of a state. But within this facade there remain very many defects. Though book learning flourishes, there are few who devote themselves to practical learning (*jitsugaku*). Though in human relations sentiments of suspicion and envy run deep, when it comes to discussing the nature of things men lack the courage to raise doubts and ask questions. Men are adept at imitative craftsmanship, but there is a dearth of original production. They know how to cultivate the old, but not how to improve it. There are accepted rules governing society, but slaves of custom that they are, they could never form rules in the true sense. This is called the semi-developed stage. It is not yet civilization in the full sense.

Thirdly, there is the stage in which men subsume the things of the universe within a general structure, but the structure does not bind them. Their spirits enjoy free play and are not credulous of old customs. They act autonomously and do not have to depend upon the arbitrary

---

* Even the obstinate Chinese have been sending students to the West in recent years. You can see how concerned they are about their country.

favors of others. They cultivate their own virtue and refine their own knowledge. They neither yearn for the old nor become complacent about the present. Not resting with small gains, they plan great accomplishments for the future and commit themselves wholeheartedly to their realization. Their path of learning is not vacuous; it has, indeed, invented the principle of invention itself. Their industrial and business ventures prosper day by day to increase the sources of human welfare. Today's wisdom overflows to create the plans of tomorrow. This is what is meant by modern civilization. It has been a leap far beyond the primitive or semi-developed stages.

Now, if we make the above threefold distinction, the differences between civilization, semi-development, and the primitive stage should be clear. However, since these designations are essentially relative, there is nothing to prevent someone who has not seen civilization from thinking that semi-development is the summit of man's development. And, while civilization is civilization relative to the semi-developed stage, the latter, in its turn, can be called civilization relative to the primitive stage. Thus, for example, present-day China has to be called semi-developed in comparison with Western countries. But if we compare China with countries of South Africa, or, to take an example more at hand, if we compare the people of mainland Japan with the Ainu, then both China and Japan can be called civilized. Moreover, although we call the nations of the West civilized, they can correctly be honored with this designation only in modern history. And many of them, if we were to be more precise, would fall well short of this designation.

For example, there is no greater calamity in the world than war, and yet the nations of the West are always at war. Robbery and murder are the worst of human crimes; but in the West there are robbers and murderers. There are those who form cliques to vie for the reins of power and who, when deprived of that power, decry the injustice of it all. Even worse, international diplomacy is really based on the art of deception. Surveying the situation as a whole, all we can say is that there is a general prevalence of good over bad, but we can hardly call the situation perfect. When, several thousand years hence, the levels of knowledge and virtue of the peoples of the world will have made great progress (to the point of becoming utopian), the present condition of the nations of the West will surely seem a pitifully primitive stage. Seen in this light, civilization is an open-ended process. We cannot be satisfied with the present level of attainment of the West.

Yes, we cannot be satisfied with the level of civilization attained by the West. But shall we therefore conclude that Japan should reject it? If we did, what other criterion would we have? We cannot rest content with the stage of semi-development; even less can the primitive stage suffice. Since these latter alternatives are to be rejected, we must look elsewhere. But to look to some far-off utopian world thousands of years hence is mere daydreaming. Besides, civilization is not a dead thing; it is something vital and advancing. As such, it must pass through sequences and stages; primitive people advance to semi-developed forms, the semi-developed advance to civilization, and civilization itself is even now in the process of advancing forward. Europe also had to pass through these phases in its evolution to its present level. Hence present-day Europe can only be called the highest level that human intelligence has been able to attain at this juncture in history. Since this is true, in all countries of the world, be they primitive or semi-developed, those who are to give thought to their country's progress in civilization must necessarily take European civilization as the criterion in making arguments, and must weigh the pros and cons of the problem in the light of it. My own criterion throughout this book will be that of Western civilization, and it will be in terms of it that I describe something as good or bad, in terms of it that I find things beneficial or harmful. Therefore let scholars make no mistake about my orientation.

Someone says that, just as the world is divided into separate lands, so also men's sentiments and social customs, as well as their national polities and governments, are different. Therefore, he argues, is it not unwise to take European civilization as the model of modernization for every country? Shall we not attain the proper balance only if Western civilization is adapted to each country's own sentiments and social customs, and only if, while preserving each national polity and government, we select what is suitable, adopting or rejecting as circumstances dictate? My reply to this is that of course we should be selective in applying foreign civilization to a semi-developed country. We can distinguish in civilization between its visible exterior and its inner spirit. It is easy enough to adopt the former, but difficult to pursue the latter. Now, when one aims at bringing civilization to a country, the difficult part must be done first and the easier left for later; then, as the difficult part is acquired, stock should be taken of how much it has taken hold, and at suitable junctures the easier part can be added to it in the same measure, in this way assuring a constant balance. But if the wrong order is followed and the easier part is adopted before the difficult, the easier part often will prove not only useless but harmful as well.

In the first place, the externals of civilization are all empirical details, from food, clothing, shelter, implements, and so forth, to government decrees and laws. If only these external things were regarded as civilization, we would naturally have to be selective in adapting them to the distinctive ways of each country. Even the nations of the West, though they border on one another, are not uniform in manners and customs. Much less can the countries of Asia, so different from the West, imitate Western ways in their entirety. And even if they did imitate the West, that could not be called civilization.

For example, can we say that the current Western styles seen more and more in daily Japanese life are a proof of civilization? Can we call those men with Western haircuts whom we meet on the street civilized persons? Shall we call a person enlightened just because he eats meat? Hardly. I am always a bit upset at the way the Japanese government is building stone buildings and iron bridges, or at the way the Chinese, in order to reform their military system all at once, are building warships, buying cannons, and so on, without regard for their national resources and at unreasonable expense. All these things can be built through manpower or purchased with money. They are the most tangible of material things and the easiest of easy things to obtain. Should we then, when adopting such things, proceed without due consideration of consequences and priorities? Due regard must always be had for the sentiments and customs of one's own nation; the resources of one's own country must always be consulted. This is what ought to be meant by those who speak of "adapting to sentiments and social customs." I have no argument with them on this score, but some of them seem to be talking about only the external forms of civilization while neglecting its spirit.

But what, then, is the spirit of civilization? It is a people's spiritual makeup. This spirit can be neither bought nor sold. Nor again can it be readily created through use of manpower. It permeates the entire lifestream of a people and is manifest on a wide scale in the life of the nation. But since it has no one visible form, it is difficult to ascertain its existence. Let me try to describe it as best as I can.

If scholars read widely into the histories of the world and compare Asia and Europe, and if they inquire into the points in which the two areas of the world differ—without going into such things as their geographies and products, their ordinances and laws, their technical skills or technical backwardness, their religious differences or similarities, and so forth—they will definitely discover a certain spiritual entity behind these respective differences. This spiritual entity is difficult to describe. But when it is nourished it grows to embrace the myriad things of the earth; if repressed or restrained, its external manifestations will also vanish. It is in constant motion, advancing or retreating, waxing or waning. It may seem a will-o'-the-wisp or an apparition, but if we look at its real manifestations within present-day Asia and Europe, we can clearly see it is not illusory.

Let us now call this the "spirit of a people." In respect to time, it may be called the "trend of the times." In reference to persons, it may be called "human sentiments." With regard to a nation as a whole, it may be called "a nation's ways" or "national opinion." These things are what is meant by the spirit of civilization. And it is this spirit of civilization that differentiates the manners and customs of Asia and Europe. Hence the spirit of civilization can also be described as the sentiments and customs of a people.

Considered in these terms, the statement of those who say that even if we intend to adopt Western civilization we must first consider the sentiments and customs of our own nation, however inadequately expressed and vague their view may be, when understood correctly means that we must not import only the outward forms of civilization, but must first make the spirit of civilization ours and only then adopt its external forms. What I mean when I say that we should take European civilization as our goal is that we should turn to Europe in order to make the spirit of civilization ours, and thus I am in complete accord with their opinion. However, there are those who, in the pursuit of civilization, would give priority to external forms. As a result, when they suddenly encounter obstacles they do not know how to handle them. I differ from them only in wanting to give priority to the spirit of civilization in order to eliminate the obstacles in advance, and thus to facilitate the assimilation of external civilization. Still others, finally, are not opposed to civilization, but they have not committed themselves to its pursuit as wholeheartedly as I have. They have simply not fully thought through their own positions.

I stated earlier that it is easy to adopt the external forms of civilization but difficult to pursue its inner spirit. Let me clarify this further. Such matters as food, clothing, shelter, implements, government decrees, and laws are all tangible things. Of course, the daily necessities differ somewhat from government decrees and laws. But the latter too are empirical matters, even though they cannot be grasped with the hand or bartered for cash. The methods of adopting them are also somewhat more difficult than those used to acquire daily material necessities. Consequently, it is comparatively easier to imitate the West by putting up stone buildings and iron bridges, but much more difficult to reform government and law. This is why, though Japan has built iron bridges and stone buildings, it still finds it difficult to reform its government and law and has yet to establish a national parliament. But it will be far, far more difficult to change the spirit of the whole nation. It is not something to be fortuitously accomplished in one day. It cannot be pushed through by government decree alone. Nor can it be urged on religious grounds alone. Still less can it be introduced through externals, merely by a revolution in the material aspects of daily life. The only effective method will be to respect the natural inclinations of man and eliminate evils and obstacles, so that the levels of knowledge and virtue in the people rise spontaneously and their opinions can be elevated to a higher plane. When we have begun to change the sentiments of the people, there shall be nothing to prevent the gradual reformation of government decrees and laws.

The cornerstone of modern civilization will be laid only when national sentiment has thus been revolutionized, and government institutions with it. When that is done, the foundations of civilization will be laid, and the outward forms of material civilization will follow in accord with a natural process without special effort on our part, will come without our asking, will be acquired without our seeking. This is why I say that we should give priority to the more difficult side of assimilating European civilization. We should first reform men's minds, then turn to government decrees, and only in the end go out to external things. It may be more difficult to follow this order, but it is the path which has no truly insurmountable obstacles. We can reverse the order and seem to have easy going, but this latter course will lead to a dead end. It will be like coming up against a stone wall, before which, unable to advance, we either will have to mark time or, if we try to push forward another inch, will be rudely hurled back a foot.

My above remarks only discuss the question of priorities in regard to importing civilization. I am hardly suggesting that the material forms of civilization are utterly useless. Between the material and the immaterial aspects, between seeking them abroad and building them internally, there are no discriminations being made. At this juncture it is merely a question of priorities. I am not at all against the external aspects of civilization. In the first place, the activities of men are boundless. Man has both physical and spiritual activities. These are broad in extent and their requirements are numerous. Since innate human nature is compatible with modern civilization, as long as a thing does not do violence to human nature, it is permissible. The only requirement of civilization is that one use one's natural endowments of body and mind to the fullest extent.

For example, in the primitive age, men so valued sheer physical prowess that the dominating factor in society was mere brute strength. Authority in society was inevitably unilateral. Man's use of his functions was extremely circumscribed. As culture made its slow advance and the spirits of men in society gradually evolved, intelligence also spontaneously came into its own to challenge the primacy of brute

24

strength. The two powers limited and balanced each other, so that the one-sided influence of the one could to some extent be checked by the other. Both factors made it possible for man's activities to enlarge their scope somewhat. However, in olden times the uses of man's physical and intellectual powers were still limited. Brute strength was almost exclusively devoted to fighting battles; to obtain food, clothing, and shelter they used only the little energy left over from fighting. This was life according to "the warlike way." In the course of time intellectual powers also gained force, but since in those days men were kept busy containing people's primitive instincts, their mental forces could not be turned to making the world a peaceful and pleasant place to live in. Mental powers had to be used almost exclusively as means to rule and control the people; with intellectual power still being complemented by the use of physical power, an independent place for the former had yet to be found.

Indeed, the present world still suffices to illustrate my point. Not only among primitive peoples, but also in the semi-developed countries as well, men of knowledge and virtue inevitably are found in the government class, serving in one kind of capacity or other. Dependent on the power of the government, they utilize their energies exclusively for the purpose of ruling the people. Any rare individual who gives himself entirely to his own private affairs merely cultivates ancient learning or devotes all his time to the polite accomplishments of poetry and prose composition. Truly, men's energies have yet to be tapped on a wide scale.

But as human affairs proliferate in the course of time, and the needs of mind and body increase, inventions and schemes are brought forth to meet those needs, the pace of industry and commerce quickens, scholarship becomes more demanding, and men can no longer rest content with the simple ways of old. Such things as warfare, government, ancient learning, and poetry are only a few facets of the totality of human life and cannot be allowed to monopolize the whole picture. A hundred thousand enterprises spring into life together to enter the struggle for the survival and development of the fittest. Finally some reach a state of relative equality and equilibrium. In this balance of forces and pressures, the conduct of men cannot help but advance to a higher plane. Only at this juncture do the powers of intellect become dominant and become the means whereby civilization can progress.

The simpler the functions of man, the more his mind will be restricted in scope and, accordingly, the more one-sided will be the use of his powers. In ancient times, human enterprises were few and outlets for man's energies were far between. As a result, man's powers developed in only one direction. But the passing of the years witnessed a changeover from a simple to a complex scene. New frontiers of human activity were opened. The West of today can with justice be described as a complex world.

Therefore, an essential feature of civilized progress lies in endeavoring to intensify and multiply human enterprises and needs, to find more and more outlets, regardless of their relative priorities, and to stimulate the activities of the human spirit. Provided there are no obstacles put in the way of human nature, man's affairs will intensify by the day and his needs will multiply. The actual experience of the world will bear this out. For human life is by nature compatible with modern civilization; the relation of the two is not accidental. In truth, their connection seems to be fulfilling the hidden design of the lord of creation.

By following this line of discussion we may discover one more thing, and that is the difference between Japanese and Chinese civilization. In both China and Japan there evolved an absolute autocracy or theocracy in which the exalted pedigree of the ruler was Heaven-bestowed and both the most sacrosanct and the most powerful were united in one person. It controlled society and, penetrating deeply into men's minds, determined the direction their thoughts were to take. Since the minds of those who lived under such a rule were always faced in one direction and they had no freedom to think for themselves, their activities of mind were always simple (and never complex). Whenever this system of social intercourse was upset by even a minor upheaval, whether a just one or not, the result each time was that a breath of freedom entered men's minds.

Toward the end of the Zhou period China fell into a condition of rule by petty princes, and several hundred years followed in which the people knew no rule by the Zhou Court. The entire country was in turmoil during this time; autocratic despotism lost considerable ground, and, as soon as there was a little room in people's minds, their thoughts naturally turned towards freedom. Throughout the three thousand and some odd years of Chinese civilization there was never a time when conflicting teachings were more loudly proclaimed or when black and white were so completely opposite than at the end of the Zhou.* These were the heresies of which Confucius and Mencius spoke. Yet, though these ideas may have been heretical from the standpoint of Confucius and Mencius, from the heretics' point of view it was Confucius and Mencius who were the heretics! Since there are very few documents extant today this may be hard to prove, but it is probably safe to conjecture that in those days the Chinese mind was quite active and filled with the spirit of freedom.

When the First Emperor of Qin unified the country and burned the books, it was not only the teachings of Confucius and Mencius that he abhorred; he thought that all the conflicting theories and disputes among the hundred schools, of Confucius and Mencius and of Yang Zhu and Mozi alike, ought to be prohibited. If in those days only the teachings of Confucius and Mencius had existed, you can be sure the First Emperor of Qin would not have had to burn the books. This is proved by the fact that, though there were tyrants the equal of the First Emperor of Qin in later times, the teachings of Confucius and Mencius were never again considered dangerous. Their teachings were no real threat to any despot. Why, then, did the First Emperor of Qin so detest the theories and disputes of the hundred schools and prohibit them? Simply because their voices were loud and they were a serious threat to his hegemony. Since his only reason was that they were a threat to his rule, this clearly shows that elements of freedom must have emerged during the disputes among the hundred schools. If you maintain only a single school of thought, no matter how pure and good, it will by its very nature hinder freedom. We know that the spirit of freedom can exist only in an atmosphere of diversity of ideas and contending views.

---

* I [Fukuzawa] am referring to the number of theories proclaimed by Laozi, Zhuangzi, Yang Zhu, Mozi, and others.

The First Emperor of Qin cut off the sources of diverse ideas; and although Chinese government long remained autocratic and one dynasty gave way to another, there was no reform in the patterns of society. The Chinese people were ruled by a combination in one person of the most sacrosanct and the most powerful, and, since the teachings of Confucius and Mencius were most convenient for the maintenance of this system, only they were propagated throughout the country.

Now, one view holds that, although Chinese government was autocratic, there were at least changes of dynasty, but since Japan has had unbroken imperial succession from antiquity, the minds of the Japanese people are even more ossified! However, this strikes only at the surface of the issue without grasping the heart of it. One who is well acquainted with the facts would see that just the opposite is true. In antiquity Japan did have a theocracy which ruled the people, and the people's minds were simple, unquestioningly believing the one in whom the most sacrosanct and the most powerful positions in the land were united. Here, of course, the Japanese people were no different from the Chinese, in that their minds were inclined in a single direction. But by the late classical times the social fabric had broken down, and the political power lay in the hands of the samurai; the most sacrosanct was not necessarily the most powerful, and the most powerful was not necessarily the most sacrosanct. The two concepts of the most sacrosanct and the most powerful were so obviously distinct that people could hold in their heads, as it were, the simultaneous existence and functioning of the two ideas. Once they did so, they could not help adding a third, the principle of reason. With the principle of reason added to the idea of reverence for the imperial dignity and the idea of military rule, none of the three concepts was able to predominate. And since no single concept predominated, there naturally followed a spirit of freedom.

This obviously was not the same as in China, where the people looked up to one completely autocratic ruler and were credulous slaves to the idea that the most sacrosanct and the most powerful were embodied in the same person. In the realm of political thought, therefore, the Chinese were impoverished and the Japanese were rich. The Chinese world was simple, the Japanese world complicated. When a man's mental processes are manifold and multifarious and his thought is rich, even his propensity to credulity will naturally turn into indifference. In an absolute theocracy the ruler may change his palace because of an eclipse, or rule by star-gazing and divination; the more people look upon the ruler as a god the more easily can they be led by their noses and the lower they will sink into folly. This is the way things are in present-day China, yet it is not so in Japan. The Japanese people are indeed foolish and extremely credulous, but this credulity comes out of themselves. The Japanese are thus not so subject to the excesses of theocracy. For example, in the age of the samurai in Japan, the emperor could move his palace because of an eclipse or engage in star-gazing and divination, but the people did not pay much attention to his activities, for the most sacrosanct emperor did not possess the most power. On the other hand, though a very powerful shogun was able to subjugate the whole country with mighty forces, the people did not revere his authority as they did that of the sacrosanct emperor, but rather looked upon him as a mere man.

It was truly Japan's great good fortune that the ideas of the most sacrosanct and of the most powerful balanced each other in such a way as to allow room between them for some exercise of intelligence and the play of reason. In today's world it is, of course, hardly desirable to revive the samurai class; had the power of the military elite been held by the Imperial House during the seven hundred years of shogunal government, or had the military elite, in turn, possessed the prestige of the Imperial House, with the most sacrosanct and the most powerful thus united and lodging simultaneously in the minds of the Japanese people, there would be no Japan as we know it today. But if today, as some Imperial Way scholars would have it, the people were to be set under a ruler who united in himself both political and religious functions, the future of Japan would be very different. We Japanese are fortunate that things have turned out the way they have.

In summary, I say that China has endured as a theocratic autocracy over the centuries, while Japan has balanced the element of military power against the element of theocracy. China has had but one element, Japan two. If you discuss civilization in these terms, China has never once changed and thus is not equal to Japan in her development. It is easier for Japan to adopt Western civilization than for China.

Earlier I mentioned the opinion that all countries ought to preserve their own national polity (*kokutai*) when adopting Western civilization. Although it was not my intention to discuss national polity here, when people discuss the adoption of a foreign civilization, the first thing that bothers them is this question of national polity. Many seem to feel that national polity and civilization are incompatible, and, indeed, at the present stage many refuse to discuss the issue. This is somewhat like both parties retreating before crossing swords; it will not resolve the matter. Only if we discuss the issues in detail shall we be sure to find the path to peace without coming to blows. Why should we skirt the issue and not discuss it? Not sparing length, I wish here to refute the argument of those who proclaim the primacy of national polity.

First off, what does the term *national polity* refer to? Let me put aside popular arguments for a moment and explain the term as I understand it. *Polity* means a framework or a format. It refers to a structure in which things are collected together, made one, and distinguished from other entities. Thus "national polity" refers to the grouping together of a race of people of similar feelings, the creation of a distinction between fellow countrymen and foreigners, the fostering of more cordial and stronger bonds with one's countrymen than with foreigners. It is living under the same government, enjoying self-rule, and disliking the idea of being subject to foreign rule; it involves independence and responsibility for the welfare of one's own country. In Western countries it is called **nationality**.

As there are many countries in the world, each has its own national polity. China has her national polity, India hers. Each of the countries of the West has its own, which it stoutly defends. The sense of national polity may originate in similarity of physical characteristics, or religion, or language, or geography. Although the reason may differ from country to country, the most important factor is for a race of people to pass through a series of social forms and share a common past. Even countries without any of the above common characteristics have national polities. The Swiss national structure is quite strong, but the various cantons within the country have different peoples, languages, and religions. Yet these people have a feeling of brotherhood. The various German states are virtually independent, but because their language and literature are the same and they share a common legacy of the past the Germans have till this day preserved a German national polity which distinguishes them from other peoples.

The national structure of a nation is not something immutable. It is subject to considerable change. It can unite or divide, expand or contract, or even vanish entirely. Its existence or disappearance does not depend upon such conditions as language, religion, and the like. Language and religion may continue, but if a nation loses its sovereignty and falls under foreign domination, then its national polity is said to have been terminated. For example, England and Scotland were combined into one government without either side losing its national polity. Holland and Belgium divided to form two governments and two national polities, but neither fell under the domination of other countries. In China at the end of the Song, the dynasty lost its national polity to Yuan. This event was the beginning of the end of Chinese sovereignty. The Ming, after destroying the Yuan dynasty, restored the pride of Chinese sovereignty. But then the Ming dynasty fell to the Manchus, resulting in the termination of China's national polity and the expansion of the Manchu national polity. Right down to the present the Chinese people have retained their heritage of language and customs, some men of talent among them have been able to rise to high positions in the governmental bureaucracy, and things outwardly look the same as in the Qing and Ming dynasties, but in reality the national polity of Southern China was taken over by the Manchus of North China. There are many other cases of loss of national polity, such as when India fell under British rule, or when the American Indians were driven off their lands by the white settlers. In short, the existence of a national polity depends on whether or not a given people retains or is deprived of its political sovereignty.

Secondly, every country has its **political legitimation**. **Political** here refers to matters of government. **Legitimation** refers to the justification of political authority. I shall translate this concept into Japanese as *seitō*. Therefore, what it refers to is the ultimate source of political authority recognized by the people. Political legitimation varies with world conditions and the times. Some accept the principle of monarchy as the criterion of political legitimation; others find it in decentralized feudalism, the parliamentary system, or religious institutions. These ideas of political legitimation originate, in the majority of cases, by dint of force of arms. But once established they no longer need to be maintained by force of arms. In fact, reference to the initial use of force of arms is usually considered taboo by those who later hold the reins of power. Justification of political authority is always grounded on some principle; that is, it is given a rational basis which is supposed to have lasting value. Therefore, as time passes rulers dispense with the use of force and ground their legitimation on principles of reason.

Since an abhorrence of force and a delight in principles of reason is natural to mankind, men take delight in seeing that government is run in accord with rational principles. With the passing of time, the national principle of legitimation is given increasing recognition. The past is forgotten, the present esteemed. Grievances eventually fade into oblivion. This is exactly what the political legitimation is. As a result, a reform of that system of legitimation will often require a clash of arms. Thus, the First Emperor of Qin destroyed the system of feudal princes at the end of the Zhou dynasty, and set up China's imperial system. With the decline of the Roman Empire in Europe, the northern barbarians poured in to set up feudal kingdoms. But with the advance of human culture and the buttressing of political authority by scholarly theories, "the balance of powers" turned again to peaceful ideas of legitimation and progress.

Consider also the case of modern England in relation to the same England of the early eighteenth century. Their political forms are so different we may be tempted to doubt it is the same England. In the latter half of the seventeenth century there were armed political insurrections in England; it was only in 1688, with the accession of William III, that the civil wars came to an end. Hence, though subsequently there occurred a great change in the principle of legitimation in the course of 160 and some odd years, the principle was changed so imperceptibly, without use of any military force, that earlier citizens felt the earlier form of government was the right course, and later citizens felt the later form of government was the right course. Again, even in uncivilized countries political legitimation sometimes changed without resort to force of arms. In ancient France the Carolingian rulers served as ministers to the French throne but held the real reins of power. In Japan the Fujiwara occupied a similar position in respect to the Imperial Family, and the Hōjō had a similar relationship with the Minamoto.

Change in political legitimation is unrelated to the existence of national polity. No matter how many times the former changes, as long as the political life of the country is internal to that country there will be no loss of national polity. Holland, which in antiquity had a federal form of government, is today a monarchy. France has changed its governmental structure some ten times in the last one hundred years. But in both cases the Dutch and French national polities have perdured intact. As I said above, the essence of preserving national polity lies in not forfeiting it to a foreign power. In the United States of America a native American has always been elected as president of the United States; this is based on the sentiment of internal self-rule.

Thirdly, blood lineage is called **line** in the West. The royal line is maintained by hereditary succession. Depending on individual national customs, the royal line may be restricted to male offspring, or to either sex exclusive of the other. The law of succession is not necessarily patrilineal. If a king or emperor has no offspring, his line may pass to a brother, or to one further down among his relatives. But the custom is generally to choose the closest eligible relative. This principle predominates in Western monarchies. There have been repeated examples of succession disputes in world history. When the king of a country dies without issue, and his closest relative happens to be the king of another country, the sovereign powers of the two countries might coalesce into one unified rule. This practice has been restricted to Europe; there have been no examples of it in China or Japan. However, in such a case the rule of two countries by one sovereign has had no effect on either national polity or political legitimation.

Therefore, national polity, legitimation, and blood lineage are separate matters. There can be a change of political legitimation without changing the blood lineage. Examples of this are the political evolution of England or the Carolingians in France. Also, political legitimation can change without effect on the national polity. Examples of this are universal in world history. Or the national polity can change without any impact on the blood lineage, as happened when the British and Dutch established colonies in parts of the Far East. They left the ruling families on the throne, but controlled the natives and their rulers as well.

In Japan, the national polity has not been changed since the dawn of her history. The lineage of the Imperial Family, also, goes back in one unbroken line to the very beginning. But there have been great political changes in the realm of political legitimation. At first there was rule by the emperor himself. Then power was monopolized by ministers of state through marriage alliances with the Imperial Family. Next it shifted to the military elite, only to fall into the hands of their retainers until there was a further shift, and direct power returned to the military elite. Finally, feudal institutions lasted to the end of the Edo period. Once the emperor lost personal power of rule, his position became that of a figurehead. In his evaluation of the Hōjō, Rai San'yō wrote that they made the august person of the emperor look like a helpless nitwit.[†] And what he says is correct. But why did such changes in Japan's political legitimation really mean no loss of national polity? Because Japan was governed by Japanese sharing a common heritage of language and customs. She never for a moment lost her sovereignty to foreign hands.

Still, there is something which deeply disturbs me. It is the tendency of people in general to focus exclusively on the imperial lineage and to confuse it with national polity; when this happens the unfortunate result is likely to be a stressing of one at the expense of the other. Of course, the Japanese imperial line has come down unbroken, together with the national polity, right to the present day. Since this is unparalleled in world history, the Japanese ruling line can even be called a kind of "national polity." However, if we think about it, the unbrokenness of the imperial line can be interpreted as a sign that our national polity has

---

[†] [Reference here is to *Nihon gaishi* (Unofficial History of Japan, 1826), written by the historian and poet Rai San'yō (1780–1832). The Hōjō held the post of shogunal regent in heredity under the Kamakura Bakufu. After fighting back the Retired Emperor Go-Toba's attack on the Bakufu in the Jōkyū War of 1221, they gained the power to determine the imperial succession.]

not been lost. If I may use an example from anatomy, national polity is like the entire body, while the imperial line corresponds to the eye. Light in the eye can be a sign that the body is still alive, but if one is interested in preserving the health of the whole it is wrong to concentrate on the eye at the expense of the rest of the body. For if the vitality of the whole body weakens, the eye, too, will naturally lose its light. The worst thing that can happen is to think the body is alive simply because the eyes are open, when in reality life has already terminated. The history of Britain's Far Eastern colonies provides many examples of the British killing the body and keeping the eyes.

From what we know of history, it is not difficult to preserve an unbroken line. This can be seen, in the case of Japan, from the time of the Hōjō right through the Nanbokuchō period.[†] Although at that time a split occurred over imperial succession, the affair has since been reconciled and is no longer a matter of great concern. The split was a temporary phenomenon. Seen by a later generation, it is clear that the emperors of the Northern and Southern Courts were both equally members of the Imperial Family, and this is sufficient to demonstrate that the imperial succession was never broken. Thus the split over lineage was once a very important matter, but if we consider the past from our present vantage point and focus only on the question of whether the imperial line was unbroken or not, regardless of the means by which it was preserved, there will be no problem of loyalty and disloyalty, of right or wrong. It is difficult to see a difference between Kusunoki Masashige and Ashikaga Takauji.[‡] However, if we take into full account the conditions of the times, we see that Kusunoki was not

---

† [The Nanbokuchō period (literally, "Northern and Southern Courts period," 1336–92) coincides with the early years of the Muromachi period under the Ashikaga shogunate. During this period, there existed two courts: namely, a Northern Imperial Court established by Ashikaga Takauji in Kyoto and a Southern Imperial Court established by Emperor Go-Daigo in Yoshino.]

‡ [Kusunoki Masashige (1294–1336), a samurai who supported Emperor Go-Daigo (Southern Court) in his struggle against the Kamakura Bakufu. He was initially criticized by the Northern Court as disloyal but eventually became renowned for his loyalty to the Emperor. Ashikaga Takauji (1305–58) was the founder and the first shogun of the Muromachi Bakufu. He was originally one of the loyalists who fought against the Kamakura Bakufu alongside Kusunoki Masashige, but ended up by establishing his own shogunal government and killing Kusunoki.]

fighting merely over lineage; he was actually fighting for political legitimation and a return of the reins of political power to the emperor. Thus he was putting the difficult task ahead of the easy. Even from what he did we should be able to see which is the more difficult task: preserving imperial lineage or preserving political power.

The common conception of people both past and present seems to be that Japan should be proud that she alone among the nations of the world has enjoyed unbroken imperial succession. But her only distinction here is that of the continuous imperial line, and yet it is not so difficult to maintain an unbroken succession. Even if the Hōjō and the Ashikaga were disloyal to the emperor, they still did not challenge imperial succession. A more important question is whether Japan has been unique in terms of political legitimation. Here too, Japanese political legitimation has frequently undergone change, and in this it is no different from other countries; thus there is no reason for boasting on this score. Japan's uniqueness lies only in the fact that she has preserved national polity intact from earliest antiquity and has never been deprived of her sovereignty by a foreign power.

Therefore, the essence of a nation is in its national polity. Both political legitimation and blood lineage will flourish or flounder depending upon the state of the national polity. In late classical times the Imperial House lost its sovereignty and a split occurred over imperial succession, but we have grounds for pride inasmuch as it was entirely an internal affair. If what Minamoto no Yoritomo, the first shogun of the Kamakura Bakufu, did had been the act of Englishmen or Russians, even were the imperial succession to have remained intact we Japanese would have no reason to be proud. Fortunately, there were no Englishmen or Russians around during the Kamakura period. Today, though, they converge on Japan from all sides! We must take heed of the way times have changed.

Now, the only duty of the Japanese at present is to preserve Japan's national polity. For to preserve national polity will be to preserve national sovereignty. And in order to preserve national sovereignty the intellectual powers of the people must be elevated. There are many factors involved in this, but the first order of business in development of our intellectual powers lies in sweeping away credulity to past customs and adopting the spirit of Western civilization. We can only enter into the world of natural science (kyūri) by completely doing away with blind credulity towards the outdated theory of yin-yang and the five elements. The same holds true for human affairs. Society cannot be preserved without getting rid of the credulity that shackles us to outdated customs. Once this credulity has been stripped away we shall be able to enter the realm of vital intellectual activity. We shall have achieved success when national sovereignty and national polity are supported by and grounded on the intellectual power of the whole nation.

It is extremely easy to preserve imperial succession. Let me ask you gentlemen of the land, isn't loyalty your topmost concern? Loyalty is indeed a good thing, but nothing less than complete loyalty will do. If we wish to preserve imperial succession, we must do so by increasing the glory of that succession. But the glory of imperial lineage will vanish if national polity is not solid. As I have said before, the eye too will lose its light when the strength of the whole body is sapped. If we value the eye, we must focus upon the health of the whole body—the light of the eye cannot be preserved merely by using an eye lotion. In view of these considerations, then, Western civilization is an incomparable means for both strengthening our national polity and increasing the prestige of our imperial line. Why, then, do we hesitate to adopt it? We should not even think twice about the matter.

I said that we must sweep away our credulity towards the outdated practices of the past. The expression *credulity* has many uses and various applications, but in regard to governmental matters it refers to the difference between true and false governmental authority. It is generally difficult to decide between things if the purposes for which they are used are not defined. A house is good for keeping out the rain and frost, and clothing for protecting against the elements. Every human thing has its purpose. However, when habits of use become ingrained over a long period of time, men tend to forget the actual purposes of things and value them for their own sakes. They become objects of adornment and affection which men may even strive mightily to protect, regardless of the inconveniences involved. This is credulity, the cause of this world's affectations.

For example, the samurai wore two swords during the Sengoku period[†] because there was no law people could rely upon and every man had to defend himself. But once the habit became ingrained, the samurai did not remove their swords even after peace reigned. It is bad enough that they did not give up their swords; worse still, they attached more and more value to swords: every samurai would squander a fortune in order to decorate his swords, and there was not a single samurai, young or old, who did not wear them. Were they really of any use? As a matter of fact, all the samurai did was inlay the outsides with gold and silver, while sheathed inside the scabbards were thin-bladed, dull-edged excuses for swords. Eight or nine out of ten samurai wearing the things knew nothing about how to use them. Still, though the swords were in reality quite useless, no one made a move to abandon them. Men had forgotten how to use swords, but the habit of making much of them had become ingrained. This is exactly what I mean by credulity towards outdated customs. If in these times of peace we were to ask a former samurai why he is wearing swords, he will defend the practice on the score that it is a custom handed down from his forefathers, that it is the samurai's badge—he will come up with no better explanation than that. Could any of them, now, answer the question by saying he really needs the swords at his belt? If the only reason for wearing them is that they are badges, this in itself is sufficient reason to abolish them! However, if there is some real reason for not abolishing them, they should be employed for that purpose, and the shallow excuses abandoned. There is no justification for the excuse that sword-bearing is a divine right of the samurai.

The same applies to matters of government. In every country in the world the reason for founding governments and establishing political institutions has been to secure national sovereignty and preserve national polity. Political authority is of course essential if sovereignty is to be preserved. We can call this the true authority of a government.

The business of government consists entirely in asserting this true

---

[†] [A period of intermittent civil war from 1467 to 1568. See the chronology in the appendix.]

authority. In the primitive age, man was still ignorant of the principles of nature and lived in awe of its external forms. Therefore rule over the people also naturally followed this pattern, and rulers could not help making use of irrational forms of authority. Let us call these false forms of government authority. They were necessary devices to contain the people of that barbarous age. Since these rulers were trying to deal with people at a time when the very first steps of human progress were being made after humanity had just emerged from the struggle for survival with other animals, it was inevitable that there were what we now would consider abuses of power. But it is a common vice of human nature to wield power arbitrarily when the opportunity arises, just as a person who likes sake, once he starts to drink, becomes slightly intoxicated and craves more, till finally the sake is driving the man on to drink more. In like manner, once a person gets his hands on the false type of power, he will become intoxicated with it and brandish it all the more recklessly, till finally the false power is wielding the man. When this practice becomes ingrained, he will dress up the outward forms of his government with even more false show in order to dazzle the people. Political institutions will lose their true purpose and the purely superficial forms will take over. When this happens, the ruler will take such government for granted, and tenaciously protect it even at the sacrifice of true benefits. He will set up a distinction between himself and the people—creating two altogether different species, as it were—and enforce this distinction by establishing differences between superiors and inferiors in regard to ranks, clothing, documents, and forms of speech, for all grades of society—witness the patterns of etiquette and social customs of the Zhou and Tang dynasties in China. Or he will not have the least hesitation about making such mad claims as, for example, his having directly received the "mandate of heaven" or his ancestors' having climbed the spirit mountain to exchange words with the gods of heaven, nor will he hesitate to recount dreams and recite divine oracles. This is what is known as theocracy. It prevails at the expense of the purposes of true authority which a government ought to implement. Thereby it creates a fabrication which leads to blind attachment to that false authority of which a government has no right to avail itself. Here is precisely where true and false governments part company.

The fabrication of theocratic governmental forms was a temporary device employed in the dark ages of the ancient past, but as human intelligence developed it lost its value. In the modern civilized world, even though a person is dressed in magnificent robes and bears some lofty title, can this any longer dazzle the eyes of the people? Such goings-on only invite the condescending smiles of the intelligent. One does not have to be a civilized intellectual. Even people who have just heard about or seen only a little of modern civilization will not accept such fabrications any more. They have risen to a higher level of intelligence. The only way to rule such people is to establish a contract based on reason and defend it by the true authority of political institutions and law.

Everyone in this day and age knows that a seven-year drought cannot be terminated by building an altar and praying for rain. They know that even if the ruler prays for a bountiful harvest this will not influence the laws of nature discovered by science. Indeed, every school child is perfectly cognizant of the fact that human prayer will not increase the harvest by so much as one millet of grain. In ancient times, a man once threw a sword into the waves to stem the tide.† But today we are in the midst of a tidal swell which cannot be stopped by superstitious practices. In the past heroes came riding on purple clouds, or so it was believed; today we can no longer look for men of talent in the clouds. The principles of things have not changed, but it means that human knowledge has become more sophisticated in modern times.

Do you not suppose it is a cause of celebration in our country that human behavior has become more sophisticated, that the intellectual prowess of the nation has increased, and that we have attained to the use of true authority in government? Consequently, it would now be the height of credulity if we were to abandon truth for fabrication, to lead men further down the path of stupidity by mere superficial display of external forms. If our aim is to assert false authority, the best strategy will indeed be to make the people ignorant and to return to the condition of

---

† [Reference here is to Nitta Yoshisada (1301–38), who is said to have parted the ocean in this way at Inamuragasaki in order to make a successful attack on Kamakura, the headquarters of the Kamakura Bakufu.]

original primitivity we were in at the dawn of our history. But if the people are reduced to such a state of ignorance, political control will gradually grow feeble. As it does so, that nation will cease to be—and that nation's national polity with it. This is hardly the way to preserve the national polity; on the contrary, it leads to its destruction. The whole thing, from beginning to end, will be a mistake.

Take again the case of England. Had they tried to preserve the old despotic customs of their former kings, they would have brought a quick end to the royal line. But the royal line has perdured. Why? Because they strengthened both the land and the royal institution by reducing the latter's false authority and giving free rein to the development of the rights of the people, thereby increasing the power of truth in national politics. This was the best strategy for preserving the royal family. You see here again how civilization is not a threat to national polity. As a matter of fact, national polity is enhanced by civilization.

In all the nations of the world, those that are credulous toward old ways take pride in things whose origins can be traced far back in history. The older a thing is, the more precious it is. Dilettantes cherish antiques this way. In Indian history there is a story about the first king of India, a certain Prathama-Rajah, who was a wise and virtuous ruler. He was said to be 2,000,000 years old when he ascended the throne. He then ruled for 6,300,000 years, before yielding the throne to his son. He lived on for another 100,000 years. In India there is also a classic called the *Code of Manu.** This classic was handed down two billion years ago, tradition

---

* An ancient Indian legend says that this book's name derived from its being handed down by Manu, son of Brahma, the god of creation. In the year 1794 it was translated by the Englishman [William] Jones. The gist of the book is a skillful recording of the despotism of the ways of the gods. But when it deals with the theme of moral cultivation, it is extremely rigorous and its doctrines are very lofty. Many of them resemble the teachings of Christianity. Besides agreement in content, their wordings are also quite similar. For example, it says in one place in the *Manu* that one should be kind to others in such a way that they are given no cause to complain; one should not injure another in act; one should not intend to harm another; one should not speak abusively to others; if spoken abusively to, one should bear it in silence; one should not repay anger with anger; etc. Sentences in the *Psalms* of Christianity resemble those of the *Manu*. For example, the **Psalmist** says: "The fool says in his heart, There is no **God**." In the *Manu* it is written: "The evil man says in his heart that no one sees his evil deeds, but God has seen into his heart and discerns his

says. You might say it was a pretty old book. But while the Indian people were preserving this revered classic and their ancient national customs, and thus living in a kind of trancelike state, their sovereignty was being snatched away by Westerners. The great spiritual land of India became England's kitchen, and the descendants of Prathama-Rajah became the slaves of the British. All this talk about six million years or two billion years, and things being as old as heaven and earth, was nothing but an absurd boast. In reality that book's origins go back no more than three thousand years. Suppose someone were to go along with their wild claim for a while, though, and claim seven million years for Africa to counter India's six million years, or claim three billion years to better their mere two billion; why, the Indians would have to close their mouths. Yet it all would come down to idiotic make-believe.

Let me add one more remark about this kind of braggadocio about the past. The scale of heaven and earth is infinite and vast. How can we argue over the age of a little book here or a family line there? The world passed through billions and billions of years in the twinkling of an eye of the Creator; the two billion years of which they speak is a mere split fraction of that second. Those who waste their energies in senseless debate over a fraction of a second have no idea about what is important in life and what is not. Let this suffice to silence the Indians. Anyway, merely being old does not make a thing valuable.

As I said above, Japan's imperial line has come down in unbroken succession, side by side with her national polity, making her unique among the nations of the world. This puts our country in a class by itself: an imperial rule enduring side by side with a national polity. Nevertheless, even if this connection with the emperors makes our national polity something special, to conserve it at the price of falling back will not be as desirable as putting it to good use and going forward. Taking the latter course will prove very effective in certain areas of modern political life. Hence we should venerate this union between the imperial rule and our national polity not because it goes back to the

---

evil spirit." Other parallel statements like this can also be found. (Above is my [Fukuzawa's] abridged translation of the listing found in Mr. Brande's encyclopedia [*A Dictionary of Science, Literature, and Art*, 3 vols, 1865–67]).

origins of Japanese history, but because its preservation will help us maintain modern Japanese sovereignty and advance our civilization. A thing is not to be valued for itself, but for its function.

For example, we do not value a house because of its shape, but because of its function of protecting us from rain and cold. If we valued architectural styles simply on the score of their being the legacy of our forefathers, we logically should make our houses out of paper. Therefore, if this national polity that goes hand in hand with imperial rule is not compatible with civilization, its incompatibility will be due to a blind attachment to mere empty show, the result of long years of custom. By eliminating such credulity we will be left with a practical utility. If we go on to a gradual reform of political institutions, the time will come when national polity, political legitimation, and blood lineage will become consistent with one another and they will keep pace with the present-day civilization.

Take, for example, the case of Russia today. If Russia were to reform her political institutions and immediately try to emulate English parliamentarianism, she would be unable to carry out her project and would cause herself great harm, to boot. Why? Because Russia's rate of development has been far slower than that of England, and the same is true of the sophistication of her people. Russia's present political institutions suit the present level of her civilization. Nevertheless, it is undesirable for Russia to maintain the empty show of ancient institutions indefinitely, completely disregarding the advantages of civilization. Russia must take careful stock of her present level of civilization; for every step she takes toward modern civilization she must also bring her government up one step, so that both march forward together. I say more on this point at the end of the next chapter, to which I refer the reader.*

---

* In this book I [Fukuzawa] equate the terms "Europe" and "the West." Although Europe and America differ geographically, the latter's civilization derives from Europe, and so I feel justified in using the general term "European civilization." The same holds true in the case of the term "Western civilization."

Chapter THREE

THE ESSENCE OF CIVILIZATION

AS A continuation of ideas introduced in the previous chapter, this should be the place to discuss the origins of Western civilization. And yet before going on to that discussion, we must first know what we mean by civilization. It is extremely difficult to describe in concrete terms, and, at one extreme, there are even some who dispute whether civilization is good or bad. Now, when we inquire into the reasons for such a dispute, we find that "civilization" can be understood in both a broad and a narrow sense. In the narrow sense "civilization" merely means the increase of what man consumes and of the superficial trappings added on to daily necessities. In its broad sense "civilization" means not only comfort in daily necessities but also the refining of knowledge and the cultivation of virtue so as to elevate human life to a higher plane. If scholars would make such a distinction between these two meanings of civilization, they would eliminate a good deal of fruitless argument.

Now civilization is a relative thing, and it has no limits. It is a gradual progression from the primitive level. Man is by nature a social animal. A man in isolation cannot develop his innate talents and intelligence. The community of the family does not exhaust the possibilities of society. The more society there is, the more people meet one another; the more human relationships broaden and their laws evolve, so much the more will human nature become civilized and human intelligence develop. Hence the term **civilization** in English. It derives from the Latin *civitas*, which means "nation." Civilization thus describes the process by which society gradually changes for the better and takes on a definite shape. It is a concept of a unified nation in contrast to a state of primitive isolation and lawlessness.

Civilization is all-important; it is the goal of all human endeavors. We can discuss civilization in terms of its various aspects, such as institutions, book learning, commerce, industry, war, government and law; but when taking all of these together and discussing their relative values, what criteria are we to use? The only criterion we have is that what advances civilization is beneficial and what retards it is harmful. Civilization is like a great stage; the institutions, learning, commerce, and so forth are the actors. These actors each play their specialized roles and thus contribute to the sentiment which the whole play attempts to express. If each plays his role effectively, the play receives the plaudits of the spectators, and the actors are considered good. But if the actors err in the timing of their entrances and exits or miss their cues, or if they are not convincing in their portrayal of emotion, the play as a whole will not hang together and the performance of the actors will be branded as clumsy. Although they may be subtle and convincing in their portrayal of emotions, if they laugh when they are supposed to cry and cry when they are supposed to laugh, their performance will still be branded as clumsy.

Civilization is also like an ocean, and its various institutions, book learning, and the like are the rivers which feed into it. There are both great and small rivers. Civilization is also like a warehouse. Everything goes into the warehouse—daily necessities, capital, human energies. The world of man contains much that ought to be abhorred, but if a thing contributes to advance in civilization, abhorrences are set aside with no questions asked. Civil insurrection and war are examples. To take an extreme case, even a tyrannical despot can contribute to the progress of society; and when his reign proves to be effective in advancing civilization, half the population will forget his former abuses and accept his authority. It is the same as spending money for something whose price is exorbitant; if the article proves exceedingly useful, most people will forget how much they lost when they bought it. This is human nature.

I should like now to take up in more detail some specific problems of civilization. Here is a certain group of people. Externally, they are happy and have things easy. Their taxes are light, they are not overworked, they enjoy just laws, and law and order are maintained in society. In a word, the basic requirements of life are so guaranteed that no one can complain. But this is merely the attainment of material well-being; it very effectively blocks the growth of human knowledge and virtue and keeps men from being free. They are treated like a herd of cows or sheep: led to pasture, fed, protected from hunger and cold. This kind of situation represents more than a simple oppression from above; they are hemmed in from all sides, just the way the Ainu once were treated within the Matsumae *han* at Hakodate. Can this be called civilization and enlightenment? Can you find signs of progress in knowledge and virtue among such people?

Now here is another group of people. Their material well-being does not compare with that of the former group, but still it is tolerable. However, their having less by way of material well-being is compensated for by their having ample room to develop in knowledge and virtue. Some of them propound lofty theories, and their religious and moral ideas are high. Yet the general principle of freedom has not been realized at all; they have concentrated only on those things which inhibit freedom. Some of them have acquired knowledge and virtue, but, like the poor who have received doles of food and clothing, their acquisitions have been due, not to their own efforts, but to a dependence on others. Though some of them seek the true way, their seeking is not of their own doing but at the prompting of others. The people of Asia are like this; fettered by theocratic governments, they have lost their vitality and have sunk to the extreme of worm-like servility. Can this be called civilization and enlightenment? Can you find signs of progress in civilization among such people?

And now here is a third group of people. They are self-sufficient in material things but have no social order and no concept of equal rights. The great control the small, the powerful oppress the weak. Society is governed by might alone. In ancient times Europe, for example, was like this. Can this be called civilization and enlightenment? True, the seeds of civilization are maturing here, but we can not call this particular stage civilization.

Now let's take a fourth group of people, free and unhindered, with no distinction between great and small or powerful and weak, so that a man can give free rein to his energies on the basis of sharing equal rights with everyone else. However, these peoples still have no appreciation of the values of social intercourse. Each person uses his energies solely for himself without considering the overall public good. Since these people have no understanding of nationhood or of social intercourse, one generation succeeds another without advancing beyond the stage of its predecessors. No matter how many generations pass, there are no traces of human vitality in this land. Present-day primitive races are like this. Though such people are not lacking in the spirit of freedom and equality, can we call this civilization and enlightenment?

In none of the above four examples can people be said to have attained civilization. What, then, does civilization mean? I say that it refers to the attainment of *both* material well-being *and* the elevation of the human spirit. It means both abundance of daily necessities and esteem for human refinement. Is it civilization if only the former is fulfilled? The goal of life does not lie in food and clothes alone. If that were man's goal, he would be no different from an ant or a bee. This cannot be what Heaven has intended for man.

On the other hand, is mere spiritual elevation to be termed civilization? In that case, everyone should be like Yan Hui, who lived in a humble hut and survived on only water. This cannot be called Heaven's will either. Therefore, there must be both material and spiritual aspects before one can call it civilization. Moreover, there is no limit to the material well-being or the spiritual refinement of man. By material well-being and spiritual refinement is meant a state in which these two aspects are really making progress, and by civilization is meant the progress of both man's well-being and his refinement. Since what produces man's well-being and refinement is knowledge and virtue, civilization ultimately means the progress of man's knowledge and virtue.

As I said above, the attainment of modern civilization is of the greatest importance. It embraces all aspects of mankind. Its potentials are boundless. We have only now reached the stage where true progress can be envisioned. Some contemporaries do not understand the implications of this and fall into grave error as a result. Such people say that there are other manifestations of civilization besides knowledge and virtue. Moreover, they say, if we look at the Westerners we see that they obviously have many vices. For they perpetrate fraud in business transactions, or squeeze profits through intimidation. We can hardly call such people virtuous. The people of Ireland live under the rule of the British, who are called the paradigms of civilization, yet they barely eke out their worm-like existence eating potatoes. To that extent the Irish cannot be called intellectually developed. Therefore, the critics add, civilization is not necessarily accompanied by knowledge and virtue. So the argument goes; but these people are looking only at present civilization as some ultimate in itself. They do not realize the great progress that has been made over the past. Nor do they realize that modern-day civilization has not even begun to reach the half-way stage of its potential development. How can we expect an immediate utopian perfection here and now?

Ignorance and lack of virtue are diseases of civilization. Looking for the ultimate level of civilization in today's world would be like seeking a person of perfect health in the world. The world population is huge; but show me even one person who has never had the slightest illness during his entire life. I do not think you will find one. Even if a man seems to be healthy, he is only relatively healthy with a couple of minor illnesses. The nation is like a person in this sense. It may be called civilized, but it has deficiencies just the same.

Others admit that civilization is all-important and that all human affairs must tend in that direction. However, they ask, are not equal rights the essence of civilization? If we survey the situation of the West, the first step in reform always is to overthrow the nobility. Witness English and French history. Or, taking an example closer at hand, we in Japan have abolished the *han* and set up prefectures, deprived the samurai of their privileges, and left the nobility bereft of their prestige. Is this not the principal idea of civilization? To formulate it in a general rule, then, it seems that in civilized countries monarchs are not allowed. Is this correct?

My answer is that this is looking at the world with one eye closed.

Civilization is something big and weighty, but it also is vast and spacious. Nothing is vaster or more spacious. Do you suppose it has no room for monarchs? Monarchs, and nobles as well, all have a place in it. Why get excited over such a small thing as titles? Guizot says in his *History of Civilization*[†] that a monarchical form of government is possible either in a country like India, where there is a rigid caste system, or in a country where class lines are blurred and people enjoy equal rights. Again, it can be exercised either in a world ruled under despotic conditions, or in a small country where enlightenment and freedom prevail. The monarch is like an extraordinary head, and the political system and social customs are like a body, and it is possible to take the very same head and tack it onto any body; again, the monarch is like an exotic fruit, and the political system and social customs are like a tree, and it is possible to graft this fruit onto any tree. This is indeed true. Every government in the world is the product of convenience. If convenient for a country's civilization, the form of government can be a monarchy or it can be a republic. For government is a pragmatic matter. Among the forms of government that have been tried in the world since the dawn of history, we can list absolute monarchies, constitutional monarchies, aristocracies, republics, and so forth. *A priori* arguments cannot decide which forms are best. An open mind is essential in this matter.

A monarchy is not necessarily unsuitable, and a republic is not necessarily good. Although the French Republic of 1848 had a reputation for impartial justice, it was in fact cruelly oppressive. Austria under Francis II was a dictatorship, but a benign one. The present-day democratic government in America may be better than China's monarchy, but the Mexican republic can hardly compare with England's monarchy. Thus, even though the governments of England and Austria are good, this need not mean we should therefore emulate the ways of China. Conversely, though we applaud the democratic government of America, we should not therefore copy the example of

---

† [Fukuzawa is referring to François Guizot's *General History of Civilization in Europe,*1828. He used the ninth American edition, based on the second English edition, with occasional notes by C. S. Henry (New York: D. Appleton and Company, 1870).]

France and Mexico. We have to consider the realities of government rather than judge by their names only. Since there are many different forms of government, when scholars discuss them they ought to be broadminded and not biased toward any one particular form. There have been numerous cases in the past of arguments over names, to the neglect of facts.

In China and Japan the ruler–subject relationship was considered inherent in human nature, so that the relationship between ruler and subject was conceived as analogous to the relationships between husband and wife and parent and child. The respective roles of ruler and subject were even thought of as predestined from a previous life. Even a man like Confucius was unable to free himself from this kind of credulity. His lifelong ambition was to help the Emperor of Zhou administer the empire; in times of extreme need, if there were any feudal lords or regional officials who would employ him, he was willing to serve them. His whole political philosophy was to serve under the emperor, ruler over the whole land and all its people. What it comes down to is that even Confucius still had no comprehension of a universal Way based on human nature! He concentrated solely upon the way things were in his own times; he was enthralled by the way of life of the people of his day; unconsciously, he was taken in by it, with the result that the teaching he handed down to later generations merely took it for granted that there was no other basis upon which to organize a country than the ruler–subject relationship. Of course, what he taught about the relationship between ruler and subject was extremely well thought out. Within its context, it not only was plausible but also seemed to offer the highest ideal in human relations.

Yet the ruler–subject relationship is essentially something that accrues to a person after his birth, so it cannot be termed an inherent part of human nature. What is part of nature is the root, and acquired characteristics are only branches. One cannot affect the root by one's argument about the branches, no matter how flawless the argument. For example, the ancients had no knowledge of astronomy and so they thought the heavens moved; then they worked out computations of the cycle of seasons on the basis of their idea that the earth was stationary and the heavens moving. The computations have a coherent logic to them; yet, since the ancients' conception of the nature of the universe was not correct, they erred, and their theories about the stars and planets were absurd and illusory. They could not even explain the cause of solar and lunar eclipses. In reality, there were innumerable inconsistencies in their geocentric theory. The ancients developed it principally on the basis of observations by the naked eye of the movements of the sun, moon, and stars. Investigation of the facts, however, revealed that these phenomena are the result of the motion of the earth relative to other heavenly bodies, and that therefore the earth's movement was the real cause for the way things looked. The earth's movement was the root, the phenomena were the branches. A mistake about a thing's branches tells one nothing about its root. Simply because the geocentric theory sounds logical is no reason for accepting it and repudiating the heliocentric theory. For such logic is not really true logic. It is really a theory that results from a strained explanation based on looking at the connection between appearances, without going into their principles. If you accept that theory as correct reasoning, then when you look at the shoreline from a moving boat, you ought to say that it is the shoreline that is moving and the boat that is stationary. Would this not be a gross mistake? Therefore, in a discussion of astronomy we must first consider what the earth is and what its rotations are. We will then be able to find out the relationship between the earth and the other heavenly bodies and explain the reasons for the changes of seasons. This is why I say theory should be based upon fact, and not vice versa. One must not do violence to the facts by proposing theories based on sheer conjecture.

The same principle applies to the theory of the relationship between ruler and subject. This relationship is a relationship between one man and another. It may be possible to discover a natural connection in such a relationship nowadays, but the close connection is the result of the fact that there just happen to be rulers and subjects in our day and age, so the relationship cannot be termed inherent in human nature. If it were an essential part of human nature, it would perforce be found throughout the world, but this is not the case. The relationships between parent and child and husband and wife, as well as the relationships between young and old and friend and friend, are universal, and so may be called innate in human nature. The relationship between ruler and subject is different, for there are countries on the globe where men do not have this relationship; countries that have established a parliamentary government are examples of this. These countries do not have a ruler-subject relationship, but various duties are divided between government and people, and the style of rule is very admirable. Mencius said that there should not be two rulers in the land any more than there should be two suns in heaven, but today there are countries without any king at all, and the conditions of the people are far superior to those of the ancient Chinese dynasties under Yao, Shun and others. If Confucius and Mencius could be brought back to life today, I wonder what kind of expressions would cross their faces when they saw these countries. We have to admit, the Sages were badly mistaken.

Thus in advocating a monarchical government, we should first seek to discover what human nature is and only then explain the principle of the ruler-subject relationship. We should then decide if that principle is inherent in human nature or just one that accrues after birth and as the result of chance circumstances. We should clarify on the basis of facts whether we should name this bond between ruler and subject a natural principle or not. If we investigate natural principles in a completely detached manner, we shall be forced to conclude that this ruler-subject relationship is not one of them. Once we do this, we shall be able to discuss the merits and demerits of this contractual bond. To be able to discuss a thing's merits and demerits is proof that it can be renewed or reformed, and a thing that can be renewed or reformed is not a natural principle. Therefore, though the child cannot become the father, and the wife cannot become the husband, for such relationships are immutable, the ruler can change into a subject. Tang and Wu, after all, overthrew their rulers. Or ruler and subject can be put on equal footing; an example of this is our recent abolition of the *han* and the establishment of prefectures. Seen in this light, then, a monarchical government is also not immune to change. However, the key criterion for whether to change it or not consists in grasping its merits or demerits in relation to civilization.*

---

* One Western scholar says that this ruler-subject principle is not limited to China and Japan; that in the West there are such terms as **master** and **servant**, and so such a system exists

According to my argument, then, monarchical government can be changed. Shall we therefore infer that it should be replaced by a democratic government, and that this latter is the best form of government? This does not follow at all.

There is a race of people in northern America. Two hundred and fifty years ago their ancestors, the founding fathers,** suffering British tyranny and unable to endure the ruler-subject relationship, left their homeland and came to North America. Despite innumerable hardships they gradually achieved self-government. The place they landed at was Plymouth, Massachusetts, a place which exists even today. Many brave souls followed their example, fled their native countries for America, selected new sites for their homes in what is now New England, and settled down there. The population and wealth of the country gradually increased, so that by 1775 there were already thirteen States. They finally rebelled against British rule; after eight years of bitter fighting, they managed to eke out a close victory over the British and then to lay the first foundation of a great independent nation. This country is the present United States of America.

Now, the reason for her gaining independence was not that her people had selfish desires or temporary ambitions; it had its basis in the natural principle of impartial justice. Defending the rights of man, these people simply tried to exercise their God-given rights fully. Their ideals can be read in the Declaration of Independence they composed at that time. Was there even the slightest thought of selfishness when those 101 founding fathers stepped forth on Plymouth Rock amidst the wind and snow on 22 December 1620? Indeed, they had nothing in their hearts but reverence for God and love of man. If today we conjecture what went on in their hearts, we can be sure that they certainly detested that tyrannical king and his corrupt ministers; but we can also suppose they

---

there too. But the Western and Eastern concepts are not the same. Because there are no Japanese words to express the Western concepts of **master** and **servant**, I [Fukuzawa] have translated them as *kunshin* 君臣, but we should not give undue weight to the word itself. The word *kunshin* is really a classical Oriental concept. In Japan, if a person killed his lord he was crucified, but a lord could cut down his retainers with impunity. This is how the lord–vassal relationship worked. And the relationship between daimyo and samurai in the feudal period was clearly a lord-vassal one.

** Called the **Pilgrim Fathers**, they were 101 in number, and they fled England in 1620.

fairly wanted to abolish all such governments from the face of the earth. They had this spirit 250 years ago, and the Revolutionary War of 1775 only bore visible witness to that spirit. When the war ended and they founded a political system, it was also based on the same spirit. The whole web of social institutions—industry, commerce, politics, law, and so on—that has grown up since then is woven around this idea. Because the government of the United States embodied the spirit of an independent people, and because it is a government based on their own desires, their social customs should be free of corruption and stain, they should have attained the best level humanly attainable, and their government should have become a model paradise on earth. Yet, when you look at the reality today, you see things are otherwise. Popular government turns out to mean that the people unite and use force, and this use of force does not differ in severity from that of an absolute monarch; the only difference is that in one case it is initiated by the whim of one man and in the other case by the masses. Moreover, the custom in America is to put a premium on simplicity. Of course simplicity is a fine thing, but if a society takes great delight in simplicity, men will use this simplicity to deceive or intimidate—like the country boy who deceives people with feigned simplicity. Further, America has rigorous laws prohibiting bribery, but the more strictly they are enforced, the more actively bribery is carried out. This somewhat resembles the earlier Japanese experience, when gambling was strictly prohibited but at the same time was extremely popular. There are innumerable other examples, which I would prefer to pass over now.

The reason why people generally consider government by the people a fair and just government is that it is based upon the united sentiments of a people acting as one—that, for example, one million people out of a total population of one million all agree and decide on one course of action. Between the ideal and the real, however, there is a big difference. As an example, take the matter of selecting representatives. In a popular government they follow the practice of simple majority vote. Since even a majority of one vote is enough, if in a population of one million the outcome is 51% to 49%, the one who is elected is biased towards one side, and right from the start 49% of the population has no say in deliberations of national affairs. If 100 elected representatives meet to decide some important government matter, and in casting their ballots the voting is 51 to 49, the 51 will decide the issue. Therefore, the decision is not made in accord with a nation-wide majority, but only by a majority within a majority. When elections are extremely close, it is possible for one-fourth to control the other three-fourths of the whole nation. You cannot call this fair (See Mill, *Considerations on Representative Government*).

In a parliamentary government there is much discussion. It is not easy to judge the merits and demerits of this form of government. In a monarchy there is the danger of the government's using its authority to abuse the people. In a democratic government there is the danger that the views of the people can put the government in a difficult position. If the government cannot stand up under this pressure and resorts to force of arms, it will end up inviting a great catastrophe. One cannot claim any special immunity from armed conflicts for a democratic form of government. Not too long ago, in 1861, America split into northern and southern factions over the slavery issue. Some one million people took up arms to fight a civil war of unprecedented scale. Brother clashed with brother, friend clashed with friend in mortal combat. The destruction of human lives and property over four years of war was incalculable. This civil war arose because the upper-class gentry in the nation detested the evil custom of slavery and protested that it violated the law of God as well as human decency. As admirable as their concerns were, once the civil war broke out, one thing led to another, and reason and morality were mingled with partisan interests and human passion, with the result that the real issues were submerged. Surveying the results of this war, one sees that on both sides the citizens of a free nation coveted power and acted in selfish interests. They were like a pack of devils fighting one another in the fields of Paradise. Their forefathers would have turned over in their graves to see their demonic struggle. If the civil war dead have gone to an afterlife, they must be red with shame before their forefathers.

The English scholar Mill wrote in his work on economics [*Principles of Political Economy*, 1848] that one theory holds that mankind's only purpose is progress—by any means available—in the struggle for supremacy, and this is the most desirable atmosphere for economic progress. Now, though everybody may regard this struggle for profit as the optimum condition, I am not at all happy with this view. The United States of America is the most perfect example in the world today of this struggle for profit. Young men of the Caucasian race (persons of white skin), uniting their efforts to cast off the shackles of injustice, opened up a new world; population and wealth increased; ever new frontiers beckoned the pioneers of civilization; the rights of independence and freedom were universally proclaimed; people were strangers to poverty. But the results of attaining the benefit of the best and the most beautiful have been disappointing. Their men spend their lives in the feverish pursuit of money. The only function of their women is feverishly to propagate dollar hunters. Can this be called the ideal society? I hardly think so. This observation of Mill suffices to give us some ideas of at least one undesirable aspect of the American character.

In view of the above, monarchy is not necessarily good, but neither is a democratic government necessarily good. The political form is only one element in society. It should not be taken as the criterion of an entire civilization. If that form proves inconvenient, it should be changed; if it does not, it can be kept. Civilization is the only purpose and goal of mankind, but there are many roads to it. Reasonable progress will come only through a long process of trial and error. Therefore men's ideas should not be turned exclusively in one direction. It is necessary to experiment on a broad front, for experimentation is the soul of progress.

But progress through experimentation does not mean achieving ultimate perfection. History has been an incessant process of trial and error. Even today world politics is in a state of experimentation, so that it is impossible to determine which is the ideal form. We can only say that a government contributing a great deal to civilized progress is a good one, and one contributing little to civilization, or even detrimental to it, is a bad one. Hence, in evaluating forms of government, our criterion must be the level of civilization to which a people has attained. There never has been a perfect civilization, and there never has been a perfect form of government. Should we ever attain a perfect civilization, government would become entirely superfluous. At such a point, there will be no need to choose one form over another or to fight over names. Because civilizations in the world today are in the midst of their progress, politics is also clearly in a state of progress. Nations differ only in the rate of their evolution. If one compares England and Mexico and England's civilization is superior to Mexico's, then England is probably more advanced politically than Mexico; and though American manners and customs leave much to be desired, if upon comparison with Chinese civilization some of them prove superior, then this means the American government is better than the Chinese government. Thus both monarchical and republican forms of government have their good and bad features. But politics is not the only source of civilization. It is only one accompanying facet, together with book learning, commerce, and so on, as I said before. Therefore if we may liken civilization to a deer, politics may be termed the hunting party. The hunting party is, naturally, composed of more than one person, and the method of shooting arrows will differ from person to person. However, they all have one objective, to shoot the deer and take it home. Whether they shoot standing up or shoot kneeling down, or, depending on circumstances, even capture the deer without using any weapons, makes no difference. But to be wedded to one determinate form of shooting and to refuse to shoot until one is in the proper position, to let the deer escape when it could have been taken, can only be described as wretched hunting.

Chapter FOUR

THE KNOWLEDGE AND VIRTUE OF THE PEOPLE
OF A COUNTRY

I N THE previous chapter I said that civilization refers to man's progress in knowledge and virtue. Does that mean if you have a man with knowledge and virtue you can call him a civilized person? My answer is, Yes, you can call him a civilized person. However, that still does not tell you if the country he lives in is a civilized country or not. Civilization should not be discussed in terms of an individual but only in terms of an entire nation. Though we here describe the Western nations as civilized and Asian countries as only semi-civilized, if we were to take only two or three individuals as samples, then there would be boorish and stupid people in the West, too, and outstandingly wise and virtuous persons in Asia, too. To say that the West is civilized and Asia uncivilized means that in the West the very stupid cannot give free rein to their stupidity, and that in Asia the very outstanding cannot give free rein to their knowledge and virtue. This is because civilization is not a matter of the knowledge or ignorance of individuals but of the spirit of entire nations. Thus we can only judge a nation civilized by considering the spirit which pervades the whole land. This "spirit" is a manifestation of the knowledge and virtue of the entire population. It goes through cycles of change and is the source of national vitality at any given moment. Once we have been able to determine the presence of this spirit, the degree of civilization of the whole nation will become clear and it will be easy to evaluate and discuss its merits and demerits, easier even than fishing a thing from one's pocket.

Since this spirit is national rather than individual, one cannot see or hear it even if one tries to; even if by chance one did see or hear it, one's visual and auditory impressions would always be contradictory and a fair judgment would be impossible. The same thing holds true when, for example, in order to determine how much of a certain province is mountainous and how much is marshland, one first of all surveys that province's mountains and marshy areas; then, on the basis of its total area, one can label it a mountainous or a marshy province. But a large mountain or two or a vast marsh here or there would not entitle one to draw a hasty conclusion and label it a marshy or a mountainous province. Hence, in seeking to discover the spirit of an entire nation and the general tenor of its knowledge and virtue, it is necessary to consider their manifestations in the people as a whole. This knowledge and virtue cannot be described as an individual's knowledge and virtue, but as the nation's. In the final analysis it is the sum total of the knowledge and virtue distributed throughout the entire country that is meant by a nation's knowledge and virtue. Once one knows more or less how much there is, it is not hard to judge its degree of advancement or backwardness, increase or decrease, and then to determine its overall trend. The movement of such knowledge and virtue resembles that of a strong wind, or the current of a river. Though the speed and direction of a strong wind blowing from the north or a current flowing from west to east can be seen clearly from a high vantage point, if one takes shelter inside a house there will seem to be no wind at all, or if one observes only the point where the river water is in contact with the bank the river will seem to be standing still. And if something is obstructing the river's flow, it might even be flowing in the opposite direction. However, since this reversal of direction would be due only to some obstacle to the river's flow, one would be unable to judge which way the river was flowing by looking at only the portion flowing backwards. One's view always has to be from a lofty vantage point.

In economic theory, for example, the basis of wealth is said to lie in honesty, diligence, and frugality. If you take a Western businessman and a Japanese businessman and compare their business practices, you may find that the Japanese businessman is certainly not lacking in honesty and diligence, and he is far more frugal than his Western counterpart.

But when you consider the conditions resulting from the business of the whole country, then Japan cannot stand comparison with any country in the West. Again, from ancient times China has laid claim to being a country of Confucian morality; though this may sound like a self-conceit, still, the reputation would not be possible if there were no foundation for it in fact. And from ancient times China has in fact had many praiseworthy gentlemen who acted in accord with Confucian ethical ideals. Even today there are not a few such honorable personages there, but a look at the situation of China as a whole reveals that murderers and thieves are rife, and, despite the severity of the laws, criminal acts are constantly on the increase. The baseness and vileness of human sentiments and social manners can be styled one indicator of the true state of affairs in an Asian country. Hence China is not a repository of Confucian morality, but a country in which there are some who live up to Confucian morality.

The workings of the human mind are complex and constantly changing. Today's gentleman is tomorrow's commoner and today's enemy tomorrow's friend. The greater the fluctuations, the more extraordinary life's transformations can be. Like a phantom or a demon, they are not subject to conceptualization or quantification. We cannot take the measure of another's mind, even among our own flesh and blood. What is more, in reality one does not have mastery over even his own mind. This is what is meant by the expression "I am not the man I used to be." It is quite like the unpredictability of the weather.

Once upon a time Kinoshita Tōkichi[†] absconded with six *ryō* of his master's gold and used the money to purchase a position as a retainer to Oda Nobunaga. As he rose in the military ranks he changed his name to Hashiba Hideyoshi—combining for his surname the names of Niwa [Nagahide] and Shibata [Katsuie],[‡] whose feats he admired—then went on to become one of Nobunaga's leading generals. Afterwards he grappled with a host of troubles, sometimes losing, sometimes winning,

---

† [An early name of Toyotomi Hideyoshi (1536?-98). He was also known as Hashiba Hideyoshi. On gaining control of Japan, Hideyoshi received the title of Taikō.]

‡ [That is, he combined the 羽 of Niwa 丹羽 and the 柴 of Shibata 柴田.]

as chance would have it, and in the end he came to dominate the whole of Japan and grip the reins of government under the title of Toyotomi Taikō. Even today everyone sings the praises of his accomplishments. But when Tōkichi first absconded with the six *ryō* of gold, how could he have even dreamed of someday dominating the entire country! Even after he was in the service of Nobunaga, did he not change his name merely because he envied the reputations of Niwa and Shibata? Thus we can infer that his original ambition was not so grandiose. Therefore, the fact that he escaped arrest when he pilfered his master's money was an unexpected stroke of luck for Tōkichi the thief. Next, when, in the service of Nobunaga, he became a high-ranking officer, it was an unexpected stroke of luck for Tōkichi the retainer. Later, when he spent years conquering the land and finally secured a hold on the whole country, it was an unexpected stroke of luck for Hashiba Hideyoshi. Hence, when the man holding the position of Taikō looked back upon his past and recalled how he stole the six *ryō* of gold, he must surely have felt that every one of his achievements was nothing but the result of chance, and just as surely must have felt he was living in a dream.

Later scholars who have evaluated Toyotomi Hideyoshi have all tried to characterize his whole life on the basis of what he said and did when he was Taikō, and have thus produced a serious distortion of the man. First he was Tōkichi, then Hashiba, and finally Taikō; these were three stages in one and the same man's life history. When he was Tōkichi he had one mentality, when he was Hashiba he had another mentality, and, finally, when he was Taikō he spontaneously took on the mentality of Taikō. The workings of his mind, therefore, had a beginning, a middle, and an end, and were not uniformly the same through all stages of his life. To speak more precisely, his mind passed through a thousand stages—thousands, even—all showing a kaleidoscopic variety of differences. Ignorant of this general principle, scholars of all ages use such expressions as the following when they sum up a person: "So-and-so was ambitious even from his early childhood," "So-and-so said some amazing things at the age of three," "At five, so-and-so was working prodigies." In extreme cases some scholars have recorded portentous signs occurring before the man's birth, or have recounted as part of the man's memoirs certain dreams people had about him. The height of fantasy and absurdity.*

Every man is either lofty or low in his integrity and aims, depending upon his education and natural endowments. Men with lofty natural endowments will aim at higher achievements than those with low endowments. But I do not here mean to say that a man of great purpose will necessarily accomplish a great task. Nor does one who accomplishes something great necessarily set out to do so from childhood. What I mean is that, even though a man's general purpose commits him to a general course of life, his purposes and deeds undergo all manner of change, and, if he happens to ride on the crest of fortune, he may end up producing something of lasting merit. Let scholars not mistake the point I am trying to make.

In the light of the above discussion, it may seem that we cannot fathom the changes of the human mind. But shall we then conclude that the workings of the human mind depend entirely on chance, and have no rhyme or reason? My reply is, By no means.

I say to those who discuss civilization that there is a way to take the measure of the changes of the human mind, and thereby to detect certain patterns of human conduct about which we can no more err than if we were looking at an object's physical shape or reading letters cut into a block of wood. What is this method? It is to take all the human sentiments in the land *en masse*, compare them over a long period of time, and draw conclusions on the basis of empirical observation. It is, for example, like predicting the weather. Sunshine in the morning does not enable one to forecast rain in the evening. It is beyond human power to lay down a determinate rule stipulating that

---

* Among the so-called "true" histories, one claims that Toyotomi Taikō's mother dreamed that the sun entered her bosom and impregnated her; Emperor Go-Daigo (r. 1318–39) is recorded as having gained the services of Kusunoki Masashige and his son because he dreamed of a southern tree [the Kusunoki name—楠—is a combination of tree and south: 木, 南]; and Emperor Gaozu of Han was said to resemble a dragon because of a dragon omen that preceded his birth. There is no end to such poppycock in Chinese and Japanese history. Scholars dupe people with these fanciful stories. What is worse, they themselves credulously believe them. Because of an excessive preoccupation with the past, they worship ancient heroes. In order to amaze the people of today and make the heroes seem beyond their reach, they make up farfetched stories of their accomplishments. They are our academic fortunetellers.

several days of sunshine will be followed by so-and-so many days of rain. But if we were to average up the number of rainy and sunny days in the course of a year, we could predict that sunny days will outnumber rainy ones. By taking statistical measurements of a whole province or country, predictions about weather patterns can be made more precise. If we widen our sample to take in worldwide weather patterns, and over several decades, then we can predict general weather patterns accurate to within a few days' difference. If we did this for a hundred, or a thousand years, we could really get it down to a difference of less than a minute. The workings of the human mind can be understood similarly. We cannot generalize from one man or one household, but in terms of the nation as a whole we can attain about the same degree of probability as in the case of the weather. In any country at any time, one can see the direction in which the country's knowledge and virtue are heading, by what causes they are advancing, and at what rate, by what obstacles they are retrogressing, and at what speed—the whole will be as tangible as a physical object.

As the Englishman Buckle wrote in his *History of Civilization in England*,[†] if we consider the spirit of a nation as a whole, it is amazing how we can find a determinate pattern in it. For example, crime is one such working of the human mind. A definite pattern cannot be found in it from studying the actions of one man, but as long as the conditions within a country remain constant, the number of criminals can be predicted. Take the case of murders. Many murders result from momentary passion, so it cannot be anticipated in advance who will murder whom at what time and place. However, the total number of murders in France can be predicted to be more or less the same every year, and even the kinds of weapons used will fall into statistical patterns. Suicide is an even stranger example. In the first place, suicide is not prompted by the orders, advice, deception, or compulsion of others. Suicide is the result of an individual's own decision. Therefore we might expect there to be no pattern to suicides. Yet between 1846 and 1850 the number of suicides in London averaged 240 a year,

---

† [Fukuzawa is referring to Henry Thomas Buckle's *History of Civilization in England*, vol.1, 1857, vol.2, 1861. He used the Appleton edition based on the second London edition (New York: D. Appleton and Company 1872–73).]

with a high of 266 and a low of 213.

Now, let me give an example closer at hand. A merchant cannot force a customer's decision. To buy a thing or not to buy it is entirely the buyer's prerogative. Therefore, when stocking goods the merchant must have a general idea of consumer wants, and avoid laying in a stock of unsalable items. In things like grains and rolls of cloth, there is no danger of their rotting even when overstocked. But in the summertime, a person who stocks up on fish and meat or steamed cakes such as *manjū*[†] runs the risk of total loss if he stocks up on them in the morning and cannot sell them by evening. Now, you can go to some Tokyo cake shops looking for such steamed cakes and you will find them on sale at any time of the day. By the end of the day the stores have sold their whole stock; you will never hear about cakes being left over, to spoil during the night. In this efficient arrangement, it is almost as if a prior agreement existed between the shop owner and his customers. For the customer who comes in at the end of the day and buys what is left over is, as it were, not doing so out of a regard for his own convenience, but almost as if he were buying the remainder because he did not want the cake-shop owner to have overstocked. Is this not an amazing arrangement? This happens all the time, yet if we go around the city and inquire of people how often and from what shops they buy cakes, none of them will be able to give a prompt, definite answer. The mind of these cake eaters cannot be determined by asking one man or another; but if the actions of the citizens as a whole are charted statistically, there will emerge a definite pattern governing the consumption of steamed cakes.

Hence, probable patterns within a country cannot be discerned from one event or one thing. Actual conditions can only be determined by taking a broad sampling and making minute comparisons. This method is called **statistics** in the West. It is an indispensable method for investigating and evaluating human affairs. Modern Western scholars, relying completely on this method, have made great advances in learning. If we chart the figures for land area and population, the prices

---

† [*Manjū* is a bean-paste cake. Bean paste spoils very quickly in hot weather.]

of commodities and wage rates, and the number of the married, the living, the sick, and those who die, the general conditions of a society will become clear at a glance, even things one ordinarily cannot calculate. For example, I have read that the number of marriages in England every year follows fluctuations in the price of grain. When grain prices go up, marriages decline, and vice versa. The ratio can be predicted unerringly. Since no Japanese has made such tables of **statistics**, we have no accurate idea of such patterns in Japan, but the number of marriages must certainly fluctuate with the price of rice and barley. Marriage is one of the fundamental human relations; people everywhere consider it important and do not enter into it lightly. The likes and dislikes of the prospective bride and groom, their social position, their relative wealth, the wishes of their parents, the advice of the matchmaker, and so forth—a hundred factors enter into the picture. For all these to be handled satisfactorily and the negotiations to be brought to a happy conclusion is, truly, nothing short of pure luck, something beyond the control of men. People say that a marriage is the result of some strange fate; you also have the Shinto idea that marriage is the work of the god of Izumo Shrine. These things show that marriage is the product of chance. And yet, if we look at the facts, marriage is not merely the result of chance, nor of the desire of the couple, nor of the wishes of the parents; and you can talk all you want about the persuasive powers of the matchmaker or about the spirits of the marriage gods, but the ultimate limiting and controlling factor on all these things, that which finally makes or breaks the settlement of the marriage negotiations, is the all-powerful rice market.

This principle will be a great help in discovering the causes for the actions of things. Every action has a cause. We can subdivide this into proximate and remote causes. The proximate are more readily visible than the remote causes. There are more of the former than of the latter. Proximate causes are apt to mislead people by their closeness, whereas remote causes, once discovered, are certain and unchanging. Therefore, the process of tracing a chain of causality is to begin from proximate causes and work back to the remote causes. The farther back the process is traced, the more the number of causes decreases, and several actions can be explained by one cause. The cause of water's boiling is the fire from the firewood. Air is the cause of human breathing. Therefore air is the cause of breathing and firewood the cause of boiling, but they still do not exhaust the possibilities. The basic reason why firewood burns is that there is a chemical combination of the carbon in the wood and the oxygen in the air, producing heat. The basic cause of human breathing is that we inhale oxygen from the air, and this joins with the carbon in the blood circulating through the lungs, only to be exhaled again. Thus firewood and air are only proximate causes and oxygen is the remote cause. Hence, although the activities of boiling water and breathing are different, and their proximate causes are too, we can make sound conclusions about them only when we trace back to their identical remote cause: oxygen. In the previous example of marriage, the proximate causes were the desires of the couple, the wishes of their parents, the advice of the matchmaker, and so forth, but they were not sufficient to explain the matter. In fact they tend to obfuscate the issue. Only when we go beyond them to look for the remote cause, and come up with the factor of the price of rice, do we unerringly obtain the real cause controlling the frequency of marriages in the country.

Let me give another example. Suppose an alcoholic fell off his horse, landed on his hip, and was afflicted with paralysis from the hips down. What method should be used to cure him? In the belief that the cause of his affliction was his fall from the horse, shall plasters be applied to his hips and only the bruised part be treated? A quack might think so, yes. Ultimately, falling from the horse was only the proximate cause of the man's affliction. Actually, his long addiction to drink had already been weakening his nervous system. Before being afflicted with paralysis, he just happened to take a spill from his horse; and the serious jolt this gave to his weakened nervous system just happened to bring on the sudden paralysis. Thus the only way to cure the sickness will be to restore the health of his weakened nervous system, the remote cause of his affliction, by prohibiting him from drinking. Now, while it may be easy for anyone with a knowledge of medicine to diagnose the causes of illness and prescribe correct remedies, it is not an easy matter for scholars to discuss civilization. These latter are all of a kind: quacks. Credulous of what they see and hear, they know nothing about going to the remote causes of things. Pulled now this way, now that, speaking out brashly, venturing grand schemes as the spirit moves them, they merely grope in the dark, tapping their canes in pitch-blackness. We have to pity such men, but we also have to fear for society. Great prudence is a must.

As I said above, because civilization is an expression of the human knowledge and virtue distributed widely among a people as a whole, political health and national prosperity also pertain to this general knowledge and virtue and are not to be limited to the abilities of a few men. The forces of a whole country cannot be put in motion or stopped at will by a handful of men. Let me show this from two or three examples in history. Even though historical examples in a discussion might make things long and boring for the reader, to include historical examples for the sake of illustration is like mixing sugar with bitter medicine to make it more palatable for a child. For it is extremely difficult to explain abstract theory to the uninitiated, and so it helps to speed up their understanding by concretizing theory with historical examples.

An examination of Chinese and Japanese history shows that rare indeed were the gentlemen of great talent and ability who were born at the right time. They themselves so lamented their fates that later scholars cannot help being deeply moved. Confucius was born before his time, and so was Mencius. Sugawara no Michizane was exiled to Northern Kyushu, Kusunoki Masashige perished at Minatogawa in Harima [Hyōgo]—to mention only two examples out of many. When a man happens to achieve something great in the world, people say it was "a chance in a thousand"; this is a commentary on how hard it is to be born at the right time. What is meant by this "right time"? Had the feudal lords of the Zhou dynasty employed Confucius and Mencius in public office, they would have been able to bring peace to the realm, but can we say that the lords' failure to employ them was a fault on the lords' part? Similarly, should the exile of Michizane and the death of Masashige be called the faults of the Fujiwara and Emperor Go-Daigo, respectively? Can "being born out of time" mean conflicting with the sentiments of a handful of men? Do the sentiments of only a handful of men suffice to produce that "right time"? If the Zhou princes had employed Confucius and Mencius, or if Go-Daigo had followed the policies of Kusunoki, would each of them have achieved that "once in a thousand years" success that scholars today imagine they would have achieved? Is not the "right time" something bigger than the sentiments of a handful of men? When men are not born at the right time, is it because their views conflict with those of their rulers? In my opinion this is not the reason. The fact that Confucius and Mencius were not employed was not the fault of the feudal lords of the Zhou; something else kept the princes from employing the two men. The death of Kusunoki was not due to the unenlightened views of Go-Daigo; the cause for his fall on the battlefield was something else. What was this "something else"? The trend of the times. The spirit of the men of those times. The level of knowledge and virtue distributed among the people of the age. Let me explain this.

Conditions within a country are like a steamship under way, and the man in charge of the country is like the navigator. A thousand-ton boat with a 500-horsepower engine, traveling a little over 12 miles an hour, can cross an ocean almost 3,000 miles wide in 10 days. This is the speed of this steamship. No navigator, no matter how he tries, can turn that 500 horsepower into 550. There is no way he can make the 3,000-mile crossing in 9 days. The navigator's sole function is to keep the engine running without a hitch and at top speed. If a person makes two crossings, and the first one takes 15 days and the second takes 10, the second voyage does not prove the skill of that navigator, but merely proves that the first navigator was incompetent and did not fully utilize the steam power he had. There is no limit to incompetence; with a steam engine a man can take 10 days, or 15 days, or not even move at all. But no matter how resourceful a man is he cannot get more out of a machine than it is built to give.

The health and prosperity of a government is similar. When it comes to shaping the times, two or three outstanding persons cannot grasp the reins of power and move the minds of the people of a whole nation, even if they try. Even less can they go against the sentiments of the people to indulge their own private wishes. This would be as impossible as sailing a ship over land. When great historical personages achieved success in their own times, it was not because they advanced the level of knowledge and virtue of the people through their own talents, but rather because the level of the people's knowledge and virtue permitted the successful achievement of their plans. Do not merchants sell ice in the summer and coal in the winter? They are simply following the moods of the people. Any merchants who opened up ice stores in the winter and sold coal on a summer evening would be called fools. If they tried to sell ice in the dead of winter and nobody bought their wares, would they have any right to complain? Could they lay the blame on those who did not buy? Ridiculous! Instead of bemoaning their misfortunes, they should store the ice in warehouses until summer, and during the interval of waiting they ought to inform people of what they will have to offer. If something fills a real need, when the time comes there will be buyers. Conversely, if there is no need and no market for an item, they should close up shop.

By the end of the Zhou dynasty, the people had grown dissatisfied with the restrictive ceremonies of the Imperial House. As the restrictions gradually lifted, the feudal princes turned against the Son of Heaven, the grandees controlled the feudal princes, ministers grasped the reins of power, control over the land was fragmented. It was a time when the prerogatives of the feudal nobility were fought over, and there were none who emulated the ways of Yao and Shun by ceding their own power. The nobility was the only thing that mattered, nobody cared about the common people. In such a situation anyone who wanted to aid the weaker nobles and control the powerful ones would have been able to seize power merely by going along with the mood of the people. This is how the hegemonies of Duke Huan of Qi and Duke Wen of Jin were gained. At this time Confucius advocated only the ways of government of Yao and Shun and proposed to transform the empire through moral principle. Of course, this actually never happened. In reality, Confucius was further removed from the trend of his times than were other contemporary officials like Guan Zhong.

Mencius's case was even more difficult. In his time there was a trend toward unification of the feudal principalities. Powerful hegemonies could never be achieved by aiding the weak and controlling the strong; it was a time when the strong and the great annihilated or swallowed up the weak and the little. Su Qin and Zhang Yi were busy in all directions, helping here, destroying there. With the entire country in turmoil, with battles being fought in all quarters, the nobles had more than enough to do to protect themselves. How could they bother about the common folk or be worried about their little half-acre plots of land? The only thing the princes were interested in was their own safety, and they used the common folk for their own political advantages. Any enlightened or benevolent princes there might have been were too afraid for their own power and their own lives to heed Mencius's advice about administering benevolent rule. Caught in a vise between the two powers of Qi and Chu, the policies of Mencius were impractical. I am not here trying to vindicate Guan Zhong and Su Qin and Zhang Yi and to repudiate Confucius and Mencius, but I am suggesting that both these Sages were out of tune with the times. By trying to apply their teachings to the policies of the times, they only courted ridicule and had to lament the fact that they could leave nothing of benefit to future generations.

Confucius and Mencius were great scholars and rare thinkers in the history of the world. Had they been able to open men's minds to a new world that transcended the political limitations of their times, and had they been able to teach a doctrine of the nature of man relevant for all ages, their merits and virtues would have won wider acclaim. But throughout their whole careers their teachings never perfectly crystallized, for they were never able to go one step beyond the confines of their own horizons. Confucianism never was a pure theory; more than half of it was a blend of political thought, and thus it lost much of its value as **philosophy**. The disciples of Confucius and Mencius possibly read 10,000 books, but since they were of no practical use except in government circles, the only thing they could do was go into retirement and complain about the injustice in the world. But why should they have cried foul? Had their policies been carried out on a wide scale in society, everyone would have been in the government and no one under it. Confucius and Mencius distinguished between the wise and the stupid, superiors and inferiors. Since their disciples were quick to feel that they, as the wise, should rule over the stupid, they were also quick in turning to politics. Their feverish anxiety only earned for them the cynical remark that they were like emaciated dogs in a house of mourning. I feel sorry for the poor Sages.

There have also been great problems in trying to apply their theory politically. The essential doctrine of both Confucius and Mencius is the Way of cultivating the mind and the five fundamental relationships. Because Confucianism taught a spiritual humanity and righteousness, it can be called a teaching of the mind. Because Confucian morality is pure and unadulterated, it should not be made light of. For the private individual, of course, its efficacy is enormous. But virtue is a matter of an individual's interior life, and it has no role to play in man's dealing with external things. In a simpler society where human beings were fewer, it may have had some value in controlling the people, but it inevitably loses its efficacy as human civilization unfolds. One would be the height of credulity to apply these immanent and spiritual moral principles to external, concrete human government, or to deal with present human affairs in terms of the ancient Way, or to rule the people by the principle of benevolence. If we ignore the times and the places, we will end up trying to sail a ship over land, or trying to purchase leather garments at the height of summer.

Confucian principles no longer work in practice. Witness the fact that for thousands of years no one has ever really succeeded in ruling an empire with Confucian principles of government. This is why I maintain it was not the fault of those feudal princes that they did not employ Confucius and Mencius; the Sages were prevented from carrying out their ideas by the current of the times. That their Way was not employed in politics in later times was not a defect of the Way; the times and the places were just not right. In the Zhou era there was no need for the talents of Confucius and Mencius, for they had nothing to offer in terms of actual practicality. Nor was their Way of any value for later government, for there is a huge gap between a moralist's **philosophy** and a politician's **political matters**. Later scholars cannot adapt their ideas to modern times either. I shall return to this matter at a later point.

Kusunoki Masashige's death was also a result of the trend of the times. The day in Japan when political authority was actually held by

CHAPTER FOUR: THE KNOWLEDGE AND VIRTUE OF THE PEOPLE OF A COUNTRY

the Imperial Family had long since passed. Political power had come under the firm control of the Minamoto and the Taira since before the Hōgen and Heiji conflicts, and all the warriors of the land were the vassals of these two families. Carrying on the work of his ancestors, Minamoto no Yoritomo rose in rebellion in the East (Kantō). No one in all Japan was able to stand up before the military might of the Kantō, led by Yoritomo, the strongest man in the realm. The emperor was a nobody, and all eyes were on the Minamoto. Then the Hōjō took over the reins of power, but they left the Kamakura shogunate intact for they depended upon the remaining influence of the Minamoto. Even when the Hōjō fell to the Ashikaga, the latter were still a branch of the Minamoto.

During the times of both the Hōjō and the Ashikaga, various militant bands rose up in the name of imperial loyalism, but in reality they were opposing the Kantō forces out of a desire for fame, or motivated by a desire to replace the Hōjō or the Ashikaga. To have such people on the imperial side would have been like fleeing from the tiger at the front gate only to run into a wolf at the back. The deeds of Oda Nobunaga, Toyotomi Hideyoshi, and Tokugawa Ieyasu are ample proof of this. From the Kamakura period on, every lord who rose in arms used imperial loyalism to cloak his own purposes. Once they achieved their own political ambitions the cause of imperial loyalty became a dead issue; it only served as an excuse while schemes were afoot; once they were realized, the excuse was soon forgotten.

The historical records say that Emperor Go-Daigo crushed the Hōjō and rewarded Ashikaga Takauji by putting him in supreme command of all his generals; he placed Nitta Yoshisada under Takauji and completely ignored Kusunoki Masashige and the other loyalist lords. As a result, eventually Takauji's private ambitions were realized and the Imperial Family once again declined in influence. To this day there has not been a historian who has not read these accounts without gritting his teeth and wringing his hands, castigating the villainy of Takauji and lamenting the blunders of Go-Daigo. But such scholars have no understanding of the trends of the times. Real power in the land was in the hands of the warriors, and the seat of power was the Kantō. It was the warriors of the Kantō who crushed the Hōjō, they who reinstated the emperor to power. The Ashikaga family was a famous and glorious house in the Kantō. True, the families in the West (Kansai) were proclaiming their loyalty to the emperor, but if the Ashikaga had not changed their stance do you think imperial authority would have been restored? When on the day of victory the emperor awarded Takauji the highest honors, he was not rewarding him because he really wanted to but because, in accord with the spirit of the times, he had to pay tribute to the glorious name of the Ashikaga house. This alone tells us what the conditions of the times really were. Takauji had never entertained thoughts of imperial loyalty, nor did his power and authority come from his loyalism. It derived from the prestige of the Ashikaga house. He served the emperor because it suited his own purpose of overthrowing the Hōjō. As soon as he overthrew them he stopped using the loyalist ruse, without loss of authority for his house. It was by using the same ruse time and time again and by setting up his base of power in Kamakura that he kept his independence.

This was not the case with Masashige. Sprung from a small feudal house in Kawachi of the Kansai, he was able to gather together under the banner of imperial loyalism only a few hundred warriors. He achieved rare success despite countless perils and narrow escapes, but how could a house so poor rank with the famous Ashikaga of the Kantō? In the eyes of the Ashikaga he was merely a lackey. The emperor, of course, recognized Masashige's merits but for personal reasons did not rank him among his top generals. The result was that the Ashikaga controlled the emperor, while the Kusunoki family was controlled by the emperor. It was unavoidable because of the circumstances of the times. Masashige had acted under the banner of imperial loyalism, and if imperial loyalism had been the overriding force of the times Masashige would have reached the heights. Since it was not, Masashige had to struggle along. But that Masashige, the great champion of imperial loyalty, had to be content with being a subordinate to the Ashikaga, and that even the emperor could do nothing about it, goes to show that imperial loyalty was at a low ebb in those times. Why was this so? It was not merely because of the unenlightened views of Go-Daigo, for all the emperors from the Hōgen and Heiji eras on were conspicuous for their lack of intelligence and virtue. Even the embellishments of later historians have not been able to conceal their faults. Fathers fought against sons, brothers battled brothers, and people used their retainers only to do battle against their own flesh and blood. In the time of the Hōjō, even rear vassals decided imperial succession. The families of the Imperial House vied for position by slandering their own blood in order to court the favor of the rear vassals. So engrossed were they in vying for power within their own families, no one had time to spare for tending to government. The emperor really did not have control of the country; he was no more than a slave shackled by the might of the warriors.*

Even though Go-Daigo was not an enlightened emperor, his words and deeds were far superior to those of his predecessors. Why should he alone bear the blame for the decline of the Imperial House? Its political power was not lost during his time; a long accumulation of events had led the Imperial House to give up actual power and hand it over to others. For this reason, in the eyes of the people the military families loomed larger than the Imperial House, and the Kantō appeared more powerful than Kyoto. Even a rare sage emperor with ten Masashiges to lead his cause would not have been able to reverse the long decline. In this light, the successes of the Ashikaga were not accidental, nor was the ultimate demise of Kusunoki Masashige and his son. They all had a cause. The death of Masashige was due, not to Go-Daigo's unenlightened views, but to the trend of the times; he fell victim to the trend of the times, not to Ashikaga Takauji.

As I mentioned before, that great men failed to come along at the right time simply means that they somehow did not jibe with the general spirit of the age in which they lived. Those "once in a thousand years" cases of great successes are also to be explained as instances in which men are able to channel the populace's energies in the direction of the trend of the times. The independence of the United States of

---

* Emperor Fushimi [r.1287–98], in a secret edict to Hōjō Sadatoki, criticized Emperor Kameyama's choice of successor and then set up his own son Go-Fushimi [r.1298–1301] to succeed him. Whereupon the Retired Emperor Go-Uda [r.1274–87], Fushimi's cousin, complained to Sadatoki, had Go-Fushimi removed from the throne, and had his own son installed as emperor.

America was not achieved in the eighteenth-century as a result of anything done by the forty-eight leaders, nor was it due to the victories of Washington. The forty-eight leaders merely gave expression to the spirit of independence spread among the people in the thirteen colonies, and Washington only channeled that spirit onto the battlefield. American independence, therefore, was not some miraculous, "once in a thousand years" event. Even had the American people been defeated and temporarily set back, they would have produced 480 great leaders and ten George Washingtons. Eventually they would have been sure to win their independence.

More recently, some say that the defeat of France in the Franco-Prussian War four years ago was due to poor strategy on the part of Napoleon III, and the victory of Prussia was due to the skill of Bismarck. But this is not true. It was not due to any difference in intelligence between Napoleon and Bismarck. The final result was the outcome of the trend of the times, according to which the Prussian people were united and strong while the French were fragmented and weak. Bismarck was able to channel the valor of the Prussian people, whereas Napoleon went against the direction in which the hearts of the French people were moving.

Let me put this more clearly. Suppose Washington were made the emperor of China, with Wellington as his general, and he were to lead the armies of China against the British troops; what would the outcome be? Even if China had warships and modern cannons, these would be destroyed by British matchlocks and schooners. For the outcome of a war does not depend on generals or weaponry, but entirely on the spirit of a people. If a defeat is suffered by a large army of valiant warriors, the fault does not lie with the troops in the field, but in the lack of expertise of the officers, who have interfered with the troops' own momentum and been unable to channel their fighting spirit properly.

Let me give another example. The present Meiji government thinks it is not being entirely successful because the various head officials are not able men; even with a great deal of shuffling of offices and functions the results always end up the same. Because of the dearth of personnel, foreigners are being employed as teachers or advisors, but the affairs of government still show no improvement. It would seem from the lack of improvement that the officials are all incompetent, and the foreigners hired as teachers and advisors are all fools. Yet the present government officials are among the most talented men in the country, and the foreigners selected are no fools. There must, then, be another reason for the failure of the government to improve, something that makes it impossible for government policies to be implemented.

That something is extremely hard to describe, but as the saying goes, "The feeble few are no match for the mighty many." The reason why government policies fail is that the feeble few are always being hindered by the mighty many. Government heads are not unaware of the failure of their policies, but what can they do about it? They are the feeble few, public opinion is the mighty many, and the feeble few are helpless. Try to trace the origins of public opinion and you will find it an impossible task; it seems to come out of nowhere, yet it has the power to control the affairs of government. The reason the government cannot handle its affairs is not some fault of a handful of officials, but this public opinion. When the mass of society is in error, one should not put the blame on the policies of officials. The ancients felt the necessity of first rectifying the ruler's mind, but my idea is different. The most urgent national task is to rectify the ills of public opinion. Since officials are the ones who have closest contact with national problems, they should naturally have the strongest concern for the country and be sufficiently worried about public opinion to seek ways to rectify this opinion. This is not what happens, however. Instead, officials sometimes themselves become proponents of these popular ideas, or at least become credulous of and tend to favor them. These men are in a position where they are supposed to worry about the people under them, but instead they do things which cause people to worry about them. The blunders of government, which often seem as if the very same people are tearing down what they built up, are the doings of such people.

Under such distressing circumstances, it is imperative that scholars who are concerned about the state of the country advocate a theory of civilization, try to rescue all men, both in government and in private circles, who are subject to credulity to false ideas, and correct the flow of public opinion. The tide of public opinion sweeps everything before it.

Why should scholars pick on the government? Why should they find fault with every little act of officials? Of its very nature government will change its course in line with public opinion. Therefore, I say, the scholars of today should not blame the government but should be concerned about the errant ways of public opinion.

Now someone might say that, if we accept the ideas expressed in this chapter, then the affairs of the nation depend entirely upon public sentiment and nothing can be done about it, as though the trends in society were as much beyond our control as the revolutions of the seasons or the life cycles of plants. It seems government does not need men to run it, and scholars are all superfluous; business and the different professions can run by themselves, and nobody has any particular function to perform. Can this be called civilization and progress?

No, of course not. As I said before, civilization is a contract between men, and the attainment thereof is mankind's essential goal. Each and every person must carry out his function in the pursuit of that goal. The government is in charge of maintaining order and handling current affairs; scholars focus upon a wide spectrum of ideas to discover future alternatives of action; both industry and commerce manage their respective enterprises to contribute to the wealth of the nation. Each function thus makes its own contribution to civilization. The government cannot focus upon the larger context, and scholars cannot handle current affairs. Since government officials sometimes spring from the ranks of scholars, the two tasks might seem to have points in common. But once we distinguish between the public and private spheres and see the essential functions of each, we cannot help but make a distinction between the present and the future. It is the duty of the government to take the initiative and make prompt decisions on immediate problems in the country. But it is normally the scholar's task to consider the future in the light of the present and suggest policies for future courses of action. Some scholars today are unaware of this principle and show an excessive concern for current affairs; forgetting their own essential function they rush into the world to solve its problems. The worst of them bring shame upon the scholarly community by their incompetence when, employed by the government, they adopt some short-sighted measures that end up in failure. How foolish can people get?

The work of government is like surgery, a scholar's task is one of education. The two functions deal with different priorities, but both are indispensable to the well-being of the nation. While government deals with the present situation and the scholar is concerned with the future, the contributions of each are equally significant and indispensable for the nation. The essential thing is that they must complement rather than contradict, so that by their mutual stimulation and encouragement the progress of civilization can continue unhindered.

Chapter FIVE

A CONTINUATION
OF THE PRECEDING CHAPTER

THE level of the civilization of a country can be measured by the knowledge and virtue of the people as a whole. "Public opinion," which I discussed in the preceding chapter, refers to the views of the common people of the land and reveals the intellectual and moral level of the people as a whole in a given period. Now, while it is possible to find out how people feel through this thing called public opinion, I'd like to make two arguments on the matter. The first point is that the force of public opinion does not always depend on the number of people, but on the level of their intellectual prowess. The second is that even if people are intelligent they do not shape public opinion, for the simple reason that they are not accustomed to coordinate their forces. I shall take up each of these views in turn.

Firstly, one man cannot win an argument against two men; three men with the same opinion can coerce two others with a different opinion; the greater the number of people, the more powerful their view. As the saying goes, "No use bucking the odds." Now, all this may be true, but only when all of the people involved are on the same intellectual level. If all the people in a country are lumped together, the power of their views will depend, not on superiority of numbers, but on the greater or lesser amount of knowledge and virtue they have. A person's knowledge and virtue are like his physical strength in this, that one man might be the equal of three, or even ten, others. Therefore, we cannot gauge the strength of a large group of people simply by counting them. We must measure the amount of strength distributed throughout the whole group.

For example, if a hundred people lift a thousand *kan*, the average will be ten *kan* per man, but that does not necessarily mean that all are equally strong. Suppose we divide the men into two groups of fifty each, one group might lift 70 *kan*, the other 30.[†] No matter how they are divided, their strengths will be unevenly balanced, since one man might have the strength of ten. Consequently, if one were to select from these one hundred men twenty stalwart lads and form them into one team, then pit the remaining eighty men against them, it may happen that the team of twenty can lift 60 *kan*, while the team of eighty can lift only 40 *kan*. If one calculates on the basis of numbers, the rate is 1 to 4, but the ratio of their relative strengths is 3 to 2. Thus, strength cannot be determined on the basis of numbers; it has to be calculated in terms of the ratio between the amount of weight lifted and the number of people doing the lifting.

The strength of intellectual and moral capacities cannot be gauged or calculated in terms of weights and measures, but it does not differ in principle from physical strength. The differences between moral and intellectual capacities are actually more pronounced than differences of physical strength, for one man may be the equal of a hundred, or a thousand, others. If we could distil the knowledge and virtue of men as we distil alcohol, we would get some amazing results. Were we to distil ten of one type, we might get one *to* of knowledge and virtue; were we to distil a hundred of another type of men, we might barely get three *gō*.[‡] The views of a nation do not derive from men's physical constitution but from men's spirits, and so even those who are spokesmen of public opinion are not necessarily influential because of their numerical strength, but because they have the lion's share of knowledge and virtue, through which they make up for their deficiency in numbers and gain a reputation as spokesmen for public opinion. Even

---

† [*Sic*. Even though here and a few lines below one would expect the figures to total a thousand, rather than a hundred. A *kan* is a measure of weight, one *kan* being approximately 3.75kg.]

‡ [One *to* was about 18 liters, and one *gō* was a hundredth of a *to*.]

in the countries of Europe, were the amount of knowledge and virtue in the people to be averaged out, the stupid and illiterate would constitute a clear majority. What we mean by national or public opinion is, in reality, the views of the intelligent minority among the middle and upper classes; the ignorant majority simply follow behind like sheep and never dare to give free rein to their ignorance.

There are endless differences of knowledge and virtue even among the people of the middle and upper classes, some of which make themselves immediately apparent, others of which emerge after a long process of competition. National or public opinion can be called that view which is formed under the pressure of numerous conflicting views. It is the view that prevails in the newspapers and the lecture halls and that is much discussed by the people at large. After all, people are urged on by their country's men of knowledge and virtue and if the latter change their objectives the people will also change theirs, if the latter divide into factions the people too will divide into factions—they will all just blindly follow the men of knowledge and virtue.*

I shall illustrate this with something that happened here in our own country. Only recently, the Meiji Restoration saw the feudal *han* abolished and prefectures established. The nobles and ex-samurai lost their political power and their feudal stipends. Why did they not dare to complain about it? Some people maintain that the Imperial Restoration was due to the influence of the Imperial House and that the setting up of the prefectures in place of the *han* system was the result of decisive steps by those in government. These are mere conjectures, by men who know nothing about the trend of the times. If the Imperial Household was so influential, why did it have to wait for its restoration until 1868?

---

* People of the middle and upper classes who take delight in paintings and calligraphy belong to the literate and refined sector of society. Their aesthetic interests derive from their ability to appreciate the heritage of ancient art and from the enjoyment they get in comparing the skills of various painters. But today the custom of valuing antiques and paintings is universal in society. Even the illiterate and foolish will invest their scant savings to buy paintings and hang them in a prominent place. They store up old curios and show them with pride to others. What they do may seem ridiculous and far-fetched, but such stupid people are simply blindly aping the tastes of more refined people of the middle and upper classes. Also, some people's tastes lead them after the latest fashions in clothes, but they too are just imitating the tastes of others.

The Tokugawa regime could have been toppled long ago. The emperor could have regained political power at the end of the Ashikaga reign. The only opportunity for restoration did not present itself just in 1868. Therefore why was it that the Imperial House was restored and the feudal *han* abolished only at that time? Not because of the influence of the Imperial House. Not because of decisive steps by those in power. The cause lay elsewhere.

The Japanese people suffered for many years under the yoke of despotism. Lineage was the basis of power. Even intelligent men were entirely dependent upon houses of high lineage. The whole age was, as it were, under the thumb of lineage. Throughout the land there was no room for human initiative; everything was in a condition of stagnation. But the creative powers of the human mind are irrepressible. Even in all that stagnation there actually was some progress, and by the end of the Edo period antipathy to lineage had started fermenting. The people who felt this most were leading inconspicuous lives as doctors or writers, or were to be found among the samurai-vassals in this *han* or that, or among Buddhist monks and Shinto priests. All of them were learned men who could not realize their ambitions in society. Another sign of what I mean was that, among the literary works that appeared from the period spanning the Tenmei and Bunka eras [i.e. 1781–1818], the writers' complaints about injustice were frequent. To be sure, they did not come out clearly against the injustices stemming from the despotism of the pedigreed class. But the Kokugaku (National Learning) scholars, for example, bemoaned the decline of the Imperial Household; Confucianists satirized the luxury of the aristocratic ministers; certain playwrights wrote farcical satires about society. They nowhere explicitly attacked the ancient system, but a feeling of discontent over the conditions of the times can be read between the lines of their texts. As a matter of fact, the complainers themselves did not know at what to direct their complaints. They were in the same condition as a man who has some inveterate disease racking his body: he cannot put a finger on where it hurts, but hurt it does.'

The scholars of National Learning were not necessarily loyal retainers of the Imperial House. Nor were the Confucian scholars genuinely concerned with society. Witness the fact that, while they had retired from society to decry its inequalities, when any of them were offered official positions they would immediately change their tune and grumble no more of inequality. If an imperial loyalist one day had the prospect of getting a "generous" salary of five *to* of rice, he would the next day become a supporter of the Bakufu.[†] Any of yesterday's local Confucianists who received a summons to the capital are there today, lording it over everyone. These are facts, proven by actual cases both past and present.

Thus, even though towards the end of the Tokugawa period scholars started writing cautious expressions of imperial loyalism and social concern, it was not because most of them were truly convinced of what they said. It was just that through such phrases as "revere the emperor" and "lamenting over the world" they could give vent to their own frustrations. Setting aside, though, the question of whether their feelings were sincere or not, or whether their views were motivated by public or personal interests, let us seek the cause of their discontent.

Their rage was stirred up by the authoritarian structure of a Tokugawa society based upon noble lineage, a structure which frustrated their talents. Their unexpressed feelings of dislike for despotic rule can be confirmed by looking at the tenor of their words. They had

---

[*] In the earlier days of the Tokugawa's reign, when the Tokugawa power was at its height, writers were overawed by its power and did not fault the times. On the contrary, some flattered the Bakufu policies. We have only to read the works of Arai Hakuseki or Nakai Chikuzan. Later, in the Bunsei era [1818–30], Rai San'yō's *Nihon gaishi* expressed dissatisfaction with the decline of imperial rule; the spirit of his language throughout the book indicates that he held the Tokugawa to blame. The reason for this was not necessarily that Hakuseki or Chikuzan were subservient to the Tokugawa Bakufu, or that San'yō was a loyal retainer of the emperor. Their views were merely products of their times. Hakuseki's and Chikuzan's brushes were restricted by the spirit of their times. San'yō was able to transcend this situation somewhat and to vent his anger against the despotic rule of his time. Other things that flourished, especially after the Tenmei and Bunka eras, were Japanese Learning, short stories, satirical poetry and prose, etc. Motoori Norinaga, Hirata Atsutane, Takizawa Bakin, Shokusanjin (Ōta Nanpo), Hiraga Gennai, and so on were all high-minded gentlemen, but because they were unable to express their talents in public life, they indulged in idle literary pursuits. Through their pursuits they championed imperial loyalism, or described the careers of loyal vassals and faithful retainers, or else satirized society in comedies. They thus satisfied their injured sense of justice.

[†] [Such a salary, in fact, amounted to a mere pittance.]

no way of expressing their feelings during the height of despotic rule. Whether or not feelings can be expressed depends on which is stronger—the power of a despotic government, or the intellectual power of the people. The physical force of the government and the intellectual power of the people are direct opposites. When one has the momentum, the other loses power, when one's fortune is riding high, the other's is low. The relation between them is like the balance of two weights on a scale. When the power of the Tokugawa family flourished, the scale was always tipped completely in its favor. But in the later Tokugawa period, human intelligence began ever so slightly to tip the scale in the other direction. From about the Tenmei and Bunka eras, the various writings (these constituted the weights on the side of the people) still had little overall effect and could not bring things to a balance, much less tip the scale the other way. If the ports had not been opened, not even a learned man could have predicted when the power of human intelligence would finally have tipped the scale in its favor. Fortunately, Commodore Perry's arrival in the 1850s provided the favorable opportunity for reform.

After Perry, the Tokugawa Bakufu concluded treaties with various foreign nations. For the first time, the people became aware of the stupidity and ineffectuality of the shogunal government. People actually set eyes on foreigners and heard them speak, read Western books and translations, increasingly broadened their horizons, and then woke up to the fact that a government, even a demonic one, could be overthrown by human powers. Metaphorically, this was somewhat like a deaf and blind man suddenly hearing sounds and seeing colors for the first time. The opening wedge was made by those who advocated expelling the barbarians (jōi-ron), which did not derive from people's private sentiments but from a sharp awareness of the distinction between oneself and others and a sincere desire to protect one's own country. Japanese met Westerners for the first time since the founding of the Japanese islands. It was a sudden leap from the silent depths of night into broad daylight. Everything they saw stupefied their minds; they had no categories for understanding anything. Theirs was not a merely private reaction. When individuals are able to form even a vague notion of the vast gap between their country and foreign countries and they feel deeply responsible for their own country's welfare, this is public sentiment.

Of course, when darkness suddenly turns into brightness, men's spirits become dazzled and no one is able to view facts in a logical, orderly fashion; actions also become impulsive and irrational. Generally speaking, patriotic sentiments are rough and undeveloped in people, but when the national welfare becomes their goal they become public-minded citizens, and when their views all focus on the one object of expulsion of foreigners, they become single-minded citizens. Propose a single, simple view to a public-minded people, and the result cannot help but be a powerful momentum. This was precisely why the cry of "expel the barbarians" gained currency from the start. People in society were taken in by it for a time. Not yet realizing the advantages of intercourse with foreign countries, people first of all regarded the foreigners with hatred and attributed all the problems of society to contacts with them. Any calamities in the land they blamed on the foreigners; they went so far as to claim the troubles were being deliberately engineered by the foreigners. Thus no one in the land was favorably disposed toward foreign intercourse. And even if someone inwardly was in favor of such contacts, he could do nothing outwardly but meekly follow the general mood of the time.

When the Bakufu was confronted with the problem of foreign relations, it could not help but be influenced to some extent by this conservative attitude. Not all the Bakufu officials favored foreign intercourse, true; however, many of them espoused a rational course of action because they saw no way to counter the foreigners' power and their arguments. But in the eyes of *jōi* advocates this rationality looked like so much temporizing. The Bakufu was caught between the *jōi* position and the foreigners. Finally, unable to strike a balance, the government exposed its weakness more and more as time went on, while at the same time *jōi* partisans grew increasingly powerful. Not hesitating to brandish such slogans as "expel the barbarians and restore the past of Imperial rule" (*jōi fukko*) and "revere the emperor and overthrow the Bakufu" (*sonnō tōbaku*), they devoted all their energies to toppling the Bakufu and expelling the foreign barbarians. Men were assassinated, houses were set to the torch, and many other acts were perpetrated that gentlemen would frown upon. In the end, public opinion coalesced around the one slogan of "overthrow the Bakufu," the intellectual powers of the whole nation were directed toward this single goal, and the end result was the successful revolution of 1868.

Immediately after the revolution and the "restoration of the past," the foreigners should have been thrown out, but this did not happen. Also, whereas the new government leaders should have stopped with the overthrow of the hated Bakufu, why did they disenfranchise the daimyo and the vassals as well? There must have been a reason; it did not happen by accident. The *jōi* argument had been the clarion call of revolution. True, but it was only the proximate cause of events. The intellectual powers of the people as a whole were moving in a different direction from the beginning. Their aim was neither imperial restoration nor expulsion of foreigners; they used these slogans merely as an opening wedge to attack inveterate privileges and despotic rule. Consequently, it was not the Imperial Household that instigated the whole movement, and the enemy was not the Bakufu. It was a battle between intellectual power and despotism. The cause behind the whole struggle was the intellectual forces at work in the country at large. This was the remote cause.

After the opening of the ports, this remote cause drew for reinforcement upon the idea of Western civilization and thereby gained greater momentum. But an opening wedge had been necessary to begin the intellectual hostilities, so forces were joined with the proximate cause, battle was engaged in, and intellectual power emerged triumphant in revolution. The *sonnō* and *jōi* theories served as the opening wedge to stir men on, but after victory was won it gradually became clear how weak and unstable these theories were; people gradually abandoned mere physical force and banded together in intellectual groups, and this is how they produced conditions as they stand now. Power was thus slowly won by the intellectual forces, causing those of uncertain allegiances to solidify behind them. Since in this way Japan's national polity was preserved, it was truly our immeasurably good fortune that things worked out this way.

In sum, I maintain that the restoration of imperial rule was not due to the influence or power of the Imperial House; the Imperial House only lent its name to the intellectual forces in the country. The dismantling of feudalism was not due to decisive steps taken by men in actual power; the government was able to carry out its functions only because it was, as it were, in the service of the intellectual forces in the country.

In my view, then, public opinion was formed by the intellectual powers of the land, and the government was reformed and feudalism abolished in accord with this public opinion. Yet, if we were to count the number of people involved in this public opinion, we would find they were very few. Let us put the entire Japanese population at approximately 30 million; the number of farmers, artisans, and merchants came to over 25 million, and the samurai-vassals barely numbered 2 million. If you add to the samurai all the Confucian scholars and physicians, Shinto priests, and Buddhist monks, plus the lordless samurai, you would have a total former aristocratic and samurai class of 5 million, as against 25 million commoners. From ancient times the common folk were accustomed to have nothing to do with government, and of course they had no knowledge of even the events of the recent past. Therefore, the "public opinion" of which I speak necessarily came from the ranks of the 5 million in the samurai group. And even in this group there were only a minority favoring revolution. The nobility were those most opposed to it; next were the ministers and elders; then the samurai with large fiefs. Since they all stood to lose by revolution, they could hardly be expected to favor it. Possessing neither talent nor virtue, amassing great wealth, occupying high government office, and enjoying a reputation among the common folk for their opulence—that such people should be willing to give up all they had for the good of the country is almost unheard of in the annals of history. You can be sure, then, that there were very few among either the samurai or the common folk who favored this revolution. The only ones who did were men who came from unpedigreed families within their *han*, or, if from pedigreed families, men who harbored resentment for never being able to achieve their ambitions, or scholars living humbly among the common people, without position or stipend. All of these stood to gain by a revolution. To generalize, then, those who favor a revolution are men with brains but no money. This is obvious in both ancient and modern history. Hence, those who engineered this revolution were perhaps a mere ten percent of the 5 million within the samurai class. If you exclude women and children, it comes down to a very few.

Out of nowhere a novel opinion suddenly appears; before you know it, it spreads around; men of intellectual power take it up; people around them are persuaded, or browbeaten, or follow along blindly, or are swept along helplessly; the number of adherents keeps swelling; finally the opinion crystallizes into the public opinion of a whole country and sweeps everything before it, overthrowing even a demonic government.

The abolition of the *han* and the setting up of central prefectures were extremely inconvenient for the former aristocratic and samurai class. Seventy to eighty percent were unhappy with these measures and only twenty to thirty percent espoused them. But the seventy to eighty percent were the so-called conservatives—men short on intellectual talents who were no match for the intellectuals in the twenty to thirty percent. Although the conservatives made up the larger percentage of the aristocratic class, the progressive-minded held the majority of intellectual talent. The reformers won out by making up for their lack of numbers through their intellectual abilities.

At present there are extremely few who can still be called conservatives of the old school. None of the former samurai-vassals advocates retention of the old feudal stipends. Half of the old-style Chinese and Japanese Learning scholars have changed their persuasions. But they still fabricate farfetched theories that serve to cover over their original positions; they seek to save face thereby and to appear in the ranks of the reformists. They are like people who talk about reconciliation when they really mean surrender. Of course, "reconciliation" and "surrender," when they have been used indiscriminately for a long time, finally come to mean the same thing. Anyway, since everyone should march down the road to civilization together, the reformist ranks deserve to increase. My point is that originally the proponents of reform were able to accomplish their plans not because they were numerous but because they overwhelmed the majority by means of their intellectual powers. If today there sprang up among the conservatives a group of intellectually capable individuals who could gain organized support and who started advocating the old conservative position in earnest, they would gain the ascendancy and bypass the reformers. But fortunately the conservative camp has few men of intellectual talent, and those it does happen to produce turn against the camp at once and are of no use to the conservative cause.

It should be clear from the above that success depends not on numbers but on intellectual abilities. Thus, all social affairs must be factored in terms of the intellectual variables involved. One wise man's criticism should not be invited in order to please ten fools. Ten wise men should not be given offense in order to garner the adulation of a hundred fools. The criticism of fools is no cause for shame, the praise of fools no cause for joy. The censure or praise of fools is no criterion for any project. There is a story told about some later rulers, imitating the custom of drinking parties described in the *Zhou Li*, who now and then distributed free drink and food to the people. However, rulers cannot divine the true sentiments of the people by watching them enjoy themselves. Now, in a society which is moving towards civilization, anyone who enjoys doles of food and drink is either starving or a fool. And anyone who enjoys watching a fool enjoying himself is also a fool.

Ancient history also tells the story of a ruler who traveled incognito among his people to learn about conditions in his land. He heard a plaintive children's song and was deeply moved to compassion by it. What a roundabout way of doing things, this! Yet we have our modern counterparts: secret agents in the employ of dictatorial governments. Fearing those who would spread discontent among the people, a despotic government sends out its minions to sound out the temper of the people, with the idea of acting on their recommendations. Now, in the first place, what are the sources of information of their minions, the secret agents? The true gentleman has nothing to hide. But someone plotting subversive activity is usually too smart for secret agents and therefore evades their efforts to gain information. Thus the outcome is that the secret agents, paid to mix among the people, come into contact only with fools; they swallow what the latter have to say, throw in their own conjectures, and report this back to the ruler. Really, they are of no use whatsoever. They only cost their employer money and invite upon him the ridicule of intelligent people. In France Napoleon III employed secret agents for many years. For all his trouble, at the time of the Franco-Prussian War was he able to fathom the true sentiments of the people? And was he not captured when France was defeated?

We should learn a lesson from this. If the government wants to find out the actual mood of the times, there is nothing better than allowing freedom of the press and listening to the opinions of learned men. Restriction of freedom of the press, obstructing the flow of intelligent ideas, and employing secret agents to observe the mood of the country, is like sealing a living thing in an airtight compartment and standing by to watch it die a slow death. How low can one stoop? If you want to kill the thing, beat or burn it to death. If the intellectual powers of the people are deemed harmful, the reading of books should be prohibited, and every budding scholar in the land should be buried alive—the policies of the First Emperor of Qin should be the guide. Even the clever Napoleon was not exempt from such base tactics. The workings of a statesman's mind can be extremely despicable.

Now for the second school of thought. Men's opinions change when they form groups. Three cowards are not afraid to venture together over a mountain road on a dark night; their courage is not to be found in each man individually, it is the product of their banding together. A hundred thousand brave soldiers may hear the enemy in every leaf that rustles, then break and run. Their cowardice is not to be found in each man individually, it grips the whole army at once. Man's intelligence and opinions are comparable to things that follow the laws of chemistry. Sodium and hydrochloric acid, when separated, are highly potent, having the power to melt metals. But in a chemical compound they form the ordinary table salt used every day in the kitchen. Conversely, lime and ammonium chloride are not potent in isolation, but as a compound they have the power to knock a man out. Now, when you take a look at the companies in present-day Japan, you find that, the larger they become, the more inefficient they become. A company of a hundred people is inferior to one of ten people, one of ten people is no match for one of three, and one of three people is surpassed in profit-making by a company where you have one man investing all the capital and making all the decisions on transactions by himself.

In the first place, those who today open companies to do business are generally among the more talented in society; they are far better equipped with intellectual abilities than those old-fashioned, stubborn skinflints who would hang on to the ways of their ancestors. Yet if all these talented people are assembled together, they will suddenly change their natures and think up some perfectly inane policy. These men will themselves be at a loss to say what went wrong. Our present government officials are also among the most talented in the land; officialdom enjoys the greatest concentration of our nation's intellectual talent. But the policies they work out in concert are not by any means the most intelligent. Their intellectual powers, when pooled together, somehow become neutralized, just as the ingredients of table salt lose their potency in chemical combination. Generally speaking, when we Japanese form a group to accomplish something, the group turns out to be far less effective than the individual talents would indicate.

The citizens of Western countries are not all intelligent. However, most of what they achieve through concerted group action proves to be the product of intelligent men. The internal affairs of these countries are all agreed upon by these groups. The governments are based on group consensus, and they have parliaments. Businesses are **companies** formed by groups. The religious and academic worlds also have their groups. Right down to the remotest village small groups of people form clubs to discuss matters of common interest. Once formed, each group has its own viewpoint. If a number of friends or two or three houses in a neighborhood form a group, they will come to share their own particular viewpoint. This is true for the village, the province, the district. As one view combines with another, the tenor of the original views changes slightly. This process is repeated many times; in the end, a national opinion takes shape.

This process is like a certain number of soldiers forming a regiment, a number of regiments forming a battalion, and a number of battalions constituting a great army. The strength of an army lies in its ability to stand up against the enemy in battle, but this does not mean every individual soldier is brave. The strength of an army does not consist in the strength of each individual soldier, but in something beyond this created by the army as a whole. The public opinion of a whole nation is also very lofty and powerful, but the reason for this is not that it is supported by lofty-minded, powerful people. The reason is that public opinion engenders self-confidence within everyone in the group as a whole, after it has gained a large number of supporters who have gone along with the view and joined the group. In sum, public opinion in a country in the West is something greater than the talent and knowledge of each individual in that country, and an individual advocates and puts into effect ideas all out of proportion to his personal capacities.

Consequently, Westerners advance ideas and develop techniques out of proportion to their intelligence. Orientals spit out stupid theories and do their best to bungle things, out of proportion to their intelligence. The explanation for such a state of affairs can be found entirely in custom. A long-ingrained custom becomes second nature, with the result that certain responses become a matter of course. Since the practice of having parliaments has been a custom in the West for several hundreds of years, everybody just takes them for granted and people spontaneously structure their activities accordingly.

This is not true of the nations of Asia. Thus, as in the **caste** system of India, human relations in Asia have evolved into definite patterns of discrimination and social imbalance, and social feelings are lukewarm. As if this were not bad enough, despotic government has also made possible the enactment of laws that prohibit political factions and public discussions. All the common people care about is to be left in peace, and they do not have even enough spirit to argue about the difference between political factions and public discussions. Completely dependent on the government, they are not interested in public affairs. Take a million people, you will find a million different opinions. Every man lives shut up in his own house; the world outside his doors is a foreign country, of no interest to him whatsoever. Just try to get him to discuss the cleaning of the village well. Repair of the roads?—do not even bother. When such people see someone dying on the road, they just hurry past; when they come upon dog droppings in the street, they just walk around and pass on. As the saying goes, they are "too busy to get involved." How will you get them to engage in public discussion? Long force of habit has created routines that have made them sink to their present state.

Suppose there are no banks in the country and everybody is storing his money in his own home. Circulation of money will come to a halt, and it will be impossible to undertake large enterprises in the country. Look into individual homes and you will find piles of cash, but it all stagnates there and is of no use for the country as a whole. The opinions of citizens are similar. Ask at each door and each man will have an opinion, but the opinions are divided into a hundred million different units. Without some way to unite them, they are of no use to the nation as a whole.

In the opinion of some contemporary scholars, public discussion among the people may be a desirable thing, but for unintelligent people, sad as it may be, there is no alternative but despotic rule; hence the time is not yet ripe for initiating such discussions. However, "the time" means the time for engendering knowledge in the people. Human intelligence is not like a plant in the summertime that will grow overnight; and when it does grow, it is rendered useless by customs, or at least its effectiveness is curtailed. The power of custom is extremely strong, and once it is encouraged its effects cannot be checked. It finally becomes capable of tyrannical control over even a man's instinct to defend his own property.

Let me give an example. Today in Japan twenty percent of the government revenue is spent on the stipends of the nobility and ex-samurai families. The ones who pay for this are none other than the peasants and the merchants. If today these stipends were abolished, the expenditures of peasants and merchants could be reduced by a fifth, and their annual taxes of five sacks of rice would be reduced to four sacks. Even stupid commoners have enough intelligence to tell the difference between four and five. However, as the farmers see it the matter is not complicated at all; they just have to divide their product into rice which they give out to others and rice which they keep for themselves. And from the point of view of the samurai, their stipends are the hereditary estate of their ancestors, something their ancestors received for meritorious service, so it is different from a daily wage. Therefore they ask why they should have to forfeit their ancestors' rewards and lose their family estates just because there is no need at present for their military services. If they are declared useless citizens and deprived of the stipends that belong to their families, then the well-fed and idle rich merchants and farmers should also be deprived of their estates. They ask why they alone should be stripped of their estates to fatten peasants and merchants who have nothing to do with them.

Their argument has a grain of truth to it. Yet you never hear this view being expressed among the samurai themselves. Both the commoners and the ex-samurai live in their separate worlds of personal gain and loss. They just sit mute and accept things passively, as men do who listen to a story of some far-off land, or as people accept the changes of natural phenomena. How really strange! If this kind of thing happened in the West, there would be a great public uproar. I am not here discussing the relative merits of abolishing or not abolishing feudal stipends; I am only expressing my dismay at the way Japanese are hindered by custom from discussing things publicly, accepting passively what they should take exception to, not opening their mouths when they should, not speaking out on matters which should be discussed. To fight for one's own advantage was prohibited by the ancients, but to fight for one's own advantage is really to fight for principles. It is high time for our country to fight with the foreigners for its own advantage and for principles.

Those who are indifferent to national affairs will be indifferent to foreign problems as well, and those who are dull-witted in internal matters cannot be active in foreign issues. Such dullness and indifference on the part of the ex-samurai and commoners had their convenience for a despotic government, but dealings with foreigners will be well-nigh hopeless if we depend upon such people. If none of the citizens in the land feels a desire to discuss local issues and men as individuals lack the courage to put priority on questions of honor, then all discussion will become useless. Since this lack of concern and courage is not a natural defect but something lost as the result of custom, methods to reactivate these attitudes must also rely on custom. The only conclusion one can come to is that changing our customs is a matter of extreme importance.

Chapter SIX

THE DISTINCTION BETWEEN KNOWLEDGE
AND VIRTUE

I N THE previous discussion I conjoined the words *knowledge* and *virtue* in my thesis that the progress of civilization refers to both the intellectual and moral development of a people as a whole. In this chapter I should like to distinguish the two and clarify the differences between them.

Virtue means morality, or probity; in the West it is called **morals**. **Morals** refers to a person's interior good behavior; they enable a person to feel ashamed of nothing within his heart and to do nothing shameful even when alone. Knowledge means intelligence; in the West it is called **intellect**. It is the function of pondering, understanding, and relating things. Morality and intelligence are in turn each divided into two types. First you have what may be called private virtue: fidelity, purity, modesty, integrity, and the like—things that pertain to an individual's own heart. Secondly you have the sense of shame, justice, fairness, courage, and the like, which appear in men's dealings with others and in social relationships; these may be called public virtues. Thirdly you have the capacity to fathom the principles of things and respond to them; this may be called private knowledge. Fourthly you have the ability to evaluate men and events, to give weightier and greater things priority, and to judge their proper times and places; let me call this public knowledge. Private knowledge might be called the lesser knowledge of know-how, while public knowledge can be called the greater knowledge of wisdom.

Of the four things distinguished here, the most important is the last one. Without wisdom, private virtue and private knowledge cannot develop into their public counterparts, or the public and the private functions can end up at odds with and even harmful to each other. There has never before been a clear discussion of these four, but by examining the views of scholars and what people commonly say one can see that they are aware of these distinctions.

Mencius teaches that there are "four beginnings" of virtue in the human heart: a sense of pity, a sense of shame and dislike concerning evil, a sense of modesty and deference to others, and a sense of right and wrong. These beginnings can expand indefinitely, just as fire, once lit, spreads furiously, and spring water, once it gushes forth, spills over in abundance. If these beginnings are brought to perfection, one can protect a whole country; if not, one cannot even care for one's own parents. Mencius no doubt was thinking of the idea that private virtue expands into public virtue. He also said that even if one has intelligence, one cannot do better than follow the trend of the times; even if one has all one's farming tools ready, one had best wait for the right season. This is again probably the idea of broadening private into public knowledge in accord with the demands of the times.

Also, a man who by common consent is considered faultless and the best man for some public office may, in regard to personal affairs, be known to be absolutely deplorable. Richelieu of France was such a man: not lacking in public knowledge and public virtue, he was known to be deficient in private virtue. Again, a person might be very good at playing go, shōgi [Japanese chess], or using the abacus, but this merely proves his good sense in games and calculations; he could still have a reputation for being deficient in true discernment. Such a man is viewed as having private, but not public, knowledge.

As we can see, then, these four distinctions are recognized by scholars and ordinary people alike. It is quite natural to call them commonplace distinctions. Let me now go on to refine the demarcations and further discuss the functions of each.

As I said, without wisdom private knowledge cannot broaden into public knowledge. For example, go, card games, and playing with bean bags are all pursuits developed by man, as are the skills involved in the natural sciences and technical appliances. They all involve mental effort, but when we evaluate which things are important and which are not, choose the more important, and make a contribution to society in this way, the latter functions of intelligence certainly are greater. Even if one does not become directly involved in doing things, the evaluation of the relative merits and demerits of things, as for example Adam Smith's discussion of the laws of economics, will serve as a guide to men's minds and in general increase the sources of wealth; this can be called the greatest function which intelligence can serve. In either case, wisdom is required in order to progress from lesser to greater knowledge.

A certain gentleman once said that he could sweep the evils from the whole country but that the area around his house was not worthy of his attention. Though such a man is talented at ruling the country and bringing peace to the land, he is unable to regulate himself and his own household. Other types of men devote all their energies to maintaining their personal integrity, but know nothing of what is going on outside their gates. Still others go so far as to kill themselves without in any way benefiting society. All of these people are lacking in wisdom and err about the order in things; unable to distinguish between what is important and what is not, they lose a proper balance in their pursuit of virtue.

Because the function of wisdom is to regulate knowledge and virtue, when speaking about morality we should really call it the supreme virtue. However, because we are here using terms according to the popular understanding of them, wisdom should not be called a virtue. From ancient times in Japan, the term "morality" has been used to refer principally to an individual's private virtue. It was expressed in the Chinese Classics in such phrases as "be gentle, honest, polite, modest, and deferring to others," or "rule by inaction," or "the holy man is not troubled by dreams," or "the gentleman of the highest virtue appears to be a fool on the surface," or "the benevolent man is like a solid mountain." These all refer to inner states which in the West would be described as merely **passive**. For the word described an attitude of passive receptivity, rather than one of active motives; virtue was conceived only in terms of letting go of one's ego. The Chinese Classics, of course, do not teach only this kind of passive virtue. Some few passages imply a more dynamic frame of mind. However, the spirit which breathes throughout those works stirs up in people an attitude of patient endurance and servility. Shinto and Buddhism are practically the same as the Chinese Classics when it comes to their teachings on the cultivation of virtue. Because we Japanese have been reared according to such teachings, the popular understanding of the concept of virtue is extremely narrow; the term does not include the function of wisdom.

When one is discussing the meanings of terms, it is safest to avoid being bound by definitions established by scholars, and to take instead the senses in which people in general employ the terms. Take for example the combination of Chinese characters "boat-enjoy-mountain" in one compound.† If you take each element literally, you will have quite a job on your hands, but in the average person's mind the word contains nothing whatsoever about "enjoying oneself in the mountains." The same can be said about the term "virtue." From the scholarly standpoint its meaning is quite broad, but not so in the minds of the people. If they see an old ascetic monk of some mountain temple, they venerate him as a person of the highest virtue. On the other hand, a man learned in physics, economics, philosophy, or the like, is not called virtuous but talented, or an intellectual. Men of all ages have honored those who accomplished great deeds as heroes. But when they refer to a person's morality, they mean his private virtue. The more important public virtue does not come under the heading of morality; on the contrary, it often seems to be overlooked altogether. The common understanding of "virtue," then, is in the narrower sense.

In their hearts, of course, people naturally know the distinctions among the four classifications of knowledge and virtue that I described above, yet sometimes they seem to know it, sometimes they seem not to. Ultimately, oppressed by the general mood in the land, people are inclined to value private virtue most. Therefore, I, too, shall go along with the common understanding of people and shall discuss the function of wisdom under the heading of intelligence, while morality I shall have to define narrowly as passive private virtue. When I discuss virtue in this

---

† [The word Fukuzawa is referring to is *funa yusan* 舟遊山, and it means an outing by boat, an excursion on water.]

and the following chapter, it will be in this sense. Hence, when I compare intelligence and morality and describe the functions of the former as more important and comprehensive, and those of the latter as less important and narrower in range, I may seem to be biased. Scholars will not misunderstand me, however, if they are clear about what I say here.

In the first place, Japan is not the only country where in an unenlightened age the superiority of private virtue has been preached and where ordinary people were swayed by such teaching. This happens in all countries. When people's spirits have not yet developed and they are barely out of the brute stage, they are preoccupied with controlling their animal appetites, moderating their inner desires, and acquiring truly human sentiments. They therefore do not have the leisure to consider the complicated relations in society. In the same way, when man lived a hand-to-mouth existence, he had no time to concern himself about housing and clothing. However, there is no natural principle dictating that, as civilization progresses and human affairs become more multifarious, human society must continue to be controlled by the single mechanism of private virtue. But as old customs and human inertia cause men to long for the past and be complacent with the present, they remain unbalanced in their views.

Now, because private virtue is a universal principle valid for all ages and all lands, the simplest and most beautiful of principles, of course later generations could never revise it. But one must choose the place to exercise it, in accord with social changes, and one must consider the proper ways to use it. For example, man's need for food has always been the same, but whereas in antiquity men simply put things directly into their mouths with their hands, men later developed numerous new styles of eating. Again, private virtue in the human heart is like the eyes, ears, nose, and mouth in the human body; nobody argues about whether they are useful or not. No human can be without them. Discussing the usefulness of these parts of the body may be relevant in a world inhabited by people with physical impediments, but such discussion is only a waste of breath where people are all normal.

Because Buddhism, Shinto, Confucianism, and Christianity were proclaimed in ancient and less civilized times ("times suffering from a cultural impediment," as it were), there is no denying that they were necessary then. Why, even today eighty to ninety percent of the world's population is, so to say, culturally impeded, and as a result moral teachings cannot be neglected. Or perhaps for that very reason there is such a drive to talk so much about them.* However, because the essence of civilization lies in moving forward in the course of time, we must not rest secure with the simple ways of antiquity. If people today are not happy with eating with their fingers, and if they realize that to have eyes, ears, nose, and mouth, is no special cause for smugness, then it should also be clear that the cultivation of private virtue is not the be-all and end-all of human attainment.

Civilization requires a great diversity in human affairs. This diversity in human affairs in turn requires a diversity of responses in the human heart. Anyone who feels that private virtue suffices for all situations should be satisfied with the decorous behavior of the women of today. Women of good families in China and Japan have all the proper virtues: meekness and modesty, sincerity and truthfulness, respectful demeanor, and most are competent at managing their households. But why, then, are these women not employed in the public sector of society? This is proof that private virtue alone is insufficient for dealing with human affairs. After all, it is not my opinion that private virtue is a trivial human attainment. It is just that I do not prefer making it the basis of any and every argumentation, as Japanese people have felt they should since ancient times. I do not say that it is useless and to be discarded. My point is simply that there also are other important

---

* Confucianism values the virtue of sincerity; Shinto and Buddhism urge single-mindedness. These are important virtues for lower-class people. Thus, when educating a child whose intellectual powers are not yet developed, or in dealing with stupid people who have no knowledge or skills, to say that morality in general is of no value to men will give rise to misunderstandings. Or to say that virtue ought to be downgraded in favor of intelligence will result in a misinterpretation of intelligence, and people will fall into the error of discarding true virtue for plain cunning. All social intercourse will then be endangered. Therefore, for these people private morality is valuable. However, to consider the private virtues of sincerity or single-mindedness as man's natural obligation and to go on from there to try to control all human affairs by means of it is also greatly to be feared. The times and places must be considered, and we must always hope that people will advance to the highest level.

functions of knowledge and virtue.

Since intelligence and morality split man's heart, as it were, into two, and each controls its own proper sphere, there is no way of saying which is the more important. Both are needed to make a complete human being. But eighty to ninety percent of the theories of the past have made the mistake of stressing morality over intelligence. Some scholars went so far as to deny the usefulness of intelligence altogether. This is a most deplorable evil in human society, and yet, when one sets out to remedy this evil, he will encounter one great obstacle. When he tries to correct the evils of the past by first of all distinguishing between intelligence and morality and clarifying the respective spheres and functions of each, shallow men will complain that the explanation belittles virtue in favor of knowledge, that the territory of morality is being encroached upon. There might even be some who, after a cursory glance at the explanation, will mistakenly conclude that morality is of no use to men. Now, knowledge and virtue, together, are as necessary for civilized society as the presence of both vegetables and grains and fish and meat is to a healthy diet for the human body. My saying that intelligence should not be overlooked is no different from suggesting meat to an undernourished vegetarian. Of course, it would be necessary to explain the value of meat and the problems of eating only vegetables and grains and why both types of food should be taken together, because if the vegetarian then goes to the other extreme of eating only fish and meat, it would be the height of folly and as great a mistake as before.

Learned men of both ancient and modern times have also distinguished between knowledge and virtue, but because they feared the harm that would result from being misunderstood, they did not speak about it openly. However, one cannot go on indefinitely knowing something and not speaking of it. When something is reasonable, ten out of ten men will not misunderstand it. Even if two or three do happen to misunderstand, it would be better to speak of it. It is unreasonable to deprive seven or eight men of an intelligent insight for fear of a misunderstanding by two or three. When you come down to it, to conceal an argument that should be discussed, or to obscure an issue for fear of being misunderstood—as they say, "adapting one's teachings to the level of one's audience"—is a course of action which belittles one's fellow human beings. Even if a person is stupid, he can still clearly tell evil from good. There can't be such an extreme intellectual gap between fellow human beings. To take it upon oneself to refrain from telling things the way they are because of the supposed stupidity of one's fellows shows a lack of due respect and love. This is not the way a true gentleman should act. If a person thinks something is true, he should speak out on the matter frankly and leave it to others to judge whether he is right or wrong. This is precisely why I myself do not hesitate to discuss the distinction between knowledge and virtue.

Morality refers to something interior to a man and not to an activity meant to be seen by others. It is called "leading a moral life" or "personal propriety." These phrases make no mention of something external. For example, freedom from avarice and dishonesty is an aspect of morality, but if one's actions are only free of avarice or dishonestly because of a fear of censure or a bad reputation, this cannot be called genuine virtue. A bad reputation and censure are external to a person. Acting because of such external things cannot be called morality. If this were morality, then there is no reason why even avarice or dishonesty cannot be morality, as long as a person succeeds in escaping the censure of others. In that case there would be no distinction between a pseudo gentleman and a true one. Hence, morality has nothing at all to do with external circumstances. It is not concerned about the praise or blame of society; it can neither be bent by intimidation nor be taken away by dire want. Firm and unwavering, it exists within the self.

Intelligence is different. It deals with external things and considers their relative merits and demerits: if carrying out one course of action proves inconvenient, you adopt another policy; if you find a thing convenient but society disagrees, then you change to something else; and if something proved convenient once and continues to be so, the intelligent course is to adopt it. For example, once carriages were more convenient than palanquins, but when men discovered the advantages of steam power they had no alternative but to build steam-driven vehicles. It is by the functioning of intelligence that men designed carriages, then invented steam-driven vehicles, and finally employed each of these to best advantage. Since intelligence thus functions in reference to external circumstances and takes measures suited to the occasion, it is the exact opposite of morality; it should be styled an outward-going function. The virtuous gentleman may do nothing but sit in silence in his own home, and he cannot be called an evil person. But if an intelligent man does not involve himself in external things, he can just as well be called a fool.

Morality is the activity of one person. Its prime sphere of influence is the family circle. If the head of the family is honest, the rest of the people in his household will tend to be honest. If the words and actions of parents are gentle, then the hearts of the children should naturally be the same. Even friends and relatives can exhort one another to do good and thus lead others to virtue, but ultimately the sphere in which moral encouragement can lead another to good is extremely limited. This is what is meant by the saying that "One cannot call on every door nor preach to every man."

Intelligence is something quite different. Once some truth is discovered and announced to others, in no time at all it moves the minds of a whole nation. If the discovery is very great, the intellectual power of a single man can change the face of the entire world. James Watt invented the steam engine, and the manufacturing industry changed all over the world as a result. Adam Smith discovered the laws of economics, and world commerce took on a new dimension. How are such ideas diffused? They are spread through word of mouth or through books. As soon as men put into actual practice ideas which they have heard or have read about in books, they are in reality no different from Watt or Smith. As a result, yesterday's ignoramus can become today's wise man, and hundreds and thousands of Watts and Smiths can be born all over the world. In speed of diffusion and breadth of influence this is in a completely different category from one man's giving lessons in morality to his family and friends.

Someone may object that Thomas Clarkson's sweeping away the evil laws of slavery in society on the strength of his inner vision, or John Howard's elimination of the evils of the prison system through his own diligence, were works of public efficacy; hence, even private virtue can have extremely vast, immeasurable effects. To this I answer: True, these two gentlemen broadened private into public virtue and thus had a vast, immeasurable influence on the world. However, these two men accomplished what they did by fearing no odds and sparing no pains in putting their ideas into effect; they wrote books, exhausted their funds, endured criticism, braved dangers, and finally succeeded in moving men's hearts. But this was not directly the fruit of private virtue. Rather, it was the work of wisdom. The two of them accomplished great things, true, but if we look at the matter exclusively in terms of morality and understand morality the way men commonly do, then the only thing they both did was sacrifice their lives for the sake of others. As far as motivation goes there is no difference between Howard's loss of his life to save countless others and the case of a benevolent man who would lose his life trying to save a child fallen into a well. The only difference is that Howard acted for the sake of countless others and left a legacy of virtue and merit for all ages, while the latter's deed is for the sake of only one child and would be of temporary influence. There is no difference in morality between the two as far as offering their lives goes. Howard's saving of countless men and his legacy to countless future generations derived from his enlarging private virtue with the aid of wisdom; it was through this means that he was able to extend his range of moral influence. Our humane man, the benevolent gentleman, possesses private virtue but is poor in public virtue and public knowledge, while Howard possessed all of them.

Private virtue may be likened to raw ore, and wisdom to ore transformed by craftsmanship. If the ore is not worked on, the iron will be nothing but a heavy, hard object. But when even a little craftsmanship is added, you can produce a hammer or a pot. If it is a little more skillfully wrought, it can become a knife or a saw. If it is even more skillfully worked on, and on a larger scale, it can be made into a steam engine, while on a smaller scale it can become the mainspring of a watch. When people compare a big pot and a steam engine, is there anyone who does not value the steam engine more highly? And why? The reason is not that a big pot, a steam engine, and the raw ore are just different materials, but that people value the craftsmanship that has gone into them. Therefore, as far as the raw ore that goes into iron instruments is concerned, the pot, the engine, the hammer, and the knife are all exactly the same, but what determines their relative values is the degree of craftsmanship involved in producing them.

The relative proportions found in knowledge and virtue are similar. There is no difference between the humane person who would save a child fallen into a well, and John Howard, in terms of the raw stuff of their virtuous actions. But Howard was able to achieve the greater result by adding greater craftsmanship, that is intelligence, to his virtue. And it is precisely because of the working of intelligence that Howard the man cannot be styled merely a virtuous gentleman. The combination of knowledge and virtue, to which was added the intellectual power of wisdom, sets him apart from ordinary men of the past and present. Without this power, he would have lived his whole life within his own family circle, a nonentity, spending all his time reading the classics and edifying his wife and children with his morality—or he might not have been able to do even that much. In such a case how would he have been able to undertake his great enterprise and sweep away the evil customs which prevailed throughout Europe? This is why I say that the influence of intelligence is broad, that of private virtue narrow. Morality can only broaden its scope and radiate its splendor in conjunction with the working of intelligence.

The things embraced by morality have always been fixed and immutable. To cite the Ten Commandments of Christianity: the first is that one should think of no other god than **God**; second, one should not bend the knee before idols; third, one should not use **God**'s name in vain: fourth, one should not violate the day of worship; fifth, honor thy father and mother; sixth, one should not kill; seventh, avoid unclean thoughts and deeds; eighth, although poor and low-born, one should not steal; ninth, one should not deceive, nor take delight in deceit; tenth, one should not covet one's neighbor's belongings. These are the Ten Commandments. There are also the Five Confucian Relationships: "love between father and son," meaning that parents and children should love each other; "duty between lord and subject," meaning that a master and his servants should observe good faith in their dealings with each other; "distinction between man and wife," meaning that a couple should not become overfamiliar and behave in an unseemly way; "precedence of the old over the young," meaning that younger people should defer in all matters and respect their elders; and "faith between friends," meaning that they should not deceive each other.[†] These Ten Commandments and Five Relationships have formed the unchanging foundation for the teachings of the sages over thousands of years. Though in the course of history many outstandingly virtuous men have come upon the world scene, they have only made commentaries on these general precepts and have not added a single new teaching. Confucianism flourished during the Song dynasty in China, but no one changed the Five Relationships into Six Relationships. This shows that the precepts of morality are few in number and cannot be changed. Because the ancient sages not only practiced these precepts themselves but also taught them to others, great men of later ages have been unable to surpass them, no matter how sedulously they have tried. It is as if the sages had said that snow was white and coal was black—what can people of later ages add to this? The ancients had, as it were, an exclusive monopoly on the paths of morality, and the men of later ages have only been able to act as their brokers. In other words, there have been no sages since Jesus and Confucius, and what pertains to morality has made no advance since their times. What was virtue in the dawn of civilization is no different from virtue today.

But this is not the case with intelligence. Knowledge has increased a hundredfold since ancient times. What the ancients feared, modern people scorn. What the ancients stood in awe of, modern people laugh at. The products of intelligence have increased day by day. Inventions are too numerous to list, and there is no foreseeable end to future progress. If we could bring back the ancient sages to live in our modern world and let them hear the theories of economics and commerce current today, or could put them aboard a steamship and send them across the ocean, or let them listen to news coming in from thousands of miles away over the telegraph, they would certainly be amazed. But we might not even need steamships or the telegraph to startle them. We need only show them the process of manufacturing writing paper, or show them printing and engraving techniques, and this should be

---

† [The quotations are all from D. C. Lau's translation of *Mencius* (New York: Oxford University Press, 1970), 102.]

enough to fill them with amazement. Steam power, the telegraph, paper manufacturing, and printing, are all products of the intelligence of people of later eras. Their inventors and designers were not listening to the teachings of the sages or practicing the way of morality. The sages never even dreamed of these inventions. Why, as far as intelligence goes, the sages of antiquity were equal to a three-year-old of today.

Morality is not something that can be taught externally. It is something attained through interior efforts on the part of the one acquiring it. For example, there is the teaching in the Classics: "Overcome yourself and observe appropriate conduct." Explaining the meaning of the words does not suffice to transmit the truth contained in this saying. When the words are explained in greater detail, the first two are seen to mean curbing one's selfish desires, while "observe appropriate conduct" means to return to one's right mind and know one's station in life. These ideas must be explained again and again, always with great care. And this is the extent of the teacher's role; he cannot transmit the Way by any other method. To go beyond this depends upon a person's own exertion, whether by reading the ancient Classics or by observing the moral actions of people around him, then following their example. It is a matter of what is called "communion of mind with mind," or "edification in morality." But edification is, of course, something spiritual, and thus there is no way to demonstrate whether one has really been influenced by a thing or not. Hence it is that there are men who, while actually giving free rein to their selfish desires, are inwardly convinced that they are in complete control of them. And there are people who think they know their proper station in life and yet they are stepping outside their station. Yet whether they think they are or not has nothing to do with their teachers. It depends entirely upon the interior efforts of the pupils.

Some men will hear the teachings about conquering oneself and reviving ritual and will be greatly enlightened thereby. Others will completely misunderstand it. Still others will scorn the precepts. Others, even though they understand them, will put on appearances to deceive people. They can be taken in a thousand different ways, and distinguishing the genuine from the false ways is extremely difficult.

Now, when someone scorns these precepts and puts on false appearances to deceive people, or when someone errs in his acceptance of them and takes as truth a false interpretation of the principles, nothing can be done by a second party. At such a time, since there are no concrete norms by which to demonstrate the truth, nothing else can be done to correct him except to tell him to fear Heaven, or tell him to look into his heart. Still, since fearing Heaven and looking into one's own heart are private affairs, there is no way for another person to know whether the man is truly fearing Heaven or not. This is why pseudo gentlemen can exist in the world. The worst of these hypocrites are not content merely to listen to moral teachings and understand them; they must also preach moral teachings to others. Thus they write commentaries on the Classics or discuss the religion of the Way of Heaven. Their discussions are extremely plausible. If we take only their books and read them, we shall think sages have appeared in our own day and age. But as soon as we take a step back and get a good look at these people in person, we shall be greatly shocked by the contradictions between their words and their actions, and shall be forced to smile at the folly of their hearts.

Han Yu wrote his memorial about the bone of Buddha to remonstrate with the emperor, for which act he seemed like a perfectly loyal subject.[†] When he was banished to the provinces, he expressed his loyal wrath in poems and other writings. But after that he wrote a letter to influential quarters in the capital, pleading to be recalled. He was nothing but a pseudo gentlemen. Neither Japan, nor China, nor the West has been lacking in men like Han Yu. Ingratiating flattery and greed for money can be discovered even in one who expounds the Confucian *Analects*. People out to deceive the ignorant, intimidate the weak, or grasp simultaneously for fame and profits can be found even among those Westerners who preach Christian doctrine. All such base characters take advantage of the fact that there are no concrete norms by

---

[†] [Han Yu (768–824) was a great essayist and poet during the Tang dynasty as well as a central figure in the Classical Prose Movement. He was a precursor of Neo-Confucianism and influenced the revival of Confucianism during the Song dynasty in the eleventh century. His memorial, the cause behind his exile, was a strong protest against the influence of Buddhism on China in which he criticized the fact that the Emperor had arranged for a bone of the Buddha to be brought to the capital.]

which to test another's real moral sincerity. They are just illicit traffickers in morality for their own selfish ends, and proof that man cannot be regulated by morality alone.*

Intelligence is not like this. The world has an abundance of intelligence, and, without its having to be taught, people learn it from one another. It transforms men on its own, attracting them into its own realm in a manner not unlike the edification process of morality. But the power of intelligence is not limited to spreading itself only by means of private edification. There are concrete methods of acquiring intelligence, and one can clearly see its effects. If the techniques of arithmetic are learned, they can be put to immediate use. When one hears about the principle of producing steam from boiling water, then learns how to make an engine and use steam power, one can produce a steam engine, an engine no different in its functioning from Watt's steam engine. This is called the concrete teaching of knowledge. Since the teaching is concrete, there are also concrete norms and measuring devices for testing it.

Thus, the skills of intelligence can be imparted to people. Applying what he has learned, a man can actually check those points about which he is uncertain. If after testing he finds he still cannot do the thing, he

---

* There are New and Old texts of the *Book of History*. When the First Emperor of Qin burned the books, the *Book of History* perished among them. In the time of Emperor Wen of Han, an old scholar, Fu Sheng, who had memorized twenty-nine volumes, transmitted from memory what is now called the New Text. Later, when they tore down the walls of Confucius's house, they found an old copy that is now called the Old Text. And thus in the present *Book of History* we have twenty-nine volumes of the Old Text and as many of the New Text. Comparison of these texts shows their styles to be quite different. The New Text is more difficult than the Old. The meanings of the sentences and the nuances of the words are clearly different. Anyone can tell that these two texts are not taken from the same book written before the burning of the books. One of them must be a forgery. Now, it was in the Jin period that the text was found in the wall. Before that there appeared a work of the Han dynasty called the *Speech of Qin*, which many Confucian writers cited. This book was itself repudiated in the Jin as a forgery. At any rate, the origins of the *Book of History* are definitely uncertain. Later on, when people's faith became stronger and they considered it written by Confucius, Cai Shen wrote in the introduction to his edition of the *Book of History* that it seems to express the mind of Confucius. Is this not odd, though? This scholar could not distinguish between the Old and New texts, but because he found certain statements that harmonized with the ideas of Confucius, he thereby concluded that it was written by Confucius! Yet one of the two texts really was written after Confucius's time by men who tried to capture the spirit of the Sage; it was a forgery. It is plain, then, that the world is full of pseudo gentlemen, pseudo sages, and pseudo sacred writings.

can learn the proper procedure for doing it. At all steps of the learning process he can be taught with concrete objects. For example, let us suppose that a mathematics teacher is teaching his pupils that twelve divided equally will give six. To see if they can actually do that or not, he can give them twelve balls, and have them divide the balls into two sets; he will thereby be able to see whether they have learned the principle or not. If the pupils make a mistake and divide that number into eight and four, they have simply not yet learned the principle. If after further explanation he tests them again, and this time they make the correct division, this step of the lesson is over. At this point, the pupil who has learned the principle is no different from the teacher as far as being able to use the principle. A second teacher, as it were, has been born. The speed of his learning process and the clarity of the testing can actually be seen and heard by any observer.

To test a man's skill in sailing a ship, one can take him on board and have him take it out to sea; to test a man's skill in commerce, one can make him do some buying and selling and see what his profits and losses are; to judge a man's medical skill, one can see if he can cure patients or not; and one can estimate a man's business acumen by the grandeur or humbleness of his dwelling. In this manner, verification of results by seeing the actual proof, item by item, is called concrete testing of intellectual skills.

Therefore, when it comes to knowledge, there is no way to deceive others. An immoral man can put on an act and assume the outward appearance of a man of virtue, but a fool cannot for long masquerade as a wise man. This is why there are many pseudo gentlemen in the world but few pseudo intellectuals. True, there are not a few people on the order of the economics expert who can discuss world economy but can not provide for his own household, or the armchair navigator who waxes eloquent on sailing but cannot step onto a ship. Such people may seem to be "pseudo intellectuals," but, because there is no universal law that says there must be a gap between theory and practice, and only in the case of morality is there a lack of clear norms by which to measure the gaps between people's theory and their practice, within the realm of intelligence it is possible to check whether such "pseudo intellectuals" are really genuine or false. Hence, if a navigator is unable to board a ship, or if an economist cannot provide for his own household, these men either do not yet have a genuine mastery of the skills, or else some other cause is impeding their use of the skills they have learned.* Since both the skills and the causes impeding their use are concretely verifiable, it is not difficult to prove whether a person has really acquired such skills or not. When one has ascertained whether a person really knows something or not, it is possible to discuss it with him and teach him, or he can by his own efforts learn from someone else. In a word, then, in the world of intelligence there is no place for pseudo intellectuals.

For all these reasons, I say: Morality cannot be taught by means of the external; its truth or falsity cannot be checked by means of the external; it can affect others only when it is not visible. Intelligence can be taught by means of the external; its truth or falsity can be checked by means of the external; it can affect others even when it is not visible.

Morality progresses or declines according to a person's interior efforts. Take, for example, the case of two young men, both born in a rural area, both endowed with natural talents and upright temperament, so that there appears to be no difference whatever between the two of them. They go off to the city for business, or study, let us say. In the beginning they find some friends with whom they constantly associate, and find a teacher to study under. They also experience the general lack of human feeling one finds among city people. This causes them a great deal of inner suffering. Six months pass, a year passes, and one of them loses his old country-like temperament, comes under the spell of the city, and falls into a profligate way of life—thus ruining his whole life. But the other young man cultivates himself more and more, his conduct never changes, and he does not lose his original country mentality. The moral conduct of the two has suddenly become as different as the sky above and the earth beneath. You will know what I mean if you just observe students in Tokyo today.

Now, if these two young men had remained in their villages, the two of them would have remained upright fellows, growing up into

---

* For example, the economist might have a penchant for extravagance, or the navigator might be physically incapacitated. In such cases, however skilled they might be, it would be impossible for them to put their skills to practical use.

virtuous adults. And yet in the prime of his life one of them turned from virtue to vice, while the other went on to perfect his gifts. Why was this? The cause lay not in different natural endowments in the two; and the people with whom they associated and the things they studied were all fairly much the same—so it cannot be ascribed to good or bad education. What, then, accounts for the difference in their moral conduct? The reason the one changed while the other remained his old self was not a difference in pressure from outside forces, but a difference in energy in their spiritual efforts, so that one fell back while the other advanced forward.

A profligate from youth, one who steals things, injures people, and stops at no evil, a man who has forsaken the company of his family and friends, and for whom there is no place in the world—even such a man can one day have a sudden change of heart, repent his past misdeeds, and, mindful of the blessings awaiting him, spend the rest of his days a diligent and hard-working citizen. If we trace the record of his spiritual life, we find it clearly divides into two phases. He really lived two lives within one life span, as it were; his case can be likened to the grafting of a plum shoot onto the stump of a peach tree, so that when the shoot grew up one could see only plum blossoms and would never guess the trunk was a peach tree. Like examples of such people in society are not hard to find, for there are frequent cases of former gamblers who have become pious chanters of the *nenbutsu*, or of notorious rogues who have become reputable townsmen. These fellows do not undergo a change of heart because of directions from others. Their conversions are entirely the result of their own interior efforts.

We find such cases in ancient times, too. Kumagai Naozane turned to Buddha after killing Atsumori in battle, and a certain hunter once gave up hunting forever after he shot a pregnant monkey. Kumagai, once converted to the Buddha, became a *nenbutsu* devotee and ceased being the fierce warrior of old.† And once the hunter threw away his

---

† [Fukuzawa's reference is to Kumagai Naozane (1141–1208), a famous retainer of Minamoto Yoritomo, who fought in the wars between the Minamoto and the Taira. Overcome with remorse when loyalty compelled him to take the life of the young Taira commander Taira no Atsumori (1169–84) at the battle of Ichi-no-tani, Naozane renounced warfare and became a Buddhist monk. The story entered Japanese literature (for example in the *Tales of the Heike*), and the Japanese imagination.]

gun and set his hand to the plow, he became a peaceful farmer and ceased being the killer of sentient beings that he used to be. These conversions of heart took place in an instant, not because of the preaching of others but because of interior workings. There is less than a hair's breadth dividing virtue from vice.

The case is entirely different with intelligence. Men are born ignorant. If they do not learn anything, they make no progress beyond ignorance. If a newborn babe is abandoned on a desolate mountain, even if he is fortunate enough to survive, he will little differ in intelligence from the beasts. Again, a nightingale can build a nest, but adroit skills such as this would be an impossible task even for a generation of men if they received no education. Human intelligence depends entirely on learning. Once a person begins to learn, there is no limit to his potential progress. And once he has made progress, there is no possibility of retrogression. If two young men start out with the same natural endowments and you teach them both, they will make progress together. If one progresses faster than the other, it must be because they differ in natural abilities, or they do not have the same education, or one studies more diligently than the other. But no matter what the circumstances, it is impossible to acquire knowledge suddenly by dint of one's interior efforts. Yesterday's gambler can become today's pious believer, but human intelligence cannot change overnight without contact with external things. Again, though last year's serious student can change into a playboy this year, with all trace of his former virtue lost, once a man has acquired knowledge he will not lose it unless he suffers an attack of amnesia.

Mencius speaks about the universal energy nurtured by the rightful mind. Zhuzi speaks about instantaneous enlightenment leading to prolific results, and about a universal energy. Zen monks talk about the realization of Buddhist truth. However, one cannot trace the evidence of those efforts, for they occur in metaphysical minds in abstract ways. On the other hand, in the realm of knowledge, there are no such things as instantaneous enlightenment or a universal energy. When Watt invented the steam engine and Adam Smith first formulated the laws of economics, they did not sit alone in the dark and experience an instantaneous enlightenment. It was because of long years of studying physical sciences that they were able to achieve their results. Even if you let Bodhidharma sit in front of a wall for ninety years, he would never be able to invent the steam engine or the telegraph.[†] You can let our present-day scholars of antiquity read the thousands of volumes of the ancient classics of both China and Japan, and let them dream up some superb methods of governing the people by means of spiritual beneficence and authority, but they will still have no idea how to conduct political and economic affairs as they are practiced in the modern world. This is why I say that, for intelligence, learning is indispensable for progress, but once intelligence is acquired it cannot be lost, while morality is difficult to teach and difficult to learn, but by dint of interior exertion one can advance in it suddenly, or lose it just as suddenly.

Present-day teachers of morality proclaim that it is the foundation of all human affairs and the prerequisite for any human enterprise. They say that if one only cultivates his personal virtue there is nothing he will not be able to accomplish. Therefore, morality must be taught and learned before anything else, even at the expense of everything else. For once morality is cultivated, the rest will take care of itself. They declare that a society without moral teaching is unable to see where it is going, like a person without a lantern on a dark night. They add that Western civilization is the product of moral teaching, and that the semi-developed civilizations of Asia and the still primitive states of Africa are the way they are entirely because of their respective levels of moral development. They liken moral teaching to the temperature, and civilization to a thermometer whose reading is an accurate gauge of the level of virtue. Consequently, these teachers of morality lament people's immorality and grieve over their lack of goodness, some proposing that Christianity be introduced into Japan, others advocating the revival of Shinto or Buddhism. Confucianists have their solutions; scholars of National Learning have theirs; and the bitter, long-winded arguments among them go on and on. The frantic way in which they bewail the ills

---

† [Bodhidharma (early fifth century A.D.), who is said to have brought the teachings of Chan (Zen) Buddhism to China, is also said to have spent nine years meditating in front of a wall before he reached enlightenment. Fukuzawa purposely multiplies this period by 10.]

of society makes one think fire or flood were about to ravage our houses. But why all the furor?

I look at things in an entirely different way. We should not bring up extreme cases and limit our discussion to them. If we set up complete lack of goodness and morality as our criterion, and think we have to save such people, then of course it will seem we are facing an emergency situation. But applying a remedy only to one faulty area is still far from solving all of society's ills, no more than merely living from hand to mouth can be called the total economy of human life. If we were to settle discussions by looking at extreme cases, even moral teaching would become powerless. Suppose for a moment we were to make moral teaching the exclusive basis of civilization, and were to make the people of the whole world read the Christian Bible and do nothing else; then what? Or what if we promoted the Zen idea of "disdaining words and letters," with the result that everyone in the nation became illiterate?† Shall we call people civilized if they can chant the *Kojiki* and the Five Classics by rote and have learned the loyal virtues, but do not even know how to make a living?‡ Or shall we call people enlightened if they eliminate their desires and emotions and live ascetic lives without any knowledge of the world of man?

By roadsides one can see stone images of three monkeys, one covering his eyes, one his mouth, and the third his ears. Representing not-seeing, not-hearing, and not-speaking, they are supposed to symbolize the morality of patient discipline. According to this idea, man's eyes, mouth, and ears are the vehicles of immorality, as though all men were endowed by their Creator with certain tools of immorality. But if there is something wrong with one's eyes, ears, or mouth, then evil can also be done with the hands and the feet. Therefore, a deaf, dumb, and blind man is still not yet a hundred-percent good man, and it would be advisable to deprive him of the use of his four limbs as well.

---

† [Zen stresses that enlightenment cannot be found through intellectual study of Buddhist texts.]

‡ [The *Kojiki* (Record of Ancient Matters) is Japan's earliest extant written record, compiled in 712 A.D., and containing tales of the gods and accounts of Japan's earliest history. It was one of the major texts of the National Learning school. The Five Classics are the basic texts of the Chinese cultural tradition and therefore of the Chinese Learning school.]

Or maybe the wisest course would be not to create such a useless being at all but to eliminate mankind from the face of the earth altogether. Can we say this is the plan of creation? I, at least, have my doubts. Still, those who contemplate the Christian Bible or adhere to the Zen doctrine that disdains words and letters or venerate the loyal virtues or eliminate their physical emotions and desires, all have an unwavering faith in moral teachings. Now, there is no reason to condemn as evil people who have an unwavering faith in a teaching, no matter how ignorant they may be. Criticizing their ignorance has to do with their intelligence and has nothing to do with their morality. In short, then, if we wish to argue in terms of extremes, as far as moral teaching is concerned anybody who lacks private virtue should be called an evil man, and the goal of moral teaching should consist entirely in reducing the number of evil men in the world. Nevertheless, if we make a wide and careful study of the workings of the human heart and accurately observe their effects, we do have grounds for refusing to equate civilization with reducing the number of evil men in the world.

If we calculate the amount of private virtue in rural people and city people today, it would be difficult to determine clearly which side has the majority of moral individuals. Yet, as far as the opinion of the general public goes, it seems people would agree that countryfolk ways are simpler. Even if some might disagree, there probably is not a man who would consider city dwellers more virtuous than countryfolk. It would be like comparing ancient with modern times, or children with adults. However, when the topic turns to civilization, everyone considers cities and modern times to be more civilized. Hence civilization is not something whose level can be divined merely by the number of bad people in society. This is clear proof that the basis of civilization does not lie solely in private virtue; and yet the virtuous men of moral conduct stop the discussion at the very extreme right from the beginning, leaving no room for objective thought. They press on in only one direction. Knowing neither the vastness nor the complexity of civilization, knowing neither how it functions nor how it progresses, little realizing the complexities of the human mind, not knowing the distinction between public and private spheres in matters of knowledge and virtue, nor their mutual complementarity and parallelism, not knowing how to examine the whole picture prior to making a judgment, their sole aim is to lessen the number of evil men in society—but at the price of turning the cities back into simple villages, adults into children, and human beings into so many stone monkeys.

Of course, in the last analysis, Shinto, Buddhism, Confucianism, and even Christianity are not so oppressive by nature. Yet if we look at the ways they are transmitted to the general public or how people feel when they are subjected to their teachings, we see that this abuse is inevitable. One might describe this phenomenon as similar to a person with an extremely acidic stomach: whatever he eats or drinks, it all turns acidic, and he cannot benefit from the food. There is nothing wrong with the food or the drink, he just has a chronic condition. Scholars should reflect on this problem of the harm that comes from certain ways of teaching.

And why do those moral sages so deplore the immorality in the world? In the final analysis it must be because they believe people are all evil and so they have to save them! This kind of grandmotherly solicitude is truly touching, but to refer to the average person as someone steeped in sin is only a way of speaking to impress simple folk. It does not necessarily express the truth. No one is entirely evil his whole life through. There has never been a saint, no matter how noble he was, who did not do wrong sometimes, and, conversely, there is no evil person who has never done some good. Were we to weigh the conditions of human life, there would always be a mixture of good and bad, with the good probably predominant. It is because good acts do predominate that civilization has progressed. And yet these virtuous deeds have certainly not all derived exclusively from the power of moral teachings. This is proof that, if plans to lure people into evil are not always successful, neither are programs to make people good.

In the long run, the good and evil of the human heart are dependent upon a person's own efforts. Good and evil are not things which can freely be given or taken away by a second party. There were good people in ancient times even before such teachings were widespread, and the majority of children who have yet to reach the age of reason are honest; so man's nature in general is good. The principal aim of moral teaching consists merely in not hindering the natural development of this good. To lay down moral laws to family and friends does not involve imparting to them something they do not have by nature, it consists in teaching them how to exclude whatever hinders their good dispositions and motivating them to attain their own good by their own efforts. Thus morality is not something that is produced through the power of human teaching alone. It must spring from the personal efforts of the learners as well.

Furthermore, so-called virtuous conduct is the purely passive private virtue I referred to at the beginning of this chapter. Since virtue only means devoting one's life to a negative rejection of personal greed, wealth, and fame, to the observance of honesty in thought, word, and deed, then what it comes down to is the spirit of enduring life's hardships. Enduring life's hardships is not wrong. It is better beyond compare than the terrible immorality of greed, lying, stealing, and complete license. Still, there are many different degrees of moral behavior between the goodness of enduring life's hardships on the one hand and the evil of such base immorality on the other.

Early in this chapter I divided intelligence and morality into four general categories. If I were to enumerate all the finer distinctions, the list would almost go on indefinitely. It is as if good and evil were the polar opposites of hottest summer and coldest winter, between which there are an unlimited number of temperature variations possible. If we were to make it possible for man to perfect his natural endowments, the most evil of men would already have shed his evil ways and advanced to a far higher plane. Just because a man is not of a mind to steal or lie, is this enough to consider him virtuous? The mere refraining from stealing or lying cannot be counted among the virtuous acts of man. A man who has committed such serious acts of immorality as greed, covetousness, lying, or stealing, is not really a man. One harboring such evil tendencies in his heart should be scorned by society, and punished by the law in society if he manifests these tendencies in external acts. The correspondence of cause and effect should be made clear in this case: the implements for correcting evil are external, while the means of exhorting to good are internal. But to teach only the diligent practice of private morality and to urge man, a spiritual creature, merely to avoid humanly degrading vices—and to take this as man's highest condition—is ultimately to belittle man, oppress him, and interfere with his innate qualities.

Once a person's spirit is oppressed, it is hard for him to recover in later life. The adherents of the Ikkō sect,† as self-appointed mundane men, rely on the power of Amida Buddha; intent on rebirth in the Pure Land, they do nothing except invoke the aid of Amida and chant the *nenbutsu* with all their heart. The Confucians, intoxicated with the Way of Confucius and Mencius, do nothing but read the Classics over and over again. Scholars of Japanese Learning devote all their energies to compiling the ancient Shinto texts. Scholars of Western Learning thrive on the teachings of Christianity, forgetting other studies; they do nothing but read the one book, the **Bible**. All of these are of a kind with the adherents of the Ikkō sect. True, these schools do benefit society in that, as a result of their beliefs and personal cultivation, they effectively improve manners and customs. Therefore there is no reason to condemn them as useless. If civilization may be likened to a burden consisting of knowledge and virtue combined, a burden to be borne by all citizens, then personal belief and moral cultivation shoulder one end of the burden; thus they cannot be faulted on all scores. Nevertheless, such adherents are open to criticism if all they do is believe, and do nothing by way of work. They are like people with brains but no nerve cells, like people developing their brains and losing the use of their arms. What it comes down to is that, not perfecting all their natural endowments, they do not attain the maturity that is man's destiny.

As I have said, private virtue is not something which is easily developed through another's help. Even when it is so developed, it cannot serve any purpose without the aid of intelligence. Virtue depends on knowledge, and vice versa. An ignorant morality is equivalent to no morality. I adduce the following as proof of this. Why do present-day scholars consider Christianity useful but regard Shintoism, Buddhism, and Confucianism as irrelevant? Is it that one is right and the others wrong? I venture to make no judgments about this question—that is not the purpose of this essay—so I shall pass on to

---

† [An alternative name for Jōdo Shinshū, a sect of Pure Land Buddhism.]

discuss the efficacy of these teachings upon people's hearts.

When one looks carefully he sees that Christianity is not always a powerful influence. Instances of European missionaries going to various islands of the Pacific and other primitive lands and converting the native inhabitants are numerous. Nevertheless, the natives still, to this day, remain as they used to be, and their state of civilization cannot, of course, compare with that of Europe. Naked natives who do not know any distinction of husband and wife herd together in the churches; the children born from these polygamous marriages are baptized into the Christian religion, but this amounts to a mere formality. The rare cases in which some civilized progress is made in these lands are always attendant upon the book learning and arts transmitted by these missionaries; it is not the result merely of the religious teaching. Religion there ought only to be called an external formality.

Let us look at it in another light as well. The Japanese people—who have been brought up on Shinto, Confucian, and Buddhist teachings—are neither entirely uncivilized nor entirely immoral; there are very many upright people around. Thus the teachings of Shinto, Confucianism, and Buddhism are not without some efficacy, and Christianity is not the only efficacious teaching. So why should Christianity be considered conducive to civilization and the other three be considered irrelevant? The ideas of scholars on this point seem to me indefensible. Their reasoning seems to be grounded on the opinion that, since Christianity is practiced in civilized countries, it must go hand in hand with civilization, whereas the other three are practiced in uncivilized countries, so they cannot accord with civilization. That is probably why they say the one is useful whereas the others are irrelevant. However, the reason the one is more suitable than the others does not lie in the strength or weakness of the teachings themselves. It lies in the different degrees of intelligence with which these teachings are accompanied and their brilliance enhanced.

In the West Christians breathe the air of civilization. Their religious teachers especially do not read only the Bible. They all receive school educations and are well versed in book learning and the arts as well. Therefore, one who used to be a missionary to a distant land can now practice law in his own country; one who today explains the Law in his church can tomorrow go to a school and teach. Trained both in religious and secular matters, a man can teach both Christian doctrine and secular learning, thus leading men to the realm of wisdom. As a result, his activities are not antagonistic to civilization. The reason why his teachings are not belittled by people is not that people believe only the Ten Commandments, but that they also believe that his activities, far from being irrelevant, contribute to the development of modern civilization. Strip these Christian missionaries of their learning and skills and make them like our own mountain monks, and, however upright their conduct, however holy their persons, even if they intoned from memory the Old and New Testaments morning and night, what civilized gentleman would believe their teachings? Yes, occasionally they might get a few country bumpkins, the kind who finger their beads and chant their *nenbutsu*. In such people's eyes there is no difference between Jesus, Confucius, Buddha, or Amaterasu-ō-mikami. To these worshippers, foxes and racoon dogs are all gods and Buddhas.[†] What good can be had from teaching anything to ignorant folk who shed tears when they hear the chanting of sutras which they do not even comprehend? You would certainly not advance the cause of civilization. Were Christianity to be forced on these ignorant, uneducated folk, discussing with them, explaining to them, maybe even giving them money as an inducement, till finally some of them came around to Christianity, the result would only be the creation of a Christian sect within Buddhism. This would not be the result originally intended by the intellectuals.

We intellectuals should have in view the introduction of such learned and multi-talented Christian teachers in order to learn, together with their religion, their methods of book learning and arts, thereby to advance our own civilization. Now, methods of book learning and arts are matters of intelligence, the teaching of which is not necessarily the exclusive domain of Christian teachers. They can be learned from anyone, provided he has intelligence. Therefore, those intellectuals are mistaken who consider Christianity beneficial but Shinto,

---

† [In Japanese folklore, foxes and raccoon dogs are frequently portrayed as tricksters with magical powers. Foxes were also the messengers of the rice deity Inari.]

Confucianism, and Buddhism irrelevant. I have nothing against Christian teachers, of course. As long as a person has intelligence, I make no qualitative distinction between a Christian teacher and an ordinary teacher. All I care about is that a person be learned, talented, and upright. If there were no upright persons in Japan other than the Christian teachers, then of course we should take only them as our teachers and learn everything from them. But Christianity does not have a monopoly on upright individuals. There ought to be many learned and upright gentlemen in this wide world. Let each person choose for himself from among them. Why should we be biased in favor of Christianity?

In any case, to be beneficial or not beneficial is not an inherent part of any teaching as such; the value of a teaching depends on the degree of intelligence of the people who believe in it. Both the teaching of Jesus and that of Buddha would, if handed over to fools, serve the purposes only of fools. Present-day Shinto, Confucianism, and Buddhism are so very irrelevant precisely because the teaching of them is in the hands of present-day Shinto priests, Buddhist monks, and Confucian scholars. If these men were well educated (I know this is asking for too much), and if they could adorn their teachings with methods of book learning and arts so as to gain the hearing of men of culture when they expound their teachings, they would increase the value of their doctrines a hundredfold. Why, they might even make others jealous of them!

To use a simile, teaching is like a cutting tool, and the people of a country where the teaching is received are the craftsmen. Even if the cutting tool be sharp, if it is put into the hands of inept craftsmen it is useless. Virtue, too, will be useless for carrying out a civilizing function if it bumps up against people who cannot even read. The sages of morality, I dare say, have misjudged the ineptness of the craftsmen and put the whole blame on the dullness of the tool.

This is why I say that private virtue shows forth its brilliance through intelligence. It is intelligence that guides private virtue and assures its good effects. Unless knowledge and virtue go hand in hand, we can hardly look forward to society's becoming civilized.

It is not my purpose here to reopen the discussion on the relative merits of introducing some religion. But since the subject has been touched on, I should like to say a few more words about it in passing. When we are looking for something, we are trying to get something we lack entirely, or something we need more of. If one is looking for two things and has to determine which of the two is more urgently needed, he must first take stock of what he already possesses and then see what he completely lacks or, if the second type, which he has the less of. It is not a question of seeking the one and considering the other unnecessary, for they both are necessary; but there is a question here of which is more urgent. I have already said that civilization is the external mark of the knowledge and virtue of a whole nation. Everyone will grant that Japan's civilization is not equal to that of the countries of the West. If this is so, it follows that here people are deficient in knowledge and virtue; these are the two things Japan must seek in order to attain civilization. Hence, unless scholars of civilization survey the entire national scene and measure the amount of both items already present, so that they can tell which is more plentiful at the moment, which not, they will not be able to judge which is more urgently needed.

Now, a person does not have to be very smart to see that in Japan there is no dearth of morality, but at the same time there is no surplus of intelligence either. Any number of instances could be adduced to prove this, but there is no need to list them all here. Let me give just one or two by way of illustration.

The moral teaching current in Japan derives from Shintoism, Confucianism, and Buddhism, whereas in the West it derives from Christianity. Each of these does not teach exactly the same thing, yet they are not all that different in their general definitions of good and evil. East or West, snow is white and coal is black. Also, in matters of moral teaching scholars from both East and West fervently propose their own teachings, sometimes writing books, sometimes attacking other teachings in ceaseless polemics. But merely from the content of these polemics we can see that there is not a great deal of difference between the teachings of East and West. Polemics arise, really, only between evenly matched opponents. You never see a fight between a cow and a cat; you never hear of a contest between a wrestler and a little boy. When battles start, they generally start between parties whose strength is even. Now, Christianity is a religion which Westerners adorn and sustain by means of intelligence. Its subtlety and elaborateness cannot be matched by Shinto, Confucianism, or Buddhism. However, the Western missionaries come to Japan, fervently propose their own teachings, reject Shinto, Confucianism, and Buddhism, and try to carve out a position for themselves. This just stirs up counterattacks from Shinto, Confucian, and Buddhist scholars. What makes this quibbling and arguing possible, if not the fact that the West's moral teaching is no cow, no wrestler, and Japan's teachings are no cats, no little boys? In other words, the moral teachings of both East and West are really evenly matched.

My main concern here is not to discuss which side is better, but I might point out that we Japanese also have ethical values we live by. Hence, when discussing the question of who has how much private virtue, no one should conclude that we are necessarily second to the West. For if we go from theory to reality we might find more morally superior individuals among us unenlightened Japanese than we could find in the West. Therefore, though a survey of the amount of virtue in our country as a whole may show we are relatively deficient in it, the deficiency clearly has not reached crisis proportions.

The question of intelligence, however, is something completely different. If we compare the levels of intelligence of Japanese and Westerners, in methods of book learning, the arts, commerce, or industry, from the biggest things to the least, in a thousand cases or in one, there is not a single area in which the other side is not superior to us. We can compete with the West in nothing, and no one even thinks about competing with the West. Only the most ignorant thinks that Japan's book learning, arts, commerce, or industry are on a par with that of the West. Who would compare a man-drawn cart with a steam engine, or a Japanese sword with a rifle? While we are expounding the theory of the yin-yang and the Five Elements, they are discovering the sixty-element atomic chart.[†] While we are divining lucky and unlucky days by astrology, they have charted the courses of comets and are

---

† [*Sic.* There were only sixty-three chemical elements discovered when Fukuzawa was writing this book in 1874.]

studying the constitution of the sun and the moon. While we think that we live on a flat, immobile earth, they know that it is round and in motion. While we regard Japan as the sacrosanct islands of the gods, they have raced around the world, discovering new lands and founding new nations. Many of their political, commercial, and legal institutions are more admirable than anything we have. In all these things there is nothing about our present situation that we can be proud of before them. The only things we Japanese can boast of are our natural products or our scenic landscapes, but we never talk about anything made by man. We feel no urge to compete with them, nor they with us. Foreigners often brag about conditions in their own lands, true, but you do not hear them talking about the superiority of steam engines over man-drawn carts. In the final analysis, the difference between our respective levels of intelligence is like the difference between the cow and cat, mentioned above. No argument is possible in such circumstances. In view of this fact, then, if Japan's most urgent need today is not intelligence, what is it? Let scholars ponder this question.

Let me adduce another example to demonstrate this further. In the countryside today there is a man of talent, an ex-samurai of one of the old feudal domains. Before the domains were abolished he used to receive a stipend of two to three hundred *koku*.[†] He has never committed any wrong. He was loyal in the service of his lord, filial to his parents, maintained the distinction between husband and wife and the precedence of the old over the young, always paid back his debts, and is devoted to his friends. Needless to say, he has never lied or stolen. Although he may on occasion have oppressed farmers or townspeople, since such conduct was appropriate to his samurai status, it is no cause for shame. In his household he is extremely frugal, and in his personal affairs very diligent. He is skilled in archery and horsemanship and in handling the sword and spear. His only weakness is that he does not know how to read. Now, what shall we do for such a person today? Shall we give him virtue, or knowledge? Suppose that, to lead him toward virtue, we suddenly gave him the Ten Commandments of

---

† [In Tokugawa Japan, revenue and stipends were measured in *koku*, one *koku* being equivalent to the amount of rice consumed by one person in a year.]

Christianity. Since he has never heard about the first four commandments, perhaps he ought to listen to them; but as for the last six he will be sure to say that he does respect his parents, that he has no thought of committing murder, that he is not licentious, does not steal, and so forth. To each of these he can object that he already observes them, and he will not be especially impressed by them. Of course, Christ's teachings cannot be exhausted by a superficial listing of the Ten Commandments. They are surely profound, based as they all are on natural laws of human behavior, either in honoring one's father and mother, or in prohibitions against murder, adultery, or theft. Therefore, in preaching the Ten Commandments to this ex-samurai the careful explanation of their import over and over again may at length move his heart. For as far as ordinary moral conduct is concerned, this ex-samurai already knows at least the rudiments.

But if we look at his intellectual gifts, we find that his whole body is like an empty vessel. Although he can, just barely, distinguish five colors, he certainly has no knowledge at all of the principles behind the seven colors of the spectrum. He knows the proper greetings to use in hot and cold weather, but has no idea of the principles involved in measuring fluctuations of temperature. He never mistakes the time for meals, but he does not know how to tell time by a clock. He is not aware that there is more to Japan than the province in which he lives, and is unaware that there are countries beyond the shores of Japan. He knows neither the domestic situation nor anything about foreign relations. He simply yearns for the past and preserves old ways. His household is like a miniature universe in itself. His range of vision does not go beyond his own four walls. He is completely in the dark about the great world that begins just one step outside his door. But the abolition of the feudal *han* has overturned this miniature universe. He now is completely at a loss in his surroundings. In sum, this person is an upright, but ignorant, man.

Such upright but ignorant people are not found only among the ex-samurai of the old *han*; they exist throughout our society. This is a widely known fact, and both scholars and government officials are concerned about it. However, are not the learned preachers of moral conduct, so busy teaching the truth of Christianity to these ignorant people and trying to improve their morality, forgetting the question of intelligence? They may be concerned about only ignorant and immoral people, but there are many ignorant but upright people in society, too. What are they doing for them? Are they trying to increase their virtue *and* their ignorance as well? They have no sense of what is more urgently needed. Scholars of Western Learning ridicule old-style Chinese and Japanese Learning as irrelevant. And for what cause? For being devoid of any intellectual functions. They criticize others, only to do the same thing. They build only to tear down again. How deluded can people be?

Religion changes its tenor in accord with the progress of civilization. In the West, Christianity first started during the Roman Empire. Although Rome was a center of civilization, compared with modern civilization it was an ignorant and primitive world. Thus Christianity in that age proclaimed mostly fallacies which were appropriate to the level of intelligence of that time, ones that would not be criticized by people nor come as a shock to them. Then, with the changes of society over several hundred years, Christianity gradually took root in men's minds. After it had gained some influence, it began to oppress their minds. The situation was exactly like a tyrannical government's despotic oppression of the common people. But the inventive power of the human intellect is like the flow of a great river; if you try to stop it up, it becomes more violent. Hence it was that religious power fell into bad repute. The Reformation that began in the 1500s developed into new **Protestant** sects that rejected the Church of Rome. From that time on, two streams of Christianity have continued apace; however, today Protestantism seems to have finally gained the upper hand. Now, both Catholicism and Protestantism derive from the same source of Christianity, and the tenets they believe in are the same for both. Yet the reason for the ascendancy of Protestantism lies in the fact that it simplified religious formalities, eliminated some of the old fallacies, and responded to the feelings of modern man, in keeping with the state of his intellectual progress. Generally speaking, the old dogmas were heavy with the past and not far removed from foolishness, while the new teachings were light and dynamic. The difference was an expression of the difference in the human spirit and in civilization as they were in the past and are in modern times.

Now, according to what I have just said, the most civilized countries of Europe ought to be Protestant, and the least civilized should be Catholic. However, this is not the case. For example, most people in Scotland and Sweden are credulous of fallacies; they are far removed from the genius and dynamism of the French. Thus we should conclude that Scotland and Sweden are uncivilized, and France civilized. Yet France believes in the old Catholicism, while Scotland and Sweden are **Protestant** countries. Therefore, either French Catholicism has changed its style to fit the spirit of the French people, or we must think of the French outside the context of religion. Also, the Protestantism in Scotland and Sweden probably changed its character to fit the level of ignorance of those peoples. In other words, this shows that religion changes its forms in accord with the progress of civilization.

Even in Japan, such old religious doctrines as those of the mountain ascetics[†] or of the Tendai and Shingon sects misled the people by preaching chiefly mysterious practices, such as the magic of uniting fire and water, or the practice of mystical offerings and prayers. In olden times people believed such fallacies. But in the medieval world, with the appearance of the Ikkō sect, such preaching of the mysterious became rarer. The Ikkō style of teaching was plain and simple, appealing to the Japanese people of the medieval world. It thus overshadowed the other sects and finally dominated the scene completely. This is proof that the simpler religion becomes with the progress of human civilization, the more it must be based on the truth. Suppose that today Kōbō Daishi[‡] were to be reborn and made to preach the esoteric doctrines with which he misled the ancients. Hardly anybody in Meiji Japan would believe him. The people of modern times must be put in touch with a modern religion; they have to be satisfied with the religion, and the religion

---

[†] [Fukuzawa is referring here to Shugendō, a sect which combined Shinto and esoteric Buddhist practices. Its practitioners traveled widely and developed a considerable following in pre-Meiji Japan.]

[‡] [Posthumous name of Kūkai (774–835), the founder of the Shingon sect of Buddhism in Japan.]

must be satisfied with them, with no complaints on either side. If Japan's civilization starts to make progress from now on, so that people will come to dislike the Ikkō sect because of its fallacies, another kind of Ikkō sect must be created to take its place. Or we must import the religious doctrines of the West.

Ultimately, however, we must put the consideration of religion outside our frame of reference completely. Neither the power of scholars nor the authority of government can do much about it. It must be left to follow its own natural course. Accordingly, anyone who writes a book debating the right or wrong of this or that religion, and tries to control the teaching of religious doctrine by establishing laws, deserves to be called the most stupid person in the land.

A man of virtue does not always do good, and an immoral man does not always do evil. Western history gives many examples of armies mobilized and people killed in the name of religion. The most extreme examples of this were the religious **persecutions** in which people of a different religious belief were tracked down and massacred. Examples of this are most numerous in old France and Spain. In the famous Bartholomew Day massacre, it is said that in eight days five thousand innocent people were slaughtered.* Unspeakably horrible as this is, the ones who actually carried out the persecutions were good men who believed wholeheartedly in their religious creed and never hesitated a moment when it came to acting in the name of religion—they felt their acts nothing to be ashamed of. How is it that these God-fearing men could do such awful things? It was certainly not private virtue they were lacking in. What they lacked was that intelligence I term wisdom. If you give a fool power, and make this power a matter of religious faith, there is no horror he will be incapable of. This is the monster men have to fear most.

Since then, civilization has bit by bit advanced to the point where today we no longer hear of religious **persecutions**. This is not because the religious teachings of past and present are different, but because of

---

* The affair is described in my [Fukuzawa's] *Seiyō jijō* (Conditions in the West), Part Two, on France.

different stages in the progress of civilization. Why, in the case of one and the same Christian teaching, were men killed for it in ancient times, while now it is being used to save men? The cause can only be found in the difference between ignorance and intelligence. Intelligence not only increases the glory of morality, it also protects it and keeps men from doing evil.

In the Mito *han* there were both orthodox and heterodox Confucian factions.[†] There is no need to go into the history behind the existence of these factions, but in essence the two parties split over a dispute about the meaning of loyalty. In character, then, the problem was equivalent to a religious controversy. Now, the words *orthodox* and *heterodox* have no meaning in themselves, since it is simply a matter of one side claiming orthodoxy for itself and calling the other side heterodox. As a matter of fact, both factions were loyal. Many individuals on both sides were sincere and true. Proof that they were not pseudo gentlemen may be known from the fact that when they erred they met death with composure. However, the Mito *han* led all others in pre-modern Japan in killing innocent people because of their differences of opinion. This is another example of good people doing evil.

Undaunted by the hardships, Tokugawa Ieyasu brought three hundred years of peace and tranquility to a war-torn land. To the present day there is no one who does not sing the praises of his glorious achievement. True, at the end of the Ashikaga's reign, when the whole of Japan was in turmoil, even the feats of Oda Nobunaga and Toyotomi Hideyoshi had been insufficient to lay a secure foundation for this. If Ieyasu had not appeared at that time, who can say when peace would have come to Japan? Ieyasu should indeed be called the father of three hundred years of peace. Yet a look at the personal morality of the man will show not a few things of which a person ought to be ashamed. In particular, he betrayed the last request of the dying Hideyoshi; he had no intention of defending Osaka Castle. He was specially entrusted with helping Toyotomi Hideyori, Hideyoshi's only son, but instead he raised

---

† [Fukuzawa is referring to the fact that the radical late Tokugawa Imperialists of Mito *han* called themselves "orthodox" and rejected other groups as "heterodox."]

him to be a weak libertine. He did not eliminate Ishida Mitsunari as he should have, but saved him in order to use Mitsunari as a tool in overturning the rule of the Toyotomi in Osaka. These were the evil machinations of the highest order.[†] In this regard, then, it would seem that Ieyasu did not have a single virtue. Yet how was it that with this lack of virtue Ieyasu was able to lead Japan down the road of three hundred years of peace and to relieve the people in their distress? The personal endowments of Minamoto Yoritomo or Nobunaga were no better. They were repeatedly cruel, ruthless, deceitful, and treacherous. Why was it that both Yoritomo and Nobunaga were able to put a halt to warfare and the slaughter of the common people? It is because evil men are not necessarily incapable of performing good deeds. Though deficient in private virtue, these heroes must be said to have achieved great good by making use of wisdom. One cannot judge a gem's total value by a single blemish.

To summarize my argument: Morality pertains to the conduct of an individual; its range of influence is narrow. Intelligence is speedily transmitted to others and its range of influence is wide. From earliest times morality has been fixed and does not change. But the workings of intelligence progress day by day, without limits. Morality cannot be taught to men through any concrete methods. Whether a man learns virtue or not depends entirely upon his own efforts. Intelligence, on the contrary, can be verified by means of tests. Morality can easily be lost, but once intelligence is acquired it is never lost. Knowledge and virtue achieve their results by complementing each other. A good man can do evil and an evil one can do good. That is the sum and substance of my argument above.

Now, even though one cannot teach a man morality by concrete methods, nor will one's moral exhortations reach beyond the narrow sphere of one's friends or relatives, the transforming power of morality

---

† [Fukuzawa is here drawing on Rai San'yō's interpretation as described in *Nihon gaishi*. Ieyasu gave shelter to Ishida Mitsunari (1560–1600), a high-ranking retainer of the Toyotomi, when his enemies attacked him in 1599. Ieyasu purposely did not kill him, even though he realized that a clash between them was inevitable. Then, when Mitsunari formed an anti-Ieyasu alliance in 1600, this gave Ieyasu the opportunity to demolish his main rivals at the battle of Sekigahara and gain undisputed control of Japan.]

can reach out over an extremely wide area. There are cases of a person's attaining great enlightenment after reading a book published many thousand miles away, or examples of people who on their own initiative change their personal philosophies after learning about the words and actions of the ancients. This is what is meant by "Hearing about Boyi and stirring oneself to action."† If, as a human being, a man does not desire to do harm to society, can he stand by and do nothing to cultivate personal morality? It is not for the sake of reputation, nor for the sake of advantage, but precisely because we are human beings that we take upon ourselves the responsibility for morality. To restrain one's own evil bent, one must be like a valiant warrior engaged in combat with the foe, and as heartless in inflicting pain as a tyrant lording over his subjects; to see good and make it one's own, one must be as tireless as a miser storing up his coins. When one has once ordered his own life, he can then educate his family; then, if he has strength left over, he can go on to direct his energies to teaching and discussing with others, leading all human beings through the portals of virtue. Thus step by step a man can strive to widen the range of morality. This too is a human enterprise. Since it makes a vast contribution to civilization, it is truly desirable that there should be preachers in the world who strive to inculcate morality. Yet what I personally find most distressing is that people try to win over the whole world to virtue only, or worse, advocate one moral teaching to the exclusion of others, at the same time invading the realm of intelligence, as if man's only business in life were moral teaching, and moral teaching of only one determinate school. And then they go on to shackle human thought and prevent it from developing freely. But this is rather to impede true civilization by encouraging men to sink into inactivity and ignorance.

To make a contribution to civilization by passive private virtue and to enable society to attain some benefit thereby would be nothing but an accidental benefit. It is like what happens, for example, when one builds a house on one's property; in so doing one also happens to build a wall for one's neighbor. Though this may be extremely convenient for the neighbor, the original intention is to build the house for oneself; the

---

† [Boyi was a famous Chinese sage whose rectitude continued to inspire later generations after his death, according to *Mencius*.]

neighbor's benefit can be called accidental. Cultivating private virtue is also originally for one's own benefit, not for that of others. Anyone who did cultivate virtue for the sake of others would be a pseudo gentleman, deplored by the moralists. Therefore, the essence of morality lies in personal cultivation; it is a mere accidental blessing if it benefits civilization.

Now, it would be a great mistake to govern a society on the basis of something accidental. When a man is born into this world, he cannot claim that taking care of his own affairs is enough; his duty as a human being does not end there. I would like to ask all virtuous gentlemen: Where do the daily necessities of life come from? Even though the blessings of the Lord on High are great indeed, clothes do not grow in the mountains and food does not rain down from heaven. And when civilization progresses, its benefits do not stop at only food and clothing. The blessings of the steam engine, the telegraph, government, business—where do they come from? They are all the gifts of intelligence. The idea that all men have equal rights does not mean that we can just sit back and receive the gifts of others. If gentlemen of virtue were merely hanging like bottle-gourds, taking no food, their words might fit their actions, but if they take food, wear clothes, enjoy the benefits of steam and the telegraph, and share in the conveniences of government and business, they have to bear their share of responsibilities, too.

Furthermore, even though a man's physical needs are fully satisfied and he is fully virtuous in his private life, he has no reason to be satisfied with stopping there. Even if such satisfaction and perfect virtue may suffice for present-day civilization, they certainly have not reached the peak of their potential. The development of the human spirit knows no limits, and man's creative capacities have no fixed boundaries. Man must fathom the fixed principles of things with his infinite spirit, so that all the things of heaven and earth, both concrete and abstract, can be comprehended by it. At that stage of human history, it will be unnecessary to distinguish between knowledge and virtue and to fight over their respective spheres. On that day man and God will stand side by side, as it were. For some future generation of men that day will surely be a reality.

Chapter SEVEN

THE PROPER TIMES AND PLACES FOR KNOWLEDGE AND VIRTUE

THE TIMES and places must be considered when discussing the merits and demerits of things. A cart is convenient on land, but it does not make much headway on the sea. Things that were convenient in yesteryear are no longer convenient today. Again, there are many things which are most useful in our modern world which would have been useless in earlier ages. If we leave time and places out of consideration, there is nothing that is not convenient, nothing that is not inconvenient. Therefore a discussion of the merits and demerits of things means nothing more nor less than a consideration of the times and places in which they are to be used. There is nothing whose merits or demerits will not become clear when it is put in its temporal and spatial context. The long spear invented in the Middle Ages was useful in medieval warfare, but it is useless in our Meiji period. A rickshaw may be useful in Tokyo, but not in London or Paris. War may be a terrible thing, but in the face of an aggressor one cannot help but fight. Killing another person may be immoral, but in time of war one cannot help but kill. Tyrannical despots may be despicable, but the accomplishments of Peter the Great suggest that we cannot fault all dictators. The deeds of loyal retainers and faithful samurai may have been admirable, but one cannot call the United States, which has no feudal lords, a country of barbarians. Everything has its own time and place. There is no single Way that embraces all things in the universe. Progress can only be made by harmonizing with the times and places.

It is extremely difficult correctly to judge the proper times and places. Whenever people have bungled things, you can be sure there was an error in judgment concerning the time or place. Successful great achievements were the result of being in accord with the time and place. But why is it so difficult to judge the proper time and place? The reason is that many places look alike, and that in regard to time one has to consider the right moment, neither too soon nor too late, and the right speed, neither too fast nor too slow.

For example, real and adopted sons are similar, but it would be a great error to treat the latter as one does the former. Again, a horse and a deer may resemble each other, but it would kill the deer to raise it like a horse. Or again, to mistake a Buddhist temple for a Shinto shrine; or to mistake a metal gong for a paper lantern; or to use cavalry in a bog; or to drag heavy cannons up a mountain road; or to confuse Tokyo with London and use rickshaws in the latter city—all these are but a few examples of the kind of blunders that are possible. Medieval and modern warfare have certain things in common, but, as I said above, you cannot use medieval long spears in a modern war.

Frequently when people say that the time is ripe for something, the real ripe moment is already passed. The time to eat is the time to eat, and the time to cook the food must precede. If you do not bother to prepare any food until you feel hunger, you may say the time has come, but that is the time to eat, not the time to cook. Sleep-lovers get up before noon, and they call that the morning; but true morning comes at dawn, while these sleep-lovers are still fast asleep. Places, then, must be chosen well, and times must not be neglected until the right moment has passed.

In the preceding chapter I pointed out the differences between intelligence and morality and discussed their respective spheres of influence. I would like to continue in this chapter to discuss the times and places appropriate to each.

After the dawn of history, when man had newly emerged from the primitive stage, the intellectual powers of ordinary people had not yet developed and were little different from those of a child today. The only things men experienced were fear and joy. They feared earthquakes, lightning, rainstorms, fires and floods, the mountains and the seas, drought, and famine. Whatever was beyond the grasp of their minds they feared as a natural calamity. If an anticipated natural calamity did not come, or if it came and passed quickly, they called it a blessing from heaven, and rejoiced. This happened when there was rain after a drought, or a bountiful harvest after a period of famine. Moreover, when these natural calamities or blessings came, since they were entirely unanticipated, primitive man attributed them to accident, and no one ever tried to devise human ways of coping with them. Since these calamities or blessings came their way without any action on their part, their sentiments led them to ascribe the cause to some agency above the human. This was the origin of the feeling that demons and gods exist. Evil gods caused calamities, and benevolent gods were the cause of blessings. Every event in the world was due to the action of some kind of demon or god. In Japan these were called the eight million gods of heaven and earth. The people prayed to the good gods for blessings, and to the evil gods for deliverance from calamities. Whether their prayers were answered or not was not a matter of their own efforts but lay entirely in the power of the gods. This was called "divine power," and imploring the assistance of the divine power was called "prayer." The prayers and imprecations of this period were of this kind.

It was not only natural blessings or calamities which stirred up joy or fear in primitive man. The situation was the same in regard to human affairs. Since man was living in an age ignorant of reason, the strong oppressed the weak, and there was no appeal to reason. The only thing the people did was fear the strong, much as they feared natural calamities. The weak could do nothing but depend upon one of the strong to defend them against the might of others. The person whom they turned to was called their chieftain. In addition to his physical power, the chieftain had a modicum of knowledge and virtue. By controlling the might of others he protected those who were weak. The more he protected them the more popular he became, until at length he came to enjoy somewhat of a privileged position, which sometimes passed on to his descendants. In all countries of the world, primitive man lived in such circumstances. In ancient Japan, the emperors held the reins of power; in medieval times the Minamoto monopolized power in the Kantō.

The power and authority gained by a chieftain were difficult to maintain, since the people were ignorant and conditions were always unstable. In communicating with such people, a chieftain could not rely on lofty reasoning, nor persuade them by speaking of far-off benefits. In order to unite the people and maintain the form of a single racial group, the only thing a chieftain could do was to play on people's innate fears and joys and present them with blessings and calamities that they could see with their own eyes. This took the form either of the lord's beneficence or of his authority. It was perhaps here that "ritual and music" came into being. Ritual essentially meant showing reverence to those above, and impressed on men the sacredness of their lord's authority. Music soothed the minds of the ignorant masses, and roused in them feelings of admiration for their lord's virtue. By both ritual and music the ruler won the hearts of the people. By armaments he controlled their forces. Before they knew it he had made them accept their places. By rewarding the good, he filled them with feelings of joy. By punishing the wicked, he reduced people's feelings of fear. By the simultaneous exercise of benevolence and authority, then, the people were apparently made strangers to suffering. However, because praise and punishment were meted out entirely at the whim of the ruler, the only thing the people did was be afraid or joyful according as they were punished or praised. They did not know why they were praised or punished. This condition was no different from their experience of blessings or calamity from heaven; things were entirely out of their hands, everything happened at random. Because the ruler of the country was the source of blessings or calamities coming to them at random, it was inevitable that he be revered by the people as one who seemed to transcend the sphere of ordinary men. The fact that the ruler in China was revered as the "son of heaven" was probably the result of such a process.

Take, for example, cases in ancient times in which peasants were occasionally exempted from rice taxes. No matter how thrifty the government was, it could not do without a great deal of public expenditure and income for the needs of the upper classes. But if for a number of years incomes were sufficient without tax revenues, this showed that in prior years taxes had been excessive, and that surpluses had been built up. Even though people were paying such excessive taxes, they had no idea why they were. Now, if they were suddenly not taxed for several years, they would have just as little idea why they were not being taxed. When taxes were excessive, they shook with fear, taking it as a calamity from heaven. When taxes were light, they rejoiced, taking it as a blessing from heaven. Both blessings and calamities came from the emperor, the son of heaven. He possessed, as it were, the power of both lightning and the lightning rod. If thunder rumbled across the skies, it was the command of the emperor; if they were not harmed by it, this too was the command of the emperor. All the people could do was pray to this being. It was not without reason, then, that their reverence for the emperor was the same as for the demons and gods.

To modern man this seems inexcusable. But it was the result of the conditions of those times, and there is no reason to censure it. With the people of those days it was impossible to discuss intellectual matters, difficult to establish laws, and difficult to keep promises. For example, if we tried to apply the laws of modern Western countries to the times of Yao and Shun, no one would be able to understand them. The reason people would not obey these laws would not be that the people were evil, but that they would not have the intelligence needed to understand the laws. If such people were given free rein to do as they pleased, it would be impossible to imagine what harm they might cause society. Only the chieftain had a good comprehension of the trends of the times. He ruled over the people of his race as though they were his children, making them happy by his benevolence or intimidating them with his authority. He held control over everything, from the power over life and death down to the minute affairs of private households. The country was like a single family or a classroom, with the ruler as the parent or teacher. To the extent that his power and virtue were inscrutable, he was like a god. He was simultaneously parent, teacher, and god. In such a situation, if the ruler of the country checked his selfish desires and cultivated virtue, even if he were not too intelligent, he was praised as a benevolent ruler or enlightened emperor. This is what was called "the tranquility of the barbarians." Of course, in such an age this was unavoidable; it could even be called admirable. The governments in the times of Yao and Shun were of this kind. On the other hand, if the ruler indulged his selfish desires, was not virtuous, and relied only upon authority and force, he was called a tyrant. This is what was called "the tyranny of the barbarians," where the people could not be secure about even their lives.

In sum, in the society of the primitive age there were only the opposite extremes of benevolent government and authoritarian power. If it wasn't virtuous benevolence, it was violent oppression; if it wasn't merciful generosity, it was rapacious plunder. There was no room for intelligence to function between these two alternatives.

The ancient books speak of two Ways. They were called the Way of Humanity and the Way of Inhumanity. These were not applicable merely to government; the two extremes were applicable to man's private affairs as well. As we read the ancient texts of Japan and China, we find that both the Confucian Classics and the Histories, when they explain the Way and evaluate human behavior, take morality as the final criterion, and they maintain a strict distinction between humaneness and its opposite, filial piety and its absence, loyalty and disloyalty, and righteousness and non-righteousness. One who is not a Boyi is a Daozhi,† and one who is not a loyal retainer is a brigand. Between the two, there is no room for intelligence to function. If someone happened to utilize his intelligence, his actions were called trivial and no one paid attention to them. In the last analysis, it is clear that what determined the social relations in the primitive and unlettered age was morality and morality alone, and nothing else could be utilized.

As human civilization finally blossomed and the power of intelligence gradually advanced, men came to entertain doubts, and things that they experienced they did not let pass unchallenged. When

---

† [The former was a model of filial piety and loyalty; the latter was the most notorious thief in Chinese history.]

they saw how things worked, they tried to find out their causes. Even if they could not fathom the true causes, once doubt had arisen in their minds, they came to become more discriminating, preferring what worked to their advantage and avoiding what proved harmful. In order to ward off the damaging effects of wind and rain, they built their houses stronger. In order to prevent floods from rivers and the ocean, they built dikes. They built ships to cross the waters. They used water to prevent fires and made drugs to cure illnesses. They made use of irrigation to prepare against drought. By relying a bit upon human power they were able to make their lives secure. Once man learned how to secure his position through his own power, anxieties caused by fear of natural calamities gradually decreased. Great numbers of people even lost that belief in the demons and gods they had relied upon so heavily before. Therefore with every step forward in the level of intelligence they likewise advanced in courage; the more intelligence progressed the more limitless man's courage became.

If we seek the essence of Western civilization, it lies in the fact that Westerners scrutinize whatever they experience with the five senses, in order to discover its essence and its functions. They go on to seek the causes of its functions, and anything they find beneficial they make use of, while whatever they find harmful they discard. The range of power of modern man is endless. He controls the energies in water and fire to power the steam engines by which he crosses the vast Pacific. He carves out roads even in the highest Alps. He invented the lightning rod, and ever since, the power of lightning has been rendered harmless. Research in chemistry gradually produced results, and now famine no longer takes such a toll of human life. The powers of electricity, no longer terrifying, are used as a substitute for couriers. The properties of light waves, subtle as they are, are used to make photographic images. When winds and waves threaten, man builds harbors and keeps his ships safe. When contagion is about to strike, man now takes preventive measures. In sum, human intelligence resists the forces of nature and step by step invades its domain in order to discover the secrets of creation. Man harnesses nature's energies so that they cannot run about freely. Intelligence and courage sweep everything before them, and nature is put into man's employ. With nature's energies harnessed and in his service, why should man fear and worship nature? Should anyone worship mountains? Or pray to rivers? Mountains, swamps, rivers, oceans, wind and rain, sun and moon—they are now all slaves of civilized men.

Once the forces of nature are harnessed, they become our puppets. Why, then, should we fear what are merely man-made forces? Why should we be the puppets of these latter? As man's intellectual powers develop, he also probes the causes behind human activities in all their aspects. He learns that not all the words of the sages and wise men can be believed, that some of the teachings in the Classics are dubious, that even the governments of Yao and Shun ought not to be emulated, that the deeds of loyal retainers and faithful samurai cannot be our models. The ancients lived in ancient times and did things that suited their age, while we live in the modern world and must act like modern people. How can we think of applying the wisdom of the ancients to modern times? We must reach the point where we do not allow even one thing to become an obstacle to freedom of mind. Once freedom of mind is ours, why should we accept shackles on the body? Sheer physical strength is gradually losing its hold, and its place is being taken by the power of intelligence. There is no longer a struggle between the two. The number of people accepting calamities and blessings in social dealings as purely the result of accident is decreasing. And anyone who resorts to force in society can be made to answer to reason; if he does not bow to reason, he can be controlled through the combined power of the people. Once the tendency to control tyranny by the use of reason is firmly established, social distinctions based upon force and authority can also be overturned.

Therefore, while we distinguish between the government and the people, this is only a distinction of names and functions; but a distinction of status between superior and inferior cannot be allowed. The government protects the people, helps the weak, and controls the unruly because these are its proper functions. It should not be given excessive credit simply for fulfilling its duty. Even though a ruler cultivates morality and uses ritual, music, and punishment to administer by benevolence and authority, the people should first consider what kind of a ruler he is and should carefully examine his benevolence and authority. They should refuse to accept private benevolence that is unacceptable and should be undaunted by intimidation. Without compromise, they should stop short of nothing less than truth as their objective. Persons in whom powers of intelligence are developed can manage themselves and can, as it were, practice benevolence and authority upon themselves; they do not have to rely upon others. For example, when one does good he experiences within himself the reward of feeling good; since he is conscious of the fact that he ought to do good, he will do good of his own accord. He does not envy others or pine after the ancients. And when one does evil he experiences in himself the punishment of shame; since he knows that he should not do evil, he will avoid doing evil. He does not hesitate because of others or fear the ancients. Why should a person react with fear or joy to that benevolence or authority of others which comes his way at random?

Asked to comment on the relation between government and people, a civilized person should respond as follows: "Even the ruler of the whole land is a mere man like myself. He holds the position of ruler only because of an accident of birth or through victory in some battle. The members of the legislature are only servants of the country, put into office by our votes. Why should one change his morality and conduct at the order of men such as that? The government is the government, and I am I. Why should the government be allowed to meddle in my private affairs? Military armament, criminal law and control of crime are of no personal use to me, so why should I have to pay taxes to support them? True, since we live in a world of many criminals, I must continue to pay such taxes for a while, but in effect this is money just thrown away on evil persons. Should I, however, have to pay taxes so that the government can control religious and educational affairs, show people how to handle agriculture, industry, and commerce, or, worst of all, give directions on how they are to run their daily household affairs, tell them what is virtuous, and teach them how to manage their lives? That is the height of absurdity. Who would bow before another to request his instruction on how to be a good man? Who would pay money to be taught how to manage his own life by some ignorant person?"

This is more or less the way civilized people feel about government.

Is it not a waste of time to try to guide such people by abstract moral influence or by private benevolence and authority? Of course, there is no country in the world today where all of the people are intelligent, but the more people leave the primitive stages (provided the level of the country's civilization does not retrogress), the more intelligence will advance on a broad front among the people. Because some people are now steeped in old practices, they still look up to the kindness and authority of their superiors and seem to lack a spirit of their own; but as their contacts with things and ideas increase, they will inevitably begin to ask questions.

For example, suppose the ruler of a country is called enlightened, but in fact he is not; suppose he claims he considers the people his own children, but in fact the "parent" and the "children" fight over the amount of taxes. An ugly situation results: the "parent" threatens his "children," who in turn deceive their "parent." Even the ignorant lower classes will start wondering about the inconsistencies between the words and the deeds of such a ruler. Though they may not struggle against him, they will look upon him with suspicion. Once feelings of doubt or suspicion arise, their faith in, and devotion to, the ruler will dwindle, and he will no longer be able to control them through the subtleties of moral persuasion.

History is proof of this. In both Japan and China, as in the West, it was only in ancient times that benevolent rulers ruled their countries well. In Japan and China right up until early modern times they have tried to set up such "moral" rulers, but this has always proved to be a mistake. In the West, since the seventeenth and eighteenth centuries such benevolent rulers have been on the wane. In this nineteenth century there are no benevolent rulers; neither are there even any enlightened ones. This is not the result of a decline in virtue among those of sovereign stock. It is due, rather, to the fact that knowledge and virtue have increased in the ranks of the general populace, so that the ruler no longer has any opportunities to dazzle with his benevolence. If I may use a metaphor, were one to set up a benevolent ruler in the West today it would only be like lighting a paper lantern on a bright moonlit night.

Thus I say that benevolent government can only be carried out in a primitive, uncivilized society. If a benevolent ruler does not deal with primitive, uncivilized people, he is not revered. As civilization progresses private virtue loses more and more of its power.

Although I am saying that morality loses its power with the gradual advance of civilization, this does not mean a decrease in the amount of morality in the world. Virtue increases in amount, in fact, with the increase in knowledge that attends the advance of civilization. Private virtue expands into public, and the extent of public knowledge and public virtue among the populace in general widens and eventually leads toward tranquility. As the art of attaining tranquility makes daily progress, wars begin to decline. In the end, a point will be reached where men do not fight for land and do not covet wealth. When this happens, do you suppose people will struggle for such ignoble things as the position of sovereign? The words *lord* and *subject* will be things of the past, and even in children's games no one will be called by these names. War will cease, and punishment will be abolished. Government will no longer be a tool for containing evil in society. It will exist only for the purpose of keeping things in order, saving time, and cutting down on useless labor. In a world where everyone is true to his word, promissory notes for loans will only be recorded as an aid to memory and never used as grounds for lawsuits. If there are no robbers in the world, doors will only be used to keep out the wind and rain and dogs and cats—locks will become obsolete. When people no longer appropriate things they find on the road, patrolmen will have nothing to occupy them except gathering up such lost articles and returning them to their owners. Instead of cannons, men will build telescopes; schools will replace jails; soldiers and criminals will be seen only in old pictures—people will be unable even to imagine them unless they visit a theater. If public manners are cultivated within the family, there will no longer be any need to listen to preachers' sermons. The whole country will be like one family, each household like a temple. The parents will be the head priests, and the children, their disciples. People in the world will be surrounded by an atmosphere of courtesy and mutual deference; they will bathe, as it were, in a sea of morality. This is what I call the tranquility of civilization.

I do not know how many thousands of years it will take us to reach such a state. It may appear to be only a dream, but if we do reach this consummation of tranquility through human effort, then the efficacy of morality must indeed be said to be vast and unlimited. Thus, the efficacy of private virtue is most marked in a primitive age, but when it finally loses its power in the wake of civilization's advance, it takes on the form of public virtue. If we surmise how things will be thousands of years from now and imagine the pinnacle of civilization, we should be able to see what a blessing it is for everyone.

Above I discussed the appropriate time for morality. Now let me turn to the question of its appropriate place. My goal is no longer the tranquility of the barbarians. It is also irrelevant to talk about the tranquility of civilization that may come thousands of years hence. The most important key to the study of civilization is to distinguish between the places in which morality can and cannot be practiced in today's civilization. As the people of a country leave their former primitive state farther and farther behind, this distinction ought to become increasingly clear. However, uneducated people are apt not to know it and to make a great error in regard to objectives. Many wish to attain to the tranquility of civilization while holding on to the tranquility of the barbarians! Scholars of antiquity yearn for the past, and the reason seems to be that they err in making these distinctions and priorities. What they are doing is as difficult as fishing in a forest or climbing onto a roof without a ladder. Because there is always a discrepancy between where they want to be and where they really are, these people obviously are unable to describe their feelings to others. They cannot even answer their own questions; their minds are completely mixed up, their whole lives are full of ambiguous credulities, and they do not know where they are heading. Now they build up, now they tear down; now they maintain a position, now they attack it. Total up their lifelong achievements, and the sum is a big zero. Such men are truly to be pitied. They do not keep morality, morality keeps them—as its slaves. Let me explain this further.

Husband and wife, parents and children in one household constitute a family. Family relationships are bound by feeling. There is no fixed ownership of things, no rules for giving and taking. Things lost are not cried over; things gained are no special cause for jubilation. Informality is not upbraided, ineptitude does not cause embarrassment. The contentment of the wife or children becomes the joy of the husband or the parents, and the suffering of the husband or parents pains the wife and children too. The values of the family take precedence over individual satisfaction, the other's contentment becomes one's own joy. For example, when a darling child is suffering from a sickness, parents would rather suffer the illness themselves if this would lessen their child's pain. Thus, between family members there is no feeling of protecting what is one's own, no matters of personal pride, not even a selfish preference of one's own life. In relationships between family members, rules and contracts are unnecessary. Intellectual devices or grand policies have even less place. Intelligence is only useful in the one area of household management. The beauty of the family structure has its basis almost exclusively in morality.

As blood relations become more distant, however, this changes. Brothers and sisters are not as close as husband and wife, parents and children; uncles and nieces are even more distant than brothers and sisters. Cousins mark the point where the sphere of "outsiders" begins. As the blood ties get further and further removed, the power of familial feeling gradually weakens. Thus, when children grow up and establish their own families, the notion of "what belongs to me" comes into play. This is even truer in the case of uncles, nieces, and cousins. In certain kinds of friendships there is a kind of feeling of camaraderie not unlike family ties, yet in modern civilization the scope of these relationships is very limited. Examples of a group of dozens of people maintaining a close friendship over a long period of time are nonexistent.

There were lord-subject relations as well, which are again close to that of a family situation. They shared common social problems together, lived and died together, and so forth. A truly loyal subject would kill his own parents and brothers and children for the sake of his lord. People in general have always thought that this attitude was due completely to the close bond of feeling between lord and subject. But this view sees only one aspect of the matter and is shrouded in the lord-subject legend. It does not go far enough. Were one to look at the matter in full light, one would see that in fact there are other important causes, namely man's innate tendency toward forming companionships, and the spirit of men in any given age.

In the beginning of the lord–subject relationship only a few persons were involved. For example, when Hōjō Sōun and his six retainers made for the east with swords as walking sticks, their feelings for one another were closer than those of parents and children, brothers and sisters.[†] But once such a person controlled an entire province, his retainers vastly increased in number. By the time he passed his position on to his heir, the original lord–subject relation had turned into quite another thing. It was then that both lord and vassals handed down legends about how things were in the days of their ancestors. The lord tried to protect his house by relying on the power of his vassals, and the vassals revered the lord's family line, attached themselves to that family, and formed a kind of companionate group. In times of emergency they did all they could to protect the lord's family, while at the same time protecting their own lives. Sometimes an occasion offered itself for them to reap some benefit for themselves, or the spirit of the times might have motivated them to win great fame. These are some of the reasons that led them to spend themselves for their lord. It was not always due to a deep bond existing between the lord and subjects. This is why loyal retainers used to say that the land was more important than their lords, and if they thought a lord was a liability, they did not hesitate to take exceptional measures to get rid of the lord even though he was the sole head of the family. This certainly cannot be called a union based on deep affection.

Again, many cases of death on the battlefield or suicide at the fall of the castle were motivated by the spirit of the times. People sacrificed their lives to avoid loss of face as warriors; or else they saw no prospect of survival if they fled. At the time of the destruction of the Hōjō in Kamakura as recorded in the *Taiheiki*, more than 870 warriors

---

† [Hōjō Sōun (1432–1519) or Ise Moritoki was the founder of the Go-Hōjō, one of the most powerful daimyo families of the Sengoku period. He was regarded as a model of the talented warrior of low birth who was able to fight his way up to daimyo rank in this period. The name of Hōjō was never used by Sōun himself but chosen by his heir (even though the family were not directly related to the renowned Hōjō of the Kamakura period).]

committed suicide with Hōjō Takatoki at the Tōshōji on the 22nd day of the fifth month, 1333. When the Hōjō partisans heard this, more than 6,000 in Kamakura followed them in death. Was Takatoki such a benevolent ruler that a familial relationship existed between him and these 6,870 vassals? Hardly. When you come down to it, it is impossible to divine the extent of Takatoki's virtue from the number of his retainers who died in battle or committed *seppuku*. Whether retainers died for tyrants or for benevolent rulers, in actual fact the number who gave their lives out of a deep devotion to their lord was surprisingly small. The main reason for such sacrifice must be sought elsewhere. Hence, the efficacy of morality had an extremely narrow area of influence even in the lord–subject relationship.

To succor the needy by building poorhouses, hospitals, and so forth are acts of morality and sympathy, but the original motive for such actions does not lie in any personal friendship between the needy and their benefactors. It happens because one party is rich while the other is poor. The benefactors may be rich and also benevolent, but those who receive their charity are poor, and only poor. It is impossible to know whether those who receive charity are virtuous or not. One can hardly be friends with others before knowing them well. Therefore, the promotion of organizations to help the needy ought not to be carried out on a wide scale in society. The only thing the human benefactor is doing is privately consoling his conscience by thus spending his superfluous money. His primary consideration is not others but himself. Thus, although his action is praiseworthy, the more such organizations to help the needy are promoted, and the longer they exist, the more the needy will come to expect charity. They will not only fail to consider its dispensation as virtuous, they will even come to expect it as their due. If their welfare dole decreases, they will harbor feelings of hate for their benefactors. Such philanthropy is simply spending money to purchase hatred. In the West intellectuals have also often discussed the question of helping the needy, but they have not yet come to any conclusion about its merits and demerits; still, in the final analysis, charity ought to be dispensed only after one has checked on the recipients' situation and personality, has come into personal contact with them, and then gives them things privately. This is another proof that morality cannot be applied to society on a broad scale.

From the above, we can see that the only place where morality can be fully practicable is the family. As soon as one steps outside the household, it would seem, there is no chance to make morality one hundred percent efficacious. However, since some people argue that family relations are the model of social tranquility, one may wonder whether the time will ever come, thousands of years hence, when the whole world will be like one big family. Moreover, since human affairs are always in a state of motion, if we were forced to decide in which direction modern civilization is moving, we would have to answer that it is, of course, progressing. In that case, even though the road ahead is long and we have taken only the first step on a thousand-mile journey, progress is still progress. There is no reason not to advance just because one fears the length of the journey ahead. When comparing present-day Western civilization and Japanese civilization, we now are only talking about this one step forward or one step backward, that is all, and all discussion by scholars is merely a debate over this one step.

Morality operates in the sphere of affection rather than that of regulations. Regulations may often produce the same results as affection, but the nature of the sphere in which they operate is different. Regulations and morality seem to be incompatible opposites. Moreover, distinctions can be made within regulations between those which aim at preserving order and those which aim at keeping men from doing evil. To violate the former kind of regulation is a case of human error, while violation of the latter stems from an evil heart. The regulations about which I am speaking are those designed to prevent men from doing evil, so let scholars not mistake my intention. Let me give an example. In order for a certain household to run smoothly, there may be some regulation established that the family members rise at six o'clock in the morning and go to bed at ten o'clock at night, but this is not designed to prevent any evil behavior in the house. A person who violates such a regulation can hardly be called a criminal. It is a regulation which has been discussed and agreed upon for the convenience of those who live in that house. It is not a written law, but one which the members of the family make mental note of and observe spontaneously. Lending and borrowing money between close relatives and friends is another such example.

Legal papers, contracts, government laws, or treaties between nations, however, involve different kinds of laws and regulations, and though they contain not a few regulations for the purpose of putting things in proper order, their main function is obviously to prevent evil. The purpose of all such documents is to lay before men the advantages and disadvantages of a course of action and make them choose the proper course on their own initiative. For example, to steal a thousand *ryō* of gold carries a penalty of ten years at hard labor, or to be ten days late in carrying out a promise carries a compensation of a hundred *ryō*. The purpose of these penalties is to make men responsibly take that course of action which they should deem better. The spirit of morality is not involved at all. It is like showing a hungry dog or cat who is master by holding out food in one hand and brandishing a stick in the other; when the animal tries to eat, you strike it. Seen merely on the surface, this clearly is not a matter of affection.

I shall give another example to clarify the difference between morality and regulations in regard to the places suitable to each and the spheres in which they operate. Here are two men involved in a loan. They are very close friends, so close that the loaning of the money is not even considered virtuous, and failure to pay back the loan would not be cause for ill feeling. Because there is such deep affection between the two men that there is almost no distinction between who owns what, their relationship is completely grounded on morality. Even though the duration of the loan and the rate of interest is agreed upon and written down for the one who made the loan to have an accurate record, the relationship has still not left the sphere of morality. However, as soon as this paper is stamped with a seal or otherwise officially marked, or some guarantor or collateral is demanded, it has left the realm of morality; both men are now dealing with each other only through the medium of regulations. In this kind of loan, since it is difficult to know if the borrower is honest or dishonest, he is presumed to be dishonest, and it is made clear to him that, if he does not return the money, it will be claimed from the guarantor. If the money is still not returned, a legal suit will be filed to prosecute the offender, or to collect the collateral. In other words, both good and bad are held out, and the dog is threatened with an upraised stick. Therefore, there is no morality to be found at all where one disposes of affairs by means of regulations. In the relationships between government and people, company president and employees, buyer and seller, lender and borrower, paid professional teacher and student, the relationship is based entirely upon regulations; it cannot be called one of morality.

For example, two persons work in the same government office. One is deeply concerned about his public duty and works so conscientiously that he almost gets no sleep at night even after returning from the office. The other is not like this at all. He has not the slightest concern for his public duty and his main interest lies in drink and dissipation. Nevertheless, from eight in the morning until four in the afternoon he works just as diligently as the first official—he says what he should, writes what he ought, keeps his accounts straight, and cannot be faulted for neglect of his duties. The sincerity of the first official is not that conspicuous by contrast.

Again, when it comes to income tax, unless the government urges payment no one will pay it. If you should pay your taxes with counterfeit money and it is accepted, the fault lies with the one who accepted it. If one errs by overpaying, it is the loss of the payer once he has already handed over the money. If one discovers that he has been overcharged, he is the loser if he has already paid for the item. If a storeowner gives too much change to a customer, once the money is out of his hands he must pay for his own blunder. In a loan, if the documents are lost, the loss is that of the one who made the loan. If, in exchanging a bond for cash, the bondholder lets the terminal date pass, he is the loser. When someone picks up something and stashes it away, if no one knows about it, it is the finder's gain. What is more, if someone steals from another person and gets away with it, the thief is that much ahead. If we consider what goes on, then, the whole of society is the gathering place of evil persons, and we see no traces of morality left. Relying on impersonal regulations, people merely maintain the barest semblance of order in things. Full of evil intentions, they are restrained by the regulations from carrying out what is in their hearts; they go as far as the regulations allow, treading carefully, as if they were walking on a sharp blade. An alarming situation, is it not?

So base is the heart of man, and so impersonal are regulations! At a superficial glance the situation appears truly alarming and intolerable. However, if we go on to weigh the reasons behind regulations and the good that can come from them, we will see that they are not at all impersonal. Indeed, they are the greatest good in the world today. Regulations are aimed at preventing evil, but they are not drawn up because the whole population of a country is evil. They are drawn up to protect the good, since good and evil people are hard to differentiate. It may be that only one in ten thousand is evil, but since we cannot eliminate such people entirely, the purpose of regulations for the whole ten thousand always must be to check the one bad person. Take, for example, the case of singling out a counterfeit one-yen coin from ten thousand: there is no need to replace all ten thousand yen. Thus, while regulations in society may appear to be too numerous and too impersonal at a superficial glance, there really is no reason to despise them. They must be further strengthened and even accorded more respect. There are no better tools in the world today for the progress of civilization than regulations. It is not the act of an intelligent man to throw away the benefits of something because he dislikes the external form. Though regulations are designed to prevent the evil acts of bad people, they certainly do not prevent good people from doing good. Even in a world with a maze of laws, the good person can do good to his heart's content.

When planning for the future we can only hope that by passing a multitude of regulations, regulations will ultimately become unnecessary. But that time is several thousand years away. There is no reason not to create regulations now while waiting for that distant utopia to come. We must observe the concrete situation of the times. In the primitive and uncivilized world of the ancient past, when ruler and the people were as one family, law was extremely simple. It was a time when benevolent rulers and wise ministers cared for the people with sincerity, loyal retainers sacrificed themselves for their lords, all groups in society were inspired by those above them, and everyone had his own place. Without depending on regulations they put a premium on sincerity of heart, and through virtue attained tranquility. However admirable this period may seem, the truth of the matter is that they did not despise law. It was simply that there was no place for it to function. In contrast, though, with the gradual progress of human intelligence human affairs have become more complex, and in proportion to this complexity regulations have increased too. Furthermore, because the techniques of violating regulations have become subtler with the progress of civilization, preventive laws have become more elaborate.

For example, in the old days the government established laws to protect the people, whereas today people establish laws to ward off government absolutism and thus to protect themselves. Looked at through the eyes of the ancients, social order has been inverted in modern times. But if we take a broader view, we will see that things are not so unreasonable. Neither the people nor the government should feel they have lost any honor. In today's world this is the only way for a nation to advance in civilization and protect its independence. The development of human intelligence over the course of history is like that of a child growing into adulthood. When a child, one does the things of a child, and one's feelings and emotions are different from those of an adult. But as the years pass and a person becomes an adult, he no longer delights in playing on stilts as he once did; he no longer is frightened by ghost stories as he once was. The concerns of a child may seem trivial and silly, but they are not to be criticized. Childhood is its own world, not to be invaded by adult values and demands. Now, a household with a large number of children cannot compete with other households. Will it not be a blessing, then, for these children to become adults? However, to try to take the values and deeds of childhood and force them on these adults, treating them like children, trying to please them with stilts and frighten them with ghost stories, and branding those who do not obey as out of line, would be to mistake the times and places proper to knowledge and virtue, and would only invite the misfortune of weakening that household.

Although the general tenor of regulations may be considered

impersonal, and though legalistic types may seem despicable, regulations are still of great benefit to human affairs. For example, there is a regulation that if you find money and return it to the owner, half of it will be given you as a reward. Of course, if the finder returns it to the owner only in order to get the reward, this would be despicable. However, if we say that this is a demeaning regulation, and abolish it, then nothing lost would ever be returned to its original owner. This "half and half" law is not necessarily desirable from a moral point of view, but it is still a good law for civilized society.

In business a man may sometimes sell his soul for a fast profit. People refer to this as the dishonesty of merchants. For example, individual Japanese may be dishonest in making silkworm-egg cards to make a fast profit,† but in the long run the value of Japanese goods will fall, the country as a whole will lose a great deal, and the dishonest persons themselves will also end up losers. Thus, such people throw away both honor and profit. Western merchants, by contrast, appear to be exact and honest in their business dealings. They show a small sample of woven goods, someone buys several thousand times as much of the material, and what is delivered differs in no wise from the sample. The buyer receives the shipment with his mind at peace; he does not even open any of the boxes to check the contents. It would seem from this that Westerners are more honest than Japanese. However, a careful consideration of the facts reveals that Westerners are not necessarily more sincere in their dispositions than Japanese. Westerners try to expand their business to gain greater profits in the long run. Because they are afraid dishonest dealings will jeopardize long-range profits, they have to be honest. This sincerity does not come from the heart, but from the wallet. To put the same idea in other words, Japanese are greedy on a small scale; foreigners are greedy on a large scale. But just because the Westerner's honesty is motivated by a more questionable love of greater profit is no reason to despise it and to emulate the blatant dishonesty of the Japanese. Whether for the sake of self-interest or for the sake of profits, the regulations of business must be scrupulously kept. By this very respect for the regulations, business will function for the

---

† [Silkworm eggs were an important export item in the early Meiji period.]

benefit of civilized progress. Except for the area of family and friends, everything in modern society—government, companies, commerce, loans—is based on regulations. A framework of regulations may be despicable, but the advantage of having them far outweighs the catastrophe that would attend their absence.

Viewing the state of the countries of the West, one sees that human intelligence has made daily progress, increasing people's courage to try new things. In effect, there are no obstacles to human thought in either the world of nature or the world of man. They have freely investigated the principles of things and freely devised means to deal with things. Once they have grasped the nature and functions of the forces of nature, they have in many instances discovered laws which harness the energies of nature. They have done the same in human affairs. By investigating the nature and functions of mankind, they finally gain insight into its laws, and according to its nature and functions they devise methods to channel it. To cite a few examples of Western progress, their laws are detailed and innocent people are hardly ever condemned unjustly; the laws of business are clear and promote the welfare of man; the laws of corporations are just, so that many are able to undertake large-scale enterprises; and the methods of taxation are skillfully worked out so that there are few who lose their private property. The laws of warfare outline techniques for killing people, but because of them there is an actual reduction in loss of human life. International law is somewhat vague and can be circumvented, but it is an expedient means to reduce human slaughter. Again, popular parliaments can serve as a balance of power in regard to the government, and books and newspapers can prevent resort to mass violence. In recent times there has been talk about creating international peace by holding an international conference in Brussels [1874]. These are all instances of the increasing refinement and development of regulations, through which great moral good is being achieved.

Chapter EIGHT

THE ORIGINS OF WESTERN CIVILIZATION

I N THIS small volume, I shall not be able to write an exhaustive treatise on the origins of Western civilization. Therefore, I shall here only summarize parts of Guizot's *History of Civilization* and other works to supplement my account.

The point of difference between Western and other civilizations is that Western society does not have a uniformity of opinions; various opinions exist side by side without fusing into one. For example, there are theories which advocate governmental authority; others argue for the primacy of religious authority. There are proponents of monarchy, theocracy, aristocracy, and democracy. Each goes its own way, each maintains its own position. Although they vie with one another, no single one of them ever completely wins out. Since the contest never is decided, all sides grudgingly are forced to live with the others. Once they start living side by side, despite their mutual hostility, they each recognize the others' rights and allow them to go their ways. Since no view is able to monopolize the whole situation and must allow the other schools of thought room to function, each makes its own contribution to one area of civilization by being true to its own position, until finally, taken together, the end result is one civilization. This is how autonomy and freedom have developed in the West.

Present-day Western civilization began with the fall of Rome. The power of the Roman Empire began to decline in the fourth century A.D.

and in the fifth century was at its nadir. The barbarians invaded from all sides, and the vast power of the Empire could not be maintained. The most powerful among these tribes was the Germans. The Franks were a German tribe. These primitive tribes trampled over the Empire, sweeping away Roman institutions hundreds of years old. Brute force reigned unchallenged in society. Countless wild tribes sacked and pillaged in herds. Nations were founded, and nations merged. At the close of the eighth century, the chieftain of the Franks, Charlemagne, extended his authority over present-day France, Germany, and Italy, thus laying the foundation of a great empire. His efforts were partially directed toward the unification of all the states of Europe; but after his death the nations split again, and his efforts were in vain. At this point, the names France, Germany, and so forth already existed, but national structures were non-existent. Individual men used brute force to attain their own desires. From a latter-day perspective, this period is called the world of barbarians, or the Dark Ages. This period of the Dark Ages lasted for some 700 years, from the fall of Rome until the tenth century.

The Power of the Church

In this period of the Dark Ages, the Christian Church was able to retain its structure intact. After the fall of Rome it seemed that the Church, too, was doomed, but this was not to be the case. It not only continued to exist amidst the barbarians, but it even strove to convert them and win them into the Church. Its courage and resourcefulness admittedly were great indeed. For it could not utilize lofty principles to direct the ignorant barbarians. Therefore it devised numerous ceremonies and external rituals to entice people and eventually stir up their faith. Although from a later historical vantage point the Church must be criticized for having deluded the people with falsehoods, it was the only source of moral and ethical precepts in this lawless age. Without its teaching at this time all of Europe would have been no better than a world of beasts. Thus the meritorious accomplishments of the Christian Church at this time cannot be called insignificant. And that it acquired power was not accidental either. In general, to regulate the body belonged to secular physical power, and to regulate the spirit pertained to the Church's authority, so that secular and religious powers were opposed to each other. However, the Church's monks had been involved in secular affairs and serving in public offices in the cities, a custom dating back to the days of the Roman Empire, and they retained their power even at this period. The participation of monks in secular assemblies in later times had its origin far back in the ancient past.

The Origin of Popular Government

When the Roman Empire was established, it was a confederation of a number of cities and towns. The jurisdiction of Rome centered on the cities and towns. Each town or city had its own laws, and it managed its own affairs in subjection to the orders of Rome; taken all together, they formed one empire. Even after the fall of Rome, the custom of citizens' assemblies was retained, and this constituted another element of later civilization.

The Origin of Monarchy

Even though the Roman Empire fell, the fact that for hundreds of years it had been known as the Roman Empire and its rulers had been called emperors left these names embedded in the minds of the people. Because the names were not forgotten, the idea of absolutism also lingered on together with them. Later theories of monarchy have their origins here.

The Spirit of Freedom and Independence of the German Barbarians

The barbarian tribes were spread across the Empire at this time. Their spirit and temperament are hard to piece together from ancient documentary evidence, but, considering the conditions of the times, we can surmise that they were fierce, violent, and strangers to humane sentiments, and their ignorance must have been almost like that of beasts. Yet if we take a more sophisticated view, they must also have had dauntless, righteous spirits and habits of self-reliance and independence. Their spirit and habits must have stemmed from the depths of human nature itself; they thought of themselves as individuals, they each sought to be happy, they each had heroic aspirations and a dauntless spirit that could not restrain the heart's aspirations even if it would. Ancient Rome had had its theories of freedom, and the Christian Church also had its proponents of freedom. But these ideas of freedom and autonomy meant freedom for a race or a tribe; they did not extend the concept of freedom to embrace the individual. The spirit of seeking the independence of the individual and the full development of his aspirations first originated in the Germanic tribes. The spirit of freedom and independence in later European civilization, even today valued as a matchless jewel, was the contribution of the Germans.

The Feudal Principalities

The Dark Ages finally came to an end, the pillaging tribes settled down, and the transition was made to the feudal principalities. This system began in the tenth century and did not decline until the seventeenth. This period is called the age of the **feudal system**. In the feudal age, the names France, Spain, and so forth were used, and each country had its own rulers, but the rulers were only figureheads. The countries were divided into various principalities independently held by warrior barons. They formed individual political units usually centering on a castle built atop a mountain, with their vassals massed around the foot of the mountain. They regarded the common people as slaves and appropriated to themselves the titles of nobility. Forming independent political structures, they stood in awe of no man, and were forever embroiled in battle with one another. In the Dark Ages freedom in society was realized in regard to individuals, but in feudal society the situation greatly changed in complexion. Freedom pertained solely to the nobles who were owners of both land and serfs. There was no universal law to check their actions. There was no popular assembly to criticize them. In his castle each baron was absolute sovereign. The only checks upon his absolutism were the external danger posed by other barons or the weakness of his own authority. This was the general situation obtaining throughout all of Europe. The people within a feudal domain had to deal with an aristocracy, not with a king. The areas known as France and Spain and so forth had not yet formed into separate nations.

The Great Power of the Church

From the above it may seem that the reins of power in the feudal period were monopolized by the aristocracy, but this was not the entire picture. For Christianity, which had won over the hearts of the barbarians and converted them to the faith, reached the height of its power from the eleventh to the thirteenth centuries. It was no accident that the Church was able to acquire such power. A consideration of man's life shows that, though man can achieve temporary glory, can annihilate a million enemies if he is powerful, assure himself of all the riches in the world if he has talent, and can do whatever he pleases by means of his talent and power, still, he is unable to fathom the mystery of life and death. Before this mystery, even the heroism and might of a Charlemagne or the sheer might of the First Emperor of Qin is completely helpless and daunted; riches and dignity dissolve like windblown clouds, and human life is no more permanent than the morning dew. Here is where the human heart's weakest point is. It is a vulnerable spot which cannot be completely protected. Once this soft spot is attacked, a man immediately panics and reveals his weakness. Since the Church claimed religion's proper function was to explain these mysteries and to clarify the wonders of creation, and since it dared to give answers to men's doubts, do you suppose anyone could keep from being beguiled? Moreover, since it was an unenlightened age in which faith was lightly given, even fallacious ideas were accepted by the people. Since the whole land was swept by a spirit of religious faith and orthodoxy, there was no room for private opinions. This despotism and oppression of the spirit were no different from the tyranny by which the feudal princes lorded it over their subjects. We can characterize the conditions of those times by saying that men were split into two parts, as it were, the flesh and the spirit. The movements of the flesh were controlled by the secular power of the feudal rulers, while the workings of the spirit were at the beck and call of the Roman religion. The secular power controlled the physical, material world, while religion controlled the spiritual, immaterial world.

Once it had control of the spiritual world and had stolen the hearts of men, so that it stood on an even footing with secular power, religion was not content with this alone, and it asked itself: "Which is more important, the spirit or the flesh? The flesh is the branch, the external; the spirit is the root, the internal. We already control the inner root;

why should we disregard the external branch? By all means, the latter too must be won over to our sway." Finally, therefore, the territories of the rulers were invaded, and, either by stealing away their lands or by stripping them of their positions, the Roman popes became sole sovereigns of heaven and earth. It was in this period that Henry IV of Germany was excommunicated by Pope Gregory, and, walking through the deep snows of severe winter to stand three days and three nights before the gates of Rome, wept and begged the pope's pardon.[†]

The Fountainhead of Popular Government

Finally the incursions of the barbarians were checked and the power of the feudal principalities firmly established. Once the barons had built their castles and safely ensconced themselves inside, they no longer rested content merely with having enough to eat and a roof over their heads. Style and refinement gradually came into fashion. They sought better-grade clothing and fine-flavored foods, thus creating a large variety of fashionable needs, and no one was content with the primitive conditions of olden times. As soon as a need arose, someone was there to fill it. Perhaps this was how the road was paved for the beginning of commerce and industry. Here and there cities and towns came into being, and men of wealth began to emerge. In other words, the age witnessed the revival of cities and towns after their Roman demise. But this does not mean that these citizens were powerful when they first banded together. The barbarian warriors could not forget their former delight in violence and pillage, but thanks to the trend of the time they did not have to venture far, for objects of prey were close at hand in the form of these citizens. Since in the eyes of the townspeople the feudal warriors were customers when they came to purchase things but thieves when they came to plunder them, even while they did business with the warriors they also had to take precautions against their rapacious tendencies. Consequently, these new bourgeoisie constructed walls behind which they pooled their energies to defend against outside invaders. Thus there arose a tendency to share benefits and hardships. When general meetings were to be held, the people gathered together at

---

† [*Sic.* Reference here is to the "Walk to Canossa" (1077).]

the sound of a bell, pledged wholehearted support for the group, and expressed their mutual fidelity. At these gatherings a number of men were selected from the group as leaders to be in charge of defense of the walls. Once these magistrates were elected, they exercised absolute power. It was almost a special form of monarchy in itself. The only limitation was that the people held the power to elect others in their stead.

Such independent cities formed by groups of citizens were called **free cities.*** Whether in resisting the commands of the monarch or fighting against the soldiers of the barons, they were continually at war. From about the eleventh century many such free cities sprang up in Europe. Among the most famous were Milan and Lombardy in Italy.† In early thirteenth-century Germany, Lübeck, Hamburg, and other cities formed a confederation called the Hanseatic League. At one time their power had increased to the point where they forged a united bloc of some 85 towns. Neither kings nor other feudal princes could control them, so finally a treaty was concluded that recognized their independence. The various cities and towns were allowed to build their own walls, maintain armies, establish laws, and govern themselves. In form they were like independent countries.

The Great Contribution of the Crusades

Thus, as stated above, from the fourth and fifth centuries the institutions of the Church, monarchies, aristocracies, and common people each came to evolve along certain lines and to exercise a degree of power. All the ingredients necessary for social organization were there, but they had not yet coalesced to the extent that one government and one country were established. What the people struggled for never extended beyond certain particular areas, and as yet was not directed toward any united whole.

Then in 1096 the Crusades began. These Crusades consisted in the nations of Europe uniting their forces for the sake of religion and setting out to conquer the lands of Asia Minor. By making all nations of Europe

---

* **Free city** means a city or town in which the citizens are independent.
† [In fact, Lombardy was not itself a free city but a region of northern Italy which contained a number of such cities, including Milan.]

allies, with Asia their common foe, the Crusades succeeded in creating in people's minds, for the first time, the image of Europe versus Asia, "our side" versus "the other side," and in uniting popular feeling toward a certain objective. Further, because the Crusades were made a matter of grave national concern for the people in each country, all of the people in each country were united in their interests and took to heart the welfare of their own country. Hence it can be said that the single factor of the Crusades was the root cause leading the peoples of Europe to become Europe-conscious and the people in each country conscious of their own country. Beginning in 1096, periodically disbanding and then again regrouping, the Crusade expeditions were launched eight times in all, finally coming to a complete halt in 1270.

Although the Crusades were originally motivated by religious fervor, after 200 years they proved unsuccessful. The people of Europe became tired of them. Even the rulers of the countries came to feel that religious wars were not as important as political wars. They found that going to Asia to conquer its lands was less advantageous than expanding their own borders in Europe. In addition, the knights no longer wanted to serve in the armies of the Crusades; the people, too, finally came around to this view. Since they realized that plans had to be laid to promote industries in their own countries, they came to dislike the thought of distant conquest. Their zeal for conquest gradually faded and, in the end, disappeared altogether. But the Crusades were not a complete failure. The rustic clods from the European states had a taste of Eastern culture and brought it back to their own countries, where it contributed greatly to their progress. At the same time they became aware of the distinction between East and West and inside and outside. Through this self-consciousness they came to establish their own national polities. This was the contribution of the Crusades.

The Unification of National Power

In the feudal age the rulers of the various countries were mere figureheads, but they could not accept that with equanimity. On the other hand, the citizens within a country were expanding their intellectual horizons; they were displeased at continually being pawns in the power struggles of the nobles. Therefore within society a kind of counter-movement welled up to check the power of the nobles. To give one example, in France in the late fifteenth century Louis XI overthrew the aristocracy to restore the power of the royal family. In the light of a later era he seems to have been a despicably sly, crafty manipulator. He was not so much deplorable, though. We must view him in terms of the changes in the temper of the times. While in olden times society had been controlled merely by force of arms, in his day this was being replaced to some extent by the power of intelligence. Cunning replaced force, and political manipulation replaced despotism. If we look at how cleverly he manipulated things, now by argument, now by enticement, we can see that, though his attitude may have been crude, his goals were a little more advanced, since he tended to value civilized ways over force of arms. At this time France was not the only country where political power was taken over by a royal house; the same thing occurred in England, Germany, and Spain as well. Of course, the monarchs in these countries had to struggle for this end. The people, as well, availed themselves of the power of the royal house to destroy their mutual enemies, the nobles. Thus it came about that the upper and lower strata combined to topple the middle stratum of society. Government orders finally became centralized, and some form of governmental structure evolved. Also at this time, the use of firearms at last spread and the old skills of archery and horsemanship slowly became obsolete. No one any longer feared the swashbuckling bluster of the knights. At the same time the art of printing was invented, opening up a new road of communication in society. Human intelligence took a leap forward, changing the values of things. The power of intelligence gained supremacy over brute force. The old feudal knights lost their power overnight, becoming stranded as it were somewhere between the upper and the lower classes. Evaluating the situation of this time, we can say that national power was finally moving in the direction of centralized government.

The Reformation as a Sign of Civilization

The Roman Church had enjoyed special privileges for a long time, and it did not hesitate to use them. Outwardly it was like an old corrupt government that kept on, refusing to be toppled. Though internally it was thoroughly corrupt, it clung to old ways with all its might, a stranger to change. In secular society, however, human intelligence was making daily progress. Now the gullibility of the past did not suffice; knowledge of letters was no longer the exclusive preserve of the monks, and laymen also learned to read. Once laymen became literate and learned to pursue the sciences, they could not help questioning things. However, doubt in any form was prohibited by the Church, thus producing friction between the two tendencies. Perhaps we can find here the origins of the Reformation. It was in 1520 that Luther, the famous leader of reform, first went against the Roman pope and advocated new theories. He influenced men's minds to an unprecedented degree. But though the pope was like an ailing lion whose strength was declining, a lion is still a lion. The old religion was like a lion, the new was like a tiger, and the battle between the two was not to be easily decided. Because of this the countries of Europe ended up in religious wars whose toll in human lives was beyond reckoning. In the end a new religious sect, the **Protestant**, came into existence, and both the new and the old religions held their ground. Although Luther's efforts were not in vain, if we calculate the number of those who died in the religious wars, the price of the new religion was not cheap. But, aside from the question of whether the new religion was costly or not, if we look at the purposes for which it was established, we shall see that the issue was not orthodoxy or heterodoxy of teaching but whether freedom of the human spirit would be allowed or not. It was not a question of whether the Christian religion was true or not, but a struggle against the political power of Rome. Consequently, this controversy can be said to have brought to the surface the spirit of freedom in the people and to have been a sign of the progress of civilization.

From the end of the fifteenth century the power in the various countries of Europe finally became centralized under individual governments. At first the people all were devoted to the royal houses and were not conscious that they themselves had power in regard to government. The kings, for their part, had to rely upon the power of the common people in order to keep down the nobility. For the sake of temporary advantage the kings and the people formed political alliances for their mutual benefit, with the result that the people either improved their positions by themselves or they were granted greater power by the government. With these developments in the sixteenth and seventeenth centuries the feudal nobility gradually disappeared. The religious controversies, though never fully resolved, settled down to live with each other; and the shaping forces in countries were reduced to the government and the people. However, to attempt to monopolize political authority is a universal vice of those in power, and the rulers of these countries were no exceptions. Perhaps here was where the struggle between the people and the royal houses began.

It was England that took the lead in this. At this time the power of the royal family was not insubstantial, but the people were also increasing the wealth of their individual households through commercial and industrial enterprises, and quite a few became landholders by buying the lands of nobles. Once they had money and land, set up enterprises, and became important figures in the nation by their monopoly of both internal and external business, they could hardly sit back and complacently observe the despotism of the royal house. In an earlier age the Protestant Reformation had broken out against Rome, and now political reformations threatened to break out against the royal houses. While these reformations differed in kind, being respectively religious and secular, they shared something in common in so far as they manifested a spirit of autonomy and freedom and symbolized the progress of civilization. Thus the seeds contained in the **free cities** of the past would seem to have finally borne fruit.

After Charles I ascended the throne in 1625, a raging debate over human rights was coupled with religious disputes. Arguments were held over whether to open or close Parliament. All kinds of controversies ensued, finally resulting in the abolition of the status of the monarch in 1649. For a time there was a type of republican government, but it proved to be short-lived. After this there were various kinds of internal insurrections. Only after William III ascended the throne in 1688 was there a major change in political trends.† Government by constitutional

---

† [*Sic.* His enthronement was in 1689.]

monarchy based upon freedom and liberty was at length established, the form that has continued until today.

In France, during Louis XIII's reign in the beginning of the seventeenth century, the prestige of the royal house reached a high point through the power of Cardinal Richelieu. When Louis XIV succeeded in 1643, he was a mere youth of five with no knowledge of national affairs; and yet, though there were many internal and external problems, the country suffered no loss of power under him. As he grew up his natural endowments matured. Taking up the tasks bequeathed him by his forefathers, he won over the allegiance of the whole country by his charm and was victorious in every battle he fought with other nations. During his long reign of seventy-two years, the power of the French royal family reached its zenith. However, in the winter of his lifetime his military power weakened, government functions slackened, and the latent buds of the degeneration of the royal house reared their heads. When Louis XIV grew old, it was more than just he himself who had grown old; kingly power in all of Europe had also grown old and feeble.

The world of Louis XV was exceedingly corrupt, almost the extreme of lawlessness. Compared with what it used to be, France was now an entirely different country. Yet the civilization of the French nation at this juncture of political decline had progressed to a point incomparably beyond that of former ages. Although ideas of freedom were present in the discussions of scholars in the seventeenth century, their opinions were inevitably narrow, whereas by the eighteenth century there was a total revolution in religious and political ideas, in philosophy, and in science. Investigation knew no bounds: men inquired, doubted, checked, tested. This new ferment of inquiry and doubt made men feel that there could be no obstacles to the eventual progress of human thought. In short, at this time the monarchy degenerated because of stagnation; the intellectual powers of the people increased in vigor, to the point where friction between the monarch and the people was inevitable. The French Revolution of 1789 was a result of this upheaval. Although there was a difference of about a hundred years between the English Revolution in the 1600s and the French Revolution, a comparison of their causes and effects shows that they fell into exactly the same pattern.

Above I have given a general outline of Western civilization. There are translations of Guizot's *History of Civilization* available, and these should be consulted for further details. Scholars can reap immense profit if they read this work in its entirety, then go over it repeatedly and assiduously.

Chapter NINE

THE ORIGINS OF JAPANESE CIVILIZATION

S I SAID in the previous chapter, in Western civilization the social fabric included various theories that developed side by side, drew closer to one another, and finally united into one civilization, in the process giving birth to freedom. To use a simile, if you take such metals as gold, silver, copper, and iron, and melt them together, you would not end up with gold, or silver, or copper, or iron, but with a compound mixture that preserves a certain balance between the various elements, and in which each adds strength to the others. This is how Western civilization is. The Japanese scene proves to be quite different. Naturally, Japanese civilization, too, does not lack its elements in the social fabric. From ancient times Japan has had a monarchy, a nobility, religions, and the common people, each of which constituted a separate species, each of which possessed its own views. But these views did not develop side by side, draw nearer to one another, and blend together into one synthesis. It was as though the elements of gold, silver, copper, and iron could not be melted into one mass. Even if combined into one mixture, it was without a balance of the elements. There was always an imbalance; one would cancel out all the others and prevent their true colors from coming through. What happened was the same as when, in making gold or silver coins, ten percent copper is added: the color of the copper does not come through, and the coins that are produced look like pure gold or silver. This is what I mean by an imbalance of things.

Now in the first place, the freedom of civilization cannot be bought at the expense of some other freedom. It can only exist by not infringing upon other rights and profits, other opinions and powers, all of which should exist in some balance. It is only possible for freedom to exist when freedom is limited. Thus, in any area of society, whether it be the government, the people, scholars, or bureaucrats, when there is one who has power, whether it be intellectual or physical, there must be a limit to that power. In general, the power wielded by human beings cannot be a pure good; there almost always is some natural evil mixed in with it. Sometimes power is abused because of a person's cowardice, at other times it is used to the detriment of others because of a person's aggressiveness. Instances of what I mean can be found in all ages and in all lands. This I call the curse of imbalance. Those in power must always take stock of themselves. Comparison of Japanese civilization with Western civilization reveals that the greatest difference between the two is this imbalance of power.

Imbalance of power pervades the entire network of Japanese society. In Chapter Two I mentioned that there is something that we can call the spirit of a nation. This imbalance of power is one element in the Japanese spirit. When today's scholars discuss the question of power, they only think in terms of the government and the people, either to rage against the despotism of the government, or to criticize the servility of the people. But if we really examine the situation in detail, we shall find this imbalance pervading every single aspect of Japanese society, from the greatest to the smallest, public or private. It is as though thousands of scales were hung in Japan, and all of them were always out of balance, none ever in equilibrium. Again, if a crystal with three corners and four faces is broken down into a thousand pieces, even into ten thousand pieces, and finally ground into powder, every single little piece will retain the shape of three corners and four faces. And if these pieces are somehow put back together, the result will again be a crystal with three corners and four faces. The imbalance of power is similar in that it penetrates down to the smallest area of society, and yet scholars pay no special attention to it. Why? Simply because most of them have considered the relationship between the government and the people as the most important, the most public, and the most conspicuous, and they have tended to concentrate on that problem alone.

Now let me discuss this imbalance as it exists in reality. You will find this imbalance in all relations between man and woman, between parents and children, between brothers, and between young and old. Turn from the family circle to society, and relations there will be no different. Teacher and student, lord and retainer, rich and poor, noble and base-born, newcomers and oldtimers, main family and branch families—between all of these there exists an imbalance of power. What is more, even larger social groups exhibit this phenomenon. In the feudal period there were large and small *han*, main and branch temples, main and branch shrines. Wherever there are social relationships, there you will find this imbalance of power. Even within the government itself the imbalance can be extremely great, depending on the position and grade of the officials. When we see a minor official brandishing his authority over some commoner we might think he is a very powerful person. But let this same official meet someone higher in the bureaucracy and he will be subjected to even worse oppression from his superior than he dealt out to the commoner. When some minor provincial official summons a village headman to speak to him, his overbearing attitude is hateful indeed. But when this minor official deals with his own superior, the scene would stir our pity. And though the way the village headman is roundly castigated by the minor official may elicit our sympathy, when we see him go back and just as roundly castigate the men under him he will earn our hatred. A is oppressed by B, B in turn is controlled by C; in this way there is an unending cycle of pressures and controls. Truly an amazing phenomenon, indeed!

The **conditions** of base and noble, poor and rich, stupid and intelligent, weak and strong allow of limitless degrees. The existence of these levels should not be a hindrance to social relations, but in most cases where there is a difference in conditions there tends to be an imbalance of **rights**. This is what I mean by an imbalance of power.

A superficial view of social affairs suggests that the government is the only holder of power. But if we try to discover what a government is and why it is so, we should be able to arrive at a more precise view.

Originally, the government is the place where people of a country come together to do something. We simply call those people who are in this place rulers, or officials. These people are not rulers and officials by birth. Even though during the feudal period ranks and offices were inherited, those who actually controlled affairs were mainly men of talent who happened to be selected. There was no reason for these men, once in public office, suddenly to change their native mentality. If some of them wielded arbitrary power when in the government, they were only expressing their true colors. As proof of this, even in the feudal period low-born commoners were sometimes raised to important government offices. But if we look at what these people accomplished we see that they were hardly extraordinary. They merely added a bit of cleverness, while following the precedents of their predecessors. Their cleverness was the cleverness of the despot; if they did not win the people with baubles and treat them as stupid, then they intimidated them and made them cower. If these people were left to live among the common people they would have done things in the same manner. Had they lived in the villages they would have acted similarly there, and the same applies if they had lived in the cities. Since this was an epidemic infecting the Japanese people as a whole, one could hardly expect these people to have been exceptions. It is only because they were in the government that their deeds had a greater impact upon society, were more obvious, and hence became the topic of men's conversation.

Therefore the government is not the only source of despotism. It is only a meeting place of despots. It is a convenient platform for them to demonstrate their true colors in carrying out policies. If this were not the case, and if the source of despotism lay particularly in the government, then this disease of imbalance would infect all the people only while they are in public office, and never before or after that. Totally illogical! Now, since to use power as one pleases is the common fault of anyone in power, once a person is in the government and has grasped the reins of power, he might become blinded by power and increasingly arrogate it to himself; it is also true that administration tends to be ineffective without a despotic grip on all power. And yet, it is simply unreasonable to think that ordinary people with ordinary backgrounds and education will, once placed in government office, suddenly take such an attitude and bring it to their tasks.

The Separation between Ruler and Ruled

According to the above argument, arbitrary use of authority and imbalance of power are not found in the government alone. They are imbedded in the spirit of the Japanese people as a whole. This spirit is a conspicuous dividing line between the Western world and Japan, and though we must now turn to seeking its causes, we are faced with an extremely difficult task. According to some Western books, the reason for the despotism in Asia lies in the fact that, with its warm climates and fertile lands, Asia has become overpopulated, and because of the geographical and topographical conditions, fears and superstitions tend to multiply. It is hard to say whether this theory truly applies to Japan or not. Even if it did apply, since the causes are all natural phenomena, what can humans do about them? Therefore, I wish here only to speak about the development of despotism and to show the way in which it has been carried out. Once this is done, we may be able to devise means to deal with it.

At the dawn of Japanese history, Japan was just like any other country in that a number of people formed a group. Within that group, the strongest and the smartest controlled everybody else, or someone came from another region to conquer the group and become its chieftain. According to our histories, the Emperor Jinmu carried his battles eastward.[†] Since the power of one man is not sufficient to gain control over a whole group of people, it was necessary for others to assist him. These people were either his close relatives or men chosen from among his friends. By joining their forces together, they naturally formed a government. Once they formed such a government, those in the government controlled the people and the people were subject to their rule. Here was created the first distinction between the rulers and the ruled, the former being the superiors, the "masters," the "insiders," while the latter were the inferiors, the "guests," the "outsiders." This kind of political division was plain for all to see. These two groups have

---

† [According to the *Kojiki*, Jinmu was the first Emperor of Japan. Chapters 47–52 of the *Kojiki* describe his progress northeastwards from Kyushu to Yamato, as he conquered all those who stood in his way.]

been the most conspicuous in Japanese society, and may be called the two basic elements of Japanese civilization. Up until now there have been a number of kinds of social interaction, but ultimately they could all be reduced to these two elements, for not a single one of them was independent enough to retain its own identity.

National Power Resting Unilaterally with the Imperial House

To rule over men is, of course, not easy. Therefore, the members of the ruling class must have both physical and intellectual powers and a certain amount of wealth. When they have a combination of intellectual and physical attributes plus sufficient wealth, they can always gain the power to control others. Consequently, those who rule must always be holders of power.

The ancient Imperial House stood above these holders of power and, by centralizing their forces, was able to control the country and never taste defeat in battle. Since the origin of the Imperial House was so ancient, the ruled—the common people—grew more and more subservient to it. Witness the fact that from the time of Empress Jingū,[†] Japan occasionally invaded foreign lands, and within the country serious troubles were averted either by use of authority or by assuring prosperity. Culture gradually blossomed; the arts of sericulture and shipbuilding, implements for weaving and farming, writings on medicine, Confucianism, Buddhism, and other cultural items were either imported from Korea or developed in Japan.

These conditions of human life gradually had an impact on the lives of the ordinary Japanese, but the authority to make use of these cultural items belonged exclusively to the government, and the people only followed its lead. In addition, all the land in the country, and even the lives of the people, belonged to the Imperial Household. Under such conditions, the ruled were simply the slaves of the rulers. Even until later times, the designations o-kuni [country], go-denchi [paddy fields], and o-hyakushō [peasants] continued to exist. As the o- and go- sounds here were honorifics directed toward the government, what the phrases

---

† [According to the Kojiki (and the Nihon shoki) Jingū was an Empress of Japan (15th ruler according to the traditional order) who invaded the Korean peninsula.]

implied was that all the land in Japan and even the lives of the people themselves were the private property of the government. In ancient times Emperor Nintoku, seeing smoke rising from the houses of the common people, remarked how rich he was; this sentiment came from his affection for the people and his being able to identify himself with them.[†] Yet, though he was a benevolent ruler, fair and unselfish, we can still see that he regarded the realm as one large family. This was a manifestation of that attitude of considering the whole land as his private property. Thus, the power of the whole realm belonged entirely to the Imperial House, and that power was always one-sided and remained so until the end of imperial dominance.

An imbalance of power, I said above, permeated all sectors of society, from the greatest to the smallest. Were one to divide society into ten million parts, there would be ten million levels of imbalance; were these to be conflated to a hundred parts, there would be a hundred levels of imbalance. Reducing it all into only two parts, the Imperial House and the people, we see once again this imbalance between them, with power one-sidedly in favor of the Imperial House.

Changes in Government without Change in the National Spirit

With the rise of the Taira and the Minamoto, the reins of authority shifted to the hands of the warriors. It seemed that they thereby created a balance of power with the Imperial House and the trend in social relations would change, but this was not to be the case. Whether the Minamoto and the Taira, or the Imperial House, they all belonged to the ruling class, and the shift of power to the warriors was really a shift of power within the ruling class. The relationship between rulers and ruled continued as before with no change. Not only was it not different, but already in the time of Emperor Kōnin [r. 770–80] an imperial edict had set up a new division between warriors and farmers; the wealthy and militarily powerful among the farmers were chosen for the militia, while the poor and weak were assigned to till the fields. According to the rationale of this edict, those who were powerful were to protect the

---

† [This anecdote about Nintoku, 16th ruler of Japan according to the traditional order, is featured in the *Nihon shoki*. It draws heavily on Chinese portrayals of the ideal ruler. Fukuzawa criticizes this benevolent attitude because of its paternalism.]

weak, while the poor and weak were to labor as farmers to provide for the warriors. As a result the weak poor sank lower and lower while the powerful rich increasingly bettered their positions, with the inevitable result that the chasm between ruler and ruled became ever wider, and the imbalance of power increasingly one-sided.

According to various historical records, when Minamoto no Yoritomo became constable-general of the sixty-odd provinces of Japan [1185], he placed constables in every province and stewards in the manors. Through them, he put an end to the power of the previous provincial governors and manor officials. From that time on, those with distinguished pedigree among the warriors of the provinces were appointed to the positions of constable or steward. Lower-ranking warriors were called go-kenin [the shogun's vassals] and came under the control of the constables and stewards. But all of these men were retainers in the service of the Kamakura Bakufu. For example, at hundred-day intervals certain numbers of them served on guard duty at Kamakura. During the time of Hōjō dominance the situation was essentially the same; everyone in provincial office was a warrior. In the time of the Jōkyū war [1221], Hōjō Yasutoki had eighteen horsemen in Kamakura on the 22nd day of the fifth month; within three days' time he had assembled all the warriors of the eastern provinces, some 190,000 horsemen in all. Judging from this, it seems clear that the warriors in the provinces spent their days in constant training for battle, and did not have time to tend to agricultural pursuits. This shows us that they were certainly living off the labors of the peasants. As the division between warrior and peasant became more and more pronounced and as the overall population increased, the numbers of the military class increased proportionately.

In the time of Yoritomo, warriors who were retainers in the Kantō were placed in the position of constables in the various provinces and generally rotated every three to five years. But some time later such positions became hereditary. Later on, when the Ashikaga replaced the Hōjō, these constables vied with each other for power. Some grew mightier, others declined; some were driven off by powerful local families, others were attacked by their own retainers—the end result was the crystallization of the feudal spirit.

To generalize about the conditions from the period of imperial dominance on down: the military men of Japan were first scattered here and there throughout the provinces and exercised power on an individual basis, while still under the authority of the Imperial Family. By the time of the Kamakura period they had coalesced into a number of small groupings so that for the first time the terms daimyo and *shōmyō* appeared.[†] By the time of the Ashikaga these had formed into even larger groups, but these groups were unable to achieve further unification. Therefore, the period of upheaval after the Ōnin War [1467–77] marked the height of the influence of the military men. In this world of military groups there was constant splitting and regrouping, advance and decline, but in the world of the common people there was no activity whatever. The latter's only function was to repeat the cyclical toils of the harvest within the world circumscribed by the military. From the standpoint of the people, there was no real distinction between the Imperial Family and the military aristocracy. War and peace, or their rising and falling in the world, meant no more to the warriors than the daily changes of weather did to the ordinary people. All they did was silently watch to see what happened.[*]

It was Arai Hakuseki's position that Japanese history evolved through nine stages before the samurai came to power, and that the period of samurai dominance then went through five more discernible changes, culminating in Tokugawa supremacy.[‡] The positions of most other thinkers generally concur with this view. But this approach focuses exclusively upon the fortunes of the politically dominant group. Thus, all the histories that have been written in Japan are either studies of the imperial lineage and discussions of the merits and demerits of the various emperors and officials, or records of victory and defeat in wars little different from the war tales spun by professional storytellers. The rare passages which relate something that does not concern the

---

† [The *shōmyō* was a feudal lord whose holdings and subjects were fewer than those of a daimyo.]

* I [Fukuzawa] dealt with the positive role of the samurai in wiping out the credulous acceptance of divine government in Chapter Two.

‡ [Confucian scholar and shogunal adviser (1657–1725). He made this influential periodization of Japanese history in *Tokushi yoron* (Lessons from History, 1712).]

government are only the meaningless fables of Buddhists, not worth reading. These histories have not really been histories of Japan, but of Japanese governments. This negligence on the part of scholars must be termed one of our country's greatest faults.

Arai Hakuseki's *Tokushi yoron* falls under this category of historiography. In it he writes about the changes in the spirit of the land, but in reality it was the same old spirit, unchanged, the same spirit that had already been deeply ingrained early in the imperial age. There was a two-level, clearcut distinction between ruler and ruled. When the warriors and farmers were divided, the split between the two classes became even more pronounced, and the split has continued unchanged to the present. Thus, although at the end of the imperial age the Fujiwara[†] came to monopolize power or the retired emperors controlled politics, these events took place within the context of the imperial structure and had nothing to do with the constitution of society around them. When the Minamoto destroyed the Taira and established the Kamakura Bakufu, or when the Hōjō took over the reins of government as the shogunal regent, or when the Ashikaga were labeled bandits for turning against the Southern Court, or even when the whole country was brought together under unified control through the efforts of Nobunaga, Hideyoshi, and Ieyasu—hegemony in all these situations was purely a matter of manipulation within the established system. The system as a whole did not change at all. The Tokugawa favored the same things the Hōjō and the Ashikaga had, and their concerns were also the same. The political aims of the Hōjō and the Ashikaga—abundant harvests and a submissive people—were the same as those of the Tokugawa. The types of rebels who troubled the Ashikaga and the Hōjō were no different from the types that vexed the Tokugawa.

We discover a great difference when we look back upon the evolution of Western political history. As the Protestant creed gained adherents, the governments, too, had to reflect this phenomenon. In an earlier age the rulers had to worry about only the feudal aristocracy. But when with the development of commerce and industry the new middle

---

[†] [A powerful family grouping who held power for much of the Heian period (794–1185) by acting as Imperial regents.]

class came to possess a certain amount of power, the rulers had to take it into account. Thus in Europe changes in national trends forced the governments to change accordingly. Japan alone seems to be an exception to this. Because religion, learning, industry, and commerce were all under the thumb of the government, the government did not need to regret or fear any changes in those areas; if there was something which did not accord with the ideas of the government, it was immediately prohibited. The only concern was that some might arise from among its own kind to attempt a change of government.[*] Therefore, throughout the whole twenty-five centuries or so of Japanese history, the government has been continually doing the same thing; it is like reading the same book over and over again, or presenting the same play time after time. Thus, when Arai Hakuseki talks about "nine stages" and "five stages" in the general spirit of the country, he is just presenting the same play fourteen times over. A certain Westerner writes that, though there have indeed been revolutions and insurrections in Asian countries, no less than in Europe, in Asia these upheavals have not advanced the cause of civilization.[†] In my opinion, this is undeniable.

The Common People of Japan Are Unconcerned with the Affairs of the Nation

As I have said above, one government has often been replaced by another, but the political trend of Japan as a whole has never changed. Power has always remained one-sided, and a great chasm divides the rulers and the ruled. Physical force, metaphysical knowledge and virtue, learning, religion—all have belonged to the ruling class. Factions of the ruling class relied upon one another to expand their own power. Wealth and talent, honor and the sense of shame were all in the possession of the ruling class. Occupying the remote upper regions of society, these rulers controlled the masses below; war and peace, the rise and fall of political fortunes, and the advance and retreat of civilization were all the story of the ruling class. The ruled were as unconcerned with

---

[*] Those "from among its own kind" means those who arose from the ranks of the ruling class.

[†] [Fukuzawa is referring to Buckle's *History of Civilization in England*.]

these things as indifferent spectators.

For example, since ancient times there have been wars in Japan. They were called "the battle between Kai and Echizen,"[†] "the struggle between the capital and the Kantō," and so on. From their names you would suppose they were wars between provinces, but this is not true. They were only wars between the warriors of different provinces; the common people had no part in them at all. Essentially, enemy countries clash as wholes, involving the total consciousness of the people in each country, so that even though not everyone bears arms, the hopes and prayers of all are for the victory of their own country and the downfall of the other, and no one on either side forgets who is the enemy. The patriotism of the people is stirred up at such a time. However, in the wars within Japan such a thing has never happened since ancient times. Wars were fought between warrior houses and not between two different peoples, between houses and not between countries. When the warriors of two houses clashed in battle, the common people merely looked on as spectators; friend or foe made no difference, they only feared whichever was stronger. Therefore, depending on the tide of battle, the same people who brought the provisions to one side one day, provided the supplies for the other side the next day. When the outcome was decided and hostilities ended, the people merely felt another storm had subsided and a change of manor stewards made. They did not regard the victory as cause for glory nor the defeat as cause for shame. Only if the regulations of the lord happened to be more lenient and he lightened their land tax burdens would they look up to and extol him.

Let me cite an example. Hōjō Sōun's descendants controlled the eight provinces of the Kantō, but one day they were decisively defeated by Hideyoshi and Ieyasu. Immediately after the Go-Hōjō's defeat, Ieyasu, previously an enemy, took over the eight provinces. As remarkable a man as Ieyasu was, how could he instantly subdue all his foes within the eight provinces? The reason was that the common people in these provinces were neither friend nor foe but mere

---

† [This refers to a series of battles fought between Takeda Shingen of Kai and Uesugi Kenshin of Echigo between 1547 and 1565, as part of the Civil War Period.]

spectators to the war between the Go-Hōjō and Hideyoshi. When the Tokugawa subjugated the remaining enemy after it moved to the Kantō, they only struck down the remaining vassals of the Go-Hōjō. All they did to the peasants and townsmen was, figuratively, pat them on the heads and set their hearts at ease. Examples of this sort of thing are too numerous to list them all, and there has been no change in the pattern from the past right down to the present.

Therefore, we might even say that Japan has never been a single country. If today an incident should break out which pitted the whole of the Japanese nation against a foreign country, even if the whole Japanese populace took up arms and went to the front, we could calculate in advance how many would actually be interested in fighting and how many would be spectators. This is precisely what I meant when I once took the position that in Japan there is a government but no **nation**.† Of course, even in the countries of the West there have often been cases of one country taking over the lands of another in war, but to take them over was extremely difficult; it could not be done without oppression by very great force of arms, or unless some agreement was made with the common people of those lands and some degree of rights allotted them. We can see from this how different are the spirits of the commoners of East and West.

The People of the Nation Do Not Value Their Position

For this reason, since it was impossible for any person of talent and virtue who happened to rise among the common people to use his talent or virtue in that position, he had to abandon his position and join the ranks of the upper stratum of society. Thus there have been numerous examples of yesterday's commoners becoming today's generals. At first glance it might seem from this that there was no great chasm between upper and lower classes; however, these people simply abandoned their own status and fled to another. One can liken it to fleeing low swampland and moving to higher, drier ground. Though it may be convenient for the person himself, it is not the same as if he were to fill in the original swampland and convert it into higher, dry land.

---

† [This idea was first expressed in his *An Encouragement of Learning,* Section Four, in 1874.]

The result is that the swampland remains as swampy as before, and the old chasm still remains between it and the upland region the man now occupies—the separation between high and low changes not a whit.

In olden times a certain Kinoshita Tōkichi of Owari became ruler of the whole land as Taikō, yet the people of Owari remained the peasants of old, their conditions unchanged. Tōkichi merely abandoned the ranks of the peasants and joined the ranks of the warriors. His new status was the status of Tōkichi alone. He did not elevate the position of the peasants as a whole. Of course, since such were the trends of those times, it would avail us little to discuss it from the perspective of the present. But if we transplanted Tōkichi to a free city in olden-day Europe, its citizens would certainly have been displeased by the conduct of this hero. Or again, if he were brought back to life today and made to repeat his deeds, and if those independent citizens were also brought back to life and made to judge his deeds, they would be sure to call him cold-hearted. They would disclaim him, saying that anyone who depended upon the warriors, only to grab for riches and honor without regard for his ancestral burial places and his own peasant comrades, was not one of their number. Ultimately, since the viewpoints of Tōkichi and these citizens are composed of different elements, even though the general tenor of their conduct seems to be somewhat similar they were, are, and always will be completely incompatible, regardless of changes in social trends or circumstances.

In Europe of the thirteenth and fourteenth centuries, the citizens of the free cities who came into positions of prominence may have been disruptive in their actions or stubborn and ignorant, but they by no means depended upon others. They concentrated exclusively upon their own businesses; they also raised a militia to protect their businesses. But they solidified their positions by themselves. In England, France, and other countries in the modern world, the people of the middle class progressively amassed wealth; with it they also elevated their own moral conduct. Although they held many heated arguments in their parliaments, they were not vying for government power in order to be able to oppress the little people. Their only intention was to secure their own position in order to combat with power the power of others. The good of their own position they referred to as **local interest** in terms of region, and **class interest** in terms of occupation. Supported by a feeling of fellowship among those of the same region or among those engaged in the same work, they each asserted their group's viewpoint and protected their group's interests, in some cases even giving their lives for the sake of their group's interests.

Seen in these terms, the Japanese are extremely petty in their ways. They have always had little regard for their own positions and have shifted from position to position as suited their own convenience. If they do not seek power under the wing of others, they will themselves take over from someone else and do what he did, simply replacing force by force. They are as different from the independent citizens of the West as clouds are from clay.

In ancient China, one Xiang Yu of Chu once saw the procession of the First Emperor of Qin and said to himself: "I can replace that man." And when Emperor Gaozu of Han saw it, he said: "This is what a real man should be like!" Plumb their inner hearts and you will see that they were not so much enraged at the First Emperor of Qin's tyranny as wanting to advance their own positions. In reality they looked upon his tyrannical rule as a splendid opportunity for them to realize their own ambitions, and all they wanted was to usurp the First Emperor of Qin's position and carry on as he did. Even if their tyranny was not as great as that of the First Emperor of Qin, all they did was buy men's hopes by skillful manipulations. There was not the slightest difference at all between the First Emperor of Qin and Emperor Gaozu of Han as regards use of power to lord it over the masses. Japan, too, has not been without its share of great heroes, but their deeds were no different from those of Xiang Yu and Emperor Gaozu of Han.[†] Right from the dawn of Japanese history, the possibility that Japan might have independent citizens has been something beyond the wildest leap of imagination.

There Is No Religious Authority

Religion works within the hearts of men. It is something absolutely free and independent, not controlled in any way by others or dependent

---

† [Xiang Yu and Emperor Gaozu of Han were major figures in the power struggle that followed the death of the First Emperor of Qin, who had unified China. Emperor Gaozu of Han was the eventual winner, becoming the first emperor of the Han dynasty.]

upon their powers. But while this is the way religion ought to be, such has not been the case here in Japan. Some people claim that, originally, religion in Japan consisted of Shinto and Buddhism. But Shinto never became a full-fledged religion. Even though it had its theories in the ancient past, for hundreds of years now—ever since it became mixed with Buddhism—its true colors have been hidden. And though one hears Shinto mentioned now and again in modern times, it has been nothing but an insignificant movement, one which barely managed at the Meiji Restoration to avail itself of the lingering glory of the Imperial House. Since it is something merely ephemeral and incidental, in my opinion we ought not to recognize it as an established religion. No matter how one looks at it, the religion that has since ancient times represented one portion of Japanese civilization is Buddhism, and only Buddhism.

However, Buddhism, too, has belonged to the ruling class, and has depended upon the patronage of the ruling class, ever since its introduction. Though there have always been many eminent and learned monks who sought the Law of Buddha in China and began new sects, taught the people, and built large temples here in Japan, almost all of them tried to spread the Law as protegés of the emperors or shoguns and while basking in their glory. The worst of them even felt proud when the government made them peers. Cases of Buddhist monks being made *sōjō* [high priests] or *sōzu* [vicar generals] go back to very ancient times; in the *Engi shiki* it says that those who were *sōzu* and above were the equivalent to third rank at Court.[†] In Go-Daigo's edict of the second year of Kenmu [1335], *daisōjō* was equivalent to a *dainagon* of second rank; a *sōjō*, to a *chūnagon* of second rank; and an assistant abbot, to a *sangi* of third rank (*Shakka kanpan ki*).[‡] Thus the famous and learned monks of those times received Court offices and ranks and vied with other high courtiers for power and position, and took it as cause

---

[†] [*sōjō* (or later *daisōjō*) was the highest rank for a Buddhist monk; *sōzu* the second. *Engi shiki* (completed in 925 and put into force in 967) was a compilation of rules related to all aspects of court government and their implementation.]

[‡] [*dainagon* was chief councilor of State; *chūnagon*, middle councilor; *sangi*, lower councilor. Fukuzawa's source is a commentary on the official ranks given to Buddhist monks, compiled in 1355.]

for pride or shame how they ranked at Court. For these reasons Japanese religion, while always in possession of a creed, has never had a truly independent religious structure.

As proof of this consider the histories of the famous temples throughout the country. In the Tenpyō era [729–48] Emperor Shōmu established a temple in every province of the country. In the beginning of the reign of Emperor Kanmu, in the seventh year of Enryaku [788], Dengyō Daishi† cleared Mt. Hiei and built the Konpon Chūdō to protect the northeast entrance to the imperial capital. In the reign of Emperor Saga, in the seventh year of Kōnin [816], Kōbō Daishi cleared Mt. Kōya and received the emperor's seal to build a huge temple. In addition to this, all the famous temples in Japan—the various mountain temples south of Nara, the temples of Kyoto, the Five Zen Temples of Kamakura in the medieval period, the Tōeizan of Ueno in early modern times, Zōjōji of Shiba, and so forth—all were products of government support. Furthermore, the emperors have, all through history, adhered to Buddhism, and a great number of imperial princes have become monks. The Emperor Shirakawa had eight sons, of whom six were said to have become monks. Here was another reason for the power of religion. Only the Ikkō sect seems to have been somewhat independent, but even it was unable to escape this dependence on the government. At the end of the Ashikaga Bakufu in the first year of Taiei [1521], Jitsunyo‡ contributed some resources for the imperial enthronement; as a reward he was made a quasi-prince of the imperial blood, and his temple was permanently accorded a corresponding rank. Although it would seem quite in keeping with a monk's calling to sympathize with the dire economic straits of the Imperial Family and so contribute spare funds, in reality this was not the truth of the situation; through the good

---

† [Posthumous name of Saichō (767–822), who established the Tendai sect of Buddhism in Japan. Konpon Chūdo is the main building of the temple complex on Mt. Hiei, where Saichō first built in 788. Hiei was northeast of the new capital at Kyoto to which Kanmu moved in 794. The northeast was thought to be an inauspicious direction, so the temple developed an imperially recognized role in providing protection for the capital.]

‡ [Jitsunyo (1458–1525) became head of the Honganji, the main Ikkō temple, on the death of his father in 1499. Since the imperial court was starved of resources at this time, Jitsunyo's contribution was very welcome.]

offices of the monk Nishisanjō[†] he was really using the money to buy office and rank. It was a contemptible practice.

Thus, all the great Buddhist temples of Japan since ancient times were either built to fulfill a vow to Buddha by an emperor or empress, or else built by a shogun or shogunal regent. They can all be called government temples. If you ask the monks about the backgrounds of these temples, they will tell you how many hundred *koku* worth of land each temple had, or recite the various offices they have held, in a manner no different from that of the warriors who like to cite their family pedigree. Just to hear the way they talk must be disgusting. They have the nerve to post signs in front of their temples ordering riders to dismount, but when they leave their gates they rally round a host of followers and have them clear a way through the crowd. Some of them could be more powerful than feudal daimyo, but if you inquire into the basis of this power, you will find it is not religion. They have simply borrowed the government's power. Ultimately, they are nothing else but a branch of secular authority.

Buddhism has flourished, true. But its teaching has been entirely absorbed by political authority. What shines throughout the world is not the radiance of Buddha's teachings but the glory of Buddhism's political authority. Hence it is not surprising that there is no independent religious structure within the Buddhist religion.

Nor is it surprising that among its adherents there is no true religious spirit. For example, the fact that there have been so few strictly religious wars in Japan's history attests to the shallowness of their faith. The only external manifestations of faith you find in Buddhism are the tears running down the faces of ignorant, uneducated peasant clods. From this we can see that Buddhism was simply an instrument in an unenlightened world, an expedient for softening up the hearts of the most ignorant of men. Beyond this, it had no efficacy, no influence at all. The extreme of this decline can be found in the Tokugawa's time, when "delinquent" monks [men who were guilty of no secular crime but who had broken some religious regulation] were seized by the government, exposed in the city streets, and exiled. Thus we can say

---

† [Sanjō-nishi Sanetaka (1455–1537), a court noble. He had taken Buddhist vows, which was not unusual for people in his position.]

that the Buddhist monks were slaves of the government. More recently, the government has passed a law which permits Buddhist priests throughout the country to eat meat and get married. The fact that prior to this law these priests were unable to eat meat or get married was not because they were keeping some kind of religious precept. Rather, they refrained from these things because they did not have the government's permission. From this, then, we can conclude that the monks have been slaves of the government; indeed, we can even conclude that at present there is no real religion in Japan.

Learning Has No Power and Is a Tool of Absolutism
I have described the situation in regard to religion. It is even worse in regard to Confucian Learning. The transmission of Confucian writings in Japan is of quite ancient origin. In the imperial age, there were Confucian doctors of learning; the emperors themselves read the Chinese Classics. In the time of the Emperor Saga, Fujiwara no Fuyutsugu built the Kangakuin for the education of the youth of his clan [in 821]. In Emperor Uda's time Ariwara no Yukihira built the Shōgakuin [in 881]. Chinese Learning gradually blossomed, and moreover the teaching of *waka* poetry continued to flourish from ancient times.† But the learning in this period was completely limited to the sons of ranking Court officials, and all the books that were published were the works of government officials. Of course, since the techniques of printing had not yet been developed, there was no convenient method for imparting education to the common people.

In the Kamakura period, Ōe no Hiromoto, Miyoshi Yasunobu, and others were employed by the government because of their Confucian learning. But they too were attached to the government, and we hear nothing of learned men among the people. There is a story related about how, in the third year of Jōkyū [1221], when Hōjō Yasutoki attacked the Imperial forces defending the capital at Uji and Seta, an edict came from the Retired Emperor Go-Toba. A search was made among the

---

† [Japanese poems as opposed to poems composed in Chinese. The earliest surviving *waka* date from the fourth century and can be found in the *Man'yōshū* (compiled late seventh to late eighth centuries).]

5,000-odd warriors in Yasutoki's entourage to see if there were someone who could read, and only one man, Fujita Saburō from Musashi Province, was found. From this we can see the extent of illiteracy in those days.[†]

From this time down to the end of the Ashikaga's reign, book learning was monopolized by the monks. Those who wished to study had no recourse other than to go to a Buddhist temple. This is why students of calligraphy used to be called *terako* [literally "temple child"]. It has been said that the printing of books in Japan began at the Five Zen Temples in Kamakura. This is probably true. At the beginning of the Tokugawa period, Ieyasu first called upon Fujiwara Seika, and next employed Hayashi Razan. As the era of peace continued, Confucian scholars have been produced in a great number right down to recent times. Thus the rise and fall of learning have paralleled the political situation in Japan, and it, too, has failed to occupy an independent position. It is a black spot on the honor of learning that during the several hundred years of civil warfare it fell completely into the hands of the monks. Even from this one fact we can see that Confucianism was not the equal of Buddhism.

However, for learning to decline in a period of warfare is not something peculiar to Japan; it is a universal phenomenon. In Europe, too, from the late classical or Dark Ages down to the end of the feudal period the power of learning was completely monopolized by the monasteries. It was only from the seventeenth century on that learning finally was opened to society as a whole.

But the spirit of learning differs between East and West. The countries of the West stress the idea of experiment; we in Japan dote on the theories of Confucius and Mencius. These approaches are totally different, but, while we cannot put them in the same category, we also cannot entirely find fault with one or the other. At any rate, we must admit that it was Buddhism and Confucianism that saved us from barbarism and raised us to the level of civilization which we do enjoy today. Indeed, during the time of the Tokugawa, when Confucianism flourished, it did much to refute the false and illusory theories of Shinto

---

† [This anecdote is related in *Tokushi yoron*. The edict contained what was effectively Go-Toba's admission of defeat.]

and Buddhism and to dispel some of the superstitions in the popular mind. For this, Confucianism should be given full credit. Its accomplishments were considerable. In this regard Confucianism can be said to have been influential.

Therefore, leaving aside the relative merits or demerits of Eastern or Western styles of learning, and just looking at the process of how learning was carried out, I shall here point out a marked difference between the two. The difference is that after the war times, learning arose in the Western countries among the people in general, whereas in Japan it arose within the government. In the West, learning was the business of the scholars, and government officials did not have their hands in it. It belonged only to the world of scholars. Learning in Japan, on the other hand, was the learning of the ruling class, so to speak. It was merely another department within the government. During the 250 years of Tokugawa rule, all schools in Japan were either established by the central government or run by the various feudal domains. There were famous scholars, and a great body of literature was produced, but the scholars were always someone's retainers, and the writings were always published by the government. Though there were some scholars among the masterless samurai, and some privately published works, these masterless samurai were men who had tried to become retainers but had failed, and the private publications were works that had been rejected by the government. One never heard of anything in the country like an organization of scholars, or the publication of debates or news. There were no places for teaching the arts, nor were there meetings for public discussion. In short, there was, in the field of learning, not a single bit of private endeavor. Some rare great Confucian scholar would open his own private school, but his students were always limited to the samurai, all of whom were receiving stipends, serving their lords, and pursuing learning only in their spare time. What is more, the various schools of learning were interested only in teaching their students how to be competent rulers, how to rule over others. Even though the students read thousands of books, if they failed to find a position in government they were of no use whatever. If any of these glorified himself with the title of "retired gentleman," actually he was probably not "retired" by free choice but because he had to, and was really sulking over his own ill fortune and envying the good fortune of his classmates, or else he had given up on the world completely in order to engage in wool-gathering.

I might illustrate this situation by saying that the scholars in Japan were closed up within a box called the government, which they considered their universe. Within this universe they were in agony. Fortunately, the number of such scholars was not great and the extent of their educational influence was not too wide. For if they had produced the great number of scholars they had a mind to, they would have become too cramped within their narrow box; and in proportion as such people had found no place for themselves their envy and anguish would have been all the greater. This would have been a rather pathetic situation, would it not? Since, in the limited confines of the box of government, there would have proliferated an unlimited number of scholars who knew nothing of the world outside their own little box, they would not have been able to make a place for themselves in that world. Completely dependent upon those in authority, these teachers would feel no shame, no matter what humiliations they were subjected to.

In the time of Tokugawa's reign those who were successful in their goal of becoming scholars were made Confucian officials in the various *han*. Although they bore the title of Confucian officials, in reality they were merely decked out in flowing robes, receiving nobody's respect at all, used as pawns, not allowed to participate in affairs of state as they would have liked to, given the meagerest of stipends, and set to instructing the *han* youngsters in how to read. Since it was a society where knowing how to read was a rare accomplishment, they were used simply to offset this handicap. Their treatment can be likened to the way the *eta* class† was restricted to working with leather. Theirs was the ultimate in degradation. What was sought from them, or what responsibility given them? It is no wonder that no independent organizations emerged from among their groups and that they developed no definite theories.

---

† [*Eta*, itself a derogatory term, was the word used to refer to outcast groups in traditional Japanese society. Members were involved in occupations that were regarded as polluting by majority society, such as work involving contact with animal carcasses. The caste itself was abolished in 1871, but prejudices against people of outcast origin lingered on.]

True, there were some Confucian scholars with at least enough mettle to complain against the government's despotic control over everyone. But when you get down to the root of the matter, you can see that these gentlemen were like farmers who plant seeds and cultivate them, but who then are greatly inconvenienced when the plants start spreading wildly. For who were the ones teaching government absolutism? Even if in essence all government contains an element of absolutism, were not those who were helping that element develop and encouraging it none other than the Confucian scholars? Of all the Confucianists who have ever been in Japan, those who enjoyed a reputation as most talented and most capable were the greatest experts on absolutism, and the greatest tools of the government. In regard to absolutism, then, the Confucianists were the teachers and the government was the pupil.

Alas, we Japanese of today are their descendants! For us to be practicing absolutism in this day and age, and to be subjected to it, is not entirely the fault of the present generation; we have inherited a disease from our distant ancestors. But who are the ones who helped spread this contagion? The contribution of the Confucian teachers was great.

As I said above, both Confucianism and Buddhism have contributed in their respective spheres to the making of Japanese civilization. But neither avoids the vice of attachment to antiquity. The essence of religion is to provide teachings for man's heart. And since it cannot change, it is natural that Buddhists and Shintoists have been preaching to men of the present day the same things they have held for thousands of years. Confucianism differs from these religions in that it speaks exclusively about the principles of society, and the six arts of the gentlemen: ritual, music, archery, horse-riding, writing, and arithmetic. Therefore, it is a doctrine which for the most part is concerned with politics. It is indeed regrettable that it does not know the meaning of change and progress!

Human learning advances day by day. Yesterday's gain becomes today's loss; last year's right becomes this year's wrong. Doubts are raised about everything; fresh inquiry creates new discoveries and change, so that the younger generation surpasses its elders. There is a cumulative process of development. When we look back to a hundred years ago, we have to smile at how crude and uncivilized much of it used to be. This is proof of how much civilization has advanced and learning progressed. However, we read in the *Analects*: "Young people are awe-inspiring; how can you be sure that they will not equal you?" And Mencius says: "Who was Shun? Who am I? Whoever would accomplish things must be like him."† Mencius also said: "King Wen is my teacher; can I go wrong by following the Duke of Zhou?"‡ From quotations such as these we can see the spirit of Confucianism. The statement about the younger generation means: "Be careful, for if people of a later generation study hard, they might be able to match you." But if that is so, the maximum height to which people of a later generation should be able to attain is only that of the present generation. Now, since people of the present generation already are in an age which cannot measure up to the men of old, even if later generations manage to reach the present level, we will have no cause for complacency. The reason later scholars push themselves hard, egg themselves on unremittingly, and then spur themselves on even more, is that they are aspiring to reach the level Shun attained several thousand years ago, or the point where they might learn from King Wen or be aided by the Duke of Zhou. They are like school children receiving a calligraphy book from their teacher and then assiduously trying to imitate the writing specimens in the book. Right from the start they are resigned to the fact that they will not measure up to their teacher; when they reach a point where they are really good, they will merely be imitating their teacher's writing but not be able to surpass him.

The Confucian genealogy is as follows: the Way was transmitted from Yao and Shun to Yu and Tang, Wen and Wu, the Duke of Zhou, and Confucius; after Confucius the breed of sages was at an end, and we no longer hear of such men in either China and Japan. Long after Mencius, Song Confucianists and the great Confucian scholars in Japan

---

† [Mencius is here quoting Yan Hui, a disciple of Confucius. Shun, a legendary early Chinese ruler, was revered as the embodiment of Confucian ideals, particularly modesty and filial piety.]

‡ [Mencius is here quoting Gongming Yi, a disciple of Zengzi. The point is that since the Duke of Zhou was a son of King Wen, he was likely to transmit the King's teachings faithfully. Both men were seen as embodiments of the Confucian ideal.]

too could look with pride to the younger generation, but not a word could be said to compare them favorably with the ancients from Confucius on back into pre-history. All they could do was lament that their learning fell far short of the sages of old. Therefore, the longer the Way of the sages is transmitted to men of later generations, the more impoverished it becomes. With the passage of time it reduces man's knowledge and virtue while increasing the number of evil and ignorant people. Since the Way has been transmitted from generation to generation until our own degenerate times, it can be shown by calculation that the world has already gone to the dogs. Fortunately, the law of the progress of human knowledge works independently of Confucian theory. That there have often been excellent men superior to the ancients, and that the present level of progress of civilization runs counter to the Confucian calculation of matters, may be called the good fortune of us Japanese. However, because the Confucianists still believe in and cherish the old, and make not the slightest effort of their own, they may be called **mental slaves**.[†] Because they put their spirits at the service of the ancient Way, because, though living in the present world, they are subject to the control of the men of old, because they pass on this control in order in turn to control present society, and because they breathe into social relations an element of stagnation, their fault is great indeed.

Nevertheless, from another point of view, if there had been no Confucian Learning in Japan in ancient times, we should not be at the level of development that we enjoy today. In respect to what the West calls **refinement**, Confucianism's meritorious achievement in disciplining and purifying men's hearts has not been insignificant. The only trouble is that, while in ancient times it performed a service, today it is useless. When goods are hard to come by, even a worn-out straw mat can be used to keep warm at night, even rice bran can be eaten as food. With all the more reason we cannot find fault with old Confucianism. In my opinion, the teaching of Confucianism to the Japanese of old was like sending a farmer's daughter to serve in the

---

† [Fukuzawa is here referring to J. S. Mill's *On Liberty*, Chapter II: "Of the Liberty of Thought and Discussion." The term that Mill himself uses is "mental slavery."]

palace. There she learned refinement in her bearing and conduct, and developed her talent and intelligence to a high degree; however, in the process she lost her sprightliness and became useless as far as household management goes. Yet, since there were no places for the education of women in those days, it was reasonable for her to enter into such service. Today, however, we would have to pass an entirely different judgment on the value of doing this.

The Lack of an Individualistic Spirit in the Sengoku Warriors

From ancient times on, Japan was called a country of loyalty and courage, and the dauntless spirit of her warriors, their loyalty, and their straightforwardness were the pride of Asia. In the last years of the Ashikaga, the country was rocked with warfare as the powerful feudal barons ceaselessly attacked one another. War had never flourished to the extent that it did in this period. In one battle a province was lost; with one victory the fortunes of a house were revived. Men with neither pedigree nor lineage could, by their exploits, gain fame and fortune overnight. Although there are differences in the degree of civilization, the situation in Japan at that time might perhaps be comparable to the period of the barbarian invasions at the end of the Roman Empire. In these circumstances, one might imagine, the Japanese warrior class would also produce its own spirit of independence and autonomy, or, just as the German barbarians left behind a legacy of autonomy and freedom, the spirit of the Japanese people would also undergo a drastic change; but that was not the case at all. For the imbalance of power that I discussed at the beginning of this chapter had, from earliest history, permeated to the minutest level of society, and it was not to be shaken by any kind of cataclysm. And although the samurai of this time seemed fiercely independent, their active spirit sprang neither from a personal, righteous attitude nor from a strong individuality that exulted in the self's freedom from all outside influences. It was always motivated by something outside the person, or at least aided by it. What was that something outside the person? It was a man's ancestors, or the glory of his house, or his lord, or his father, or his own status.

The martial heroism of that period was always motivated by one or other of these considerations. There developed a custom for those who had no famous ancestor, or whose house, lord, or father were not of important pedigree, to invent such names. No matter how powerful or intelligent the medieval warrior heroes were, there was not one who attempted to do things by relying upon only his intelligence and power. Let me give a few examples of what I mean.

The famous warriors at the end of the Ashikaga Bakufu, in order to follow their lords, revenge their fathers, revive the fortunes of their ancestral houses, or establish their fame as warriors, gathered partisans around themselves and seized lands, thereby fiercely competing with each other to control local regions. But the one thing they were really aiming at was to go up to the capital, Kyoto. Now if we investigate just what this meant, we find that they wanted to have an audience with the emperor or the shogun, win his support, and gain control of some land. Those who had not yet had the opportunity to go up to the capital used the technique of receiving office and rank from the Imperial Family *in absentia*, thus increasing the glory of their own houses, and using that to control their subjects. This particular method was a standard one employed from of old by Japanese warriors—the chieftains of the Minamoto and Taira all used it. The Hōjō, however, did not directly seek the highest rank and office. Rather, for appearances' sake they allowed the shogun to remain in office and they ruled the land [as shogunal regents] from their lower positions of fifth rank in the Court. Thus they used not only the Imperial Family but the shogun as well. Superficially this may appear a decent, clever stratagem, but a closer look into the matter shows it ultimately stemmed from the baseness of their hearts, and contained an element that is despicable and hateful.

Again, take the case of Ashikaga Takauji, who, following the strategy of Akamatsu Enshin, obtained an edict from Emperor Go-Fushimi which allowed him to put the latter's son on the throne as the Emperor Kōmyō.† No matter how you look at it, this was hardly motivated by

---

† [*Sic.* The reference here is to an edict from the Retired Emperor Kōgon, not Go-Fushimi, to put his (Kōgon's) brother on the throne as Emperor Kōmyō in 1336 (Fukuzawa is probably following a similar error in Arai Hakuseki's *Tokushi yoron*). By claiming to lead Emperor Kōmyō's army, Takauji tried to evade any accusation that he was in fact rebelling against Emperor Go-Daigo. However, Go-Daigo set up a rival court in Yoshino, thus beginning the turbulent period of the two rival northern (at Kyoto) and southern (at Yoshino) courts known as Nanbokuchō (1336–92).]

true imperial loyalty. In the beginning, Oda Nobunaga controlled the shogun Ashikaga Yoshiaki. But realizing that the prestige of the shogun was inferior to that of the emperor, he got rid of Yoshiaki and immediately set the emperor ahead of him.[†] This act, too, was hardly motivated by deep feeling. Both cases were obvious examples of deceitful trickery. Anyone in the land with eyes to see or ears to hear could have discerned their true motivations. Yet outwardly these men professed their loyalty and sincerity, while gaining their ends on the pretext of moral duty, a pretext no more grounded in fact than children's games. Why did people go along with such men? Because there was great profit to be had by all concerned. The Japanese warriors were raised amidst this kind of imbalance of power, the definitive rule of social relations right from the dawn of our history. They did not consider it shameful to be constantly subservient to someone else. We can see a marked difference between these men and the peoples of the West, who valued their own positions and status and who proclaimed their individual rights.

Thus, even in the period of violent warfare between the samurai, this principle of social relationships could not be broken. At the head of one family was a general, and under him household elders; then came the knights, the foot soldiers, and lastly the *ashigaru* and *chūgen*.[‡] The duties of upper and lower were clearcut, and equally clear were the rights that went with these duties. Every man submitted to overbearance from those above and demanded subservience from those below. Every man was both unreasonably oppressed and unreasonably oppressive. While bowing before one man, he was lording it over another. For example, if there were ten people in A, B, C order, B in his relation to A expressed subservience and humility, to a point where the humiliation he suffered ought to have been intolerable. But in his relation with C he was able to be regally high-handed. Thus his humiliation in the former case was compensated for by the gratification he derived from the latter. Any dissatisfaction evened itself out. C took compensation from D, D

---

† [Nobunaga advanced on Kyoto in order to install Yoshiaki as shogun in 1568, but refused the title of shogunal deputy and drove Yoshiaki out of Kyoto in 1573.]

‡ [In times of war *ashigaru* fought (on foot and in an auxiliary capacity), while *chūgen* carried weapons for their masters and acted as guards.]

demanded the same from E, and so on down the line. It was like dunning the neighbor on one's east for the sum loaned to the neighbor on one's west.

Comparing these social patterns to material objects, power in the West is like iron; it does not readily expand or contract. On the other hand, the power of the Japanese warriors was as flexible as rubber, adapting itself to whatever it came in contact with. In contact with inferiors, it swelled up immensely; in contact with those above, it shriveled up and shrank. The sum total of this elasticity of power constituted that whole known as the prestige of the military houses; those oppressed by it were the ordinary people who had no political voice. This may seem to be unfortunate from the standpoint of such persons of the lower classes, but within the military groups themselves, from the generals right on down to the lowest *ashigaru* and *chūgen*, this general pattern was advantageous to everyone. Not only was it advantageous, it also was a beautifully well-organized hierarchical system. That is, while within the group this system did have the evil aspect of one man being subservient to another, yet the glory of the whole could be considered by an individual warrior as his personal glory, and, conversely, he could disregard its evil aspect by abandoning his own individual interests. Having built this system, the warriors became accustomed to it. Raised within this custom of subservience, it became second nature to them. Nothing could shake this system, no matter what happened; authority or armed might could not overcome it, dire need could not wrest it from them. Here we can see the glorious spirit of the warriors.

In a specific situation or function, there were many truly admirable facets to this feudal custom. The way the warriors of Mikawa Province attached themselves to the Tokugawa is one example of this.[†]

Because warrior relationships were organized in this way, maintenance of the system required that there be some kind of supreme spiritual authority. This authority supposedly rested in the Imperial Family, and yet in reality authority in the world of men depends on

---

[†] [The first Tokugawa Shogun, Ieyasu, originally came from Mikawa. Fellow Mikawa samurai played an important role in his rise to power and formed hereditary vassal families with crucial roles in the adminstration and maintenance of the Tokugawa system.]

knowledge and virtue. If the Imperial Family lacked the requisite knowledge and virtue, then real authority could not lie in its hands. Because of this, it seems, there developed the policy of leaving the Imperial Family authority in name only, letting it retain a meaningless status while the military houses tried to grip the reins of actual power. This was why various illustrious men of the time were eager to go up to the capital and why they deliberately used moral duty as an excuse—as patent a sham as a children's game. In sum, the fundamental reason for this was that Japanese warriors had no **individuality**. They did not consider it shameful to function in a structure of subservience.

Though this is something people from ancient times have paid little attention to, since I have brought up the matter here, there is another point in which we can see that the warriors of Japan lacked this individualistic spirit. That is the matter of names. Essentially, a man's name is something given him by his parents. Even if he changes his name when he becomes an adult, he should not have to do this at the bidding of others. Though daily necessities seem to be entirely up to people's free choices, many of them actually are influenced by others, for people follow the fads of the times. However, names are different from food, clothing, and shelter. They are not only obviously not subject to the bidding of others, they also are not things which other people, be they even close relatives or friends, can meddle in without prior consultation with the person concerned. We can say that this is one of the most completely free areas of human life. In a country which by law prohibits the changing of a name, a man's freedom is not being curtailed if he abides by the law. But in a country where there is freedom to change names, the freedom to change the name Gensuke to Heikichi, or not to change it, is entirely a matter of individual decision. It is like a man's freedom to sleep on the right side or the left side at night. It is nobody else's business at all. However, in samurai families of Japan there have always been instances in which someone is permitted to take part of an illustrious name and form a new one for himself. This is a base and contemptible custom, yet even a hero as great as Uesugi Kenshin could not escape doing it. Granted permission to use part of the name of the shogun Ashikaga Yoshiteru, he changed his name to

Terutora. A more extreme case was when after the battle of Sekigahara the reins of power fell to the Tokugawa and all of those who had called themselves Toyotomi[†] either changed back to their original names or else even took the name of the victorious Matsudaira, the former surname of Ieyasu. These changes of names occurred either at their own request or by conferral from above, but in either case we must say that it was truly a base practice.

Perhaps someone might say that this matter of changing names was simply a custom at that time and should not be censured from our present historical vantage point. But this is not true. The human repugnance to taking over the name of another is the same then as it is now. As proof of this, in the time of the Ashikaga the son of the Kamakura *kubō* Mochiuji[‡] came of age in the sixth year of Eikyō [1434] and took the name Yoshihisa.[††] Despite the remonstrances of his advisor Uesugi Norizane that he abide by custom and request part of the name of the Shogun for his son, Mochiuji refused. For at that time Mochiuji already aspired after independence.[‡‡] Whether his aspiration was right or wrong, he must have considered the practice of taking another's name a base one. Again in the time of the Tokugawa, because the family name of Matsudaira was declined by the Hosokawa, the common people spoke of the act with approval. Whether it is true or not is uncertain, but the fact that it was considered worthy of praise is proof that human nature was the same then as now. This matter of names may not be as important as the next point I shall bring up, but through it we can learn of the surprising baseness of the samurai of old—despite their reputations for loyalty and courage. At the same time it shows the terrifying power of the government, which was strong enough to violate the inner sanctum of men's hearts in order to control them.

---

† [Until his death in 1598, power had been concentrated in the hands of Toyotomi Hideyoshi. Ieyasu's victory at Sekigahara signified the ruin of the supporters of Hideyoshi's son, Hideyori.]

‡ [Kamakura *kubō* was the title given by Takauji to his fourth son, Motouji (and from then to his descendants). The *kubō* governed the eastern part of Japan around Kamakura on behalf of the Shogun, who was based in Kyoto.]

†† [*Sic.* The actual date was the tenth year of Eikyō (1438).]

‡‡ [In 1438 Mochiuji tried to oust Uesugi but the latter was supported by the Shogun and Mochiuji was defeated.]

Because of the Imbalance of Power, No Advance in Japanese Civilization, Either in Peace or in War

As I have mentioned above, Japanese society since ancient times exhibits this division between rulers and ruled. This imbalance of power has perdured right up to the present time. Needless to say, the common people never asserted their own rights. Both religion and learning were under the control of the ruling class and never succeeded in becoming independent. Although in the wartime period the warriors seem to have been loyal and courageous, they never knew the taste of individuality. Whether in war or in peace, the whole fabric of social relationships, from the highest to the lowest, exhibited this imbalance of power. Like using a single medicine for ten thousand different illnesses, by the efficacy of this one medicine the power of the ruling class was augmented and centralized, and the rulers maintained authority in their own hands. As I also said above, the governments of the imperial age and of the shoguns, and again the policies of the Hōjō, the Ashikaga, and the Tokugawa, were in essence the same. The only criterion for considering one rule better than another can be the skill or ineptitude with which this imbalance of power was utilized. Once someone succeeded in regaining supreme power for his house by a clever use of this imbalance of power, everything was settled and he had nothing more to desire.

The term *kokka* (nation) has been in use since ancient times.† The character *ka* (house) does not refer to the houses of the people, but seems to mean the family or family name of the rulers. Therefore the country equals the family and the family equals the country. Such extreme slogans have even been used as: "The enrichment of the government is the benefit of the country." In this way the country was reduced to ruin for the sake of some family. Because the basic principles of government were defined in terms of such ideas, all policies were for the sake of retaining the one-sided power within one family. Rai San'yō, in his *Nihon gaishi*, judged the government of the Ashikaga to be like a pin-headed dog that couldn't move its heavy tail, and claimed that

---

† [*Kokka* is formed by joining the character meaning "country" (*koku*) to the character meaning "house/family" (*ka*).]

its policies were a failure. He was simply saying that the Ashikaga did not enjoy one-sided power and therefore did not have full control. Although this was quite natural for a Confucianist of that time, when you come right down to it, San'yō's was a view which recognized only a family and not a country.

If San'yō judged the weakness of the Ashikaga a political failure, he should have been satisfied with the swollen-headed nature of Tokugawa power, for the imbalance was never more skillfully employed than by the Tokugawa. After unifying the whole country, the shogunate gradually increased the lands held by its own house, exhausted the resources of the other feudal lords, destroyed strongholds in all quarters, put a halt to the repair of castles in the domains, and prohibited the building of large ships. No firearms were allowed into Edo; none of the lords' women or children were allowed out. The shogunate required the daimyos to build luxurious mansions and live expensively, to the neglect of their other affairs. If it saw that they had excessive wealth, the shogunate asked for contributions to the shogunate—it invented all manners of excuses to exhaust their resources. Everything was carried out according to Tokugawa orders. It was a one-sided contest of strength against men whose arms and legs had first been broken. The Tokugawa family was truly the finest exemplar of one-sided government, for they most skillfully worked for the advantage of their own house, and achieved the most singular results.

Of course, for a government to exist there must be a nucleus which has a hold on power at the center and controls the whole. This nucleus is necessary not only in Japan but in any country. Even in ancient Japan, when the level of civilization was still primitive, this principle was understood. Precisely for that reason, perhaps, the principle of absolutism has been an enduring political tradition. Indeed, ever since the first beginnings of civilized society, would anyone ever expect civilization to exist if the power of government were taken away? Even school children know that government power is necessary.

However, in the civilized nations in the West this power does not spring from one source alone. Even if the government decides upon a certain course of action, its orders either are merely voicing the consensus of the people or, if a consensus could not be had, are voicing a compromise representing a variety of opinions held by the people. In Japan, though, the relation between the government and the people has always been not merely that of master and guest, but we may even say that of enemies. The Tokugawa shogunate's policy of exhausting the resources of the daimyos was no different in principle from exacting tribute from an enemy defeated in battle, and the prohibition of shipbuilding and the repair of castles was equivalent to destroying the forts of a defeated enemy. We certainly cannot call this relationship between government and people that of one between fellow countrymen.

In all human affairs there is a first step and a second step. When one takes the first step, one must make sure it will suit the second step. Thus in a sense it can be said that the second step regulates the first. For example, there is a saying that pain precedes pleasure, and another that good medicine is bitter to the taste. It is human nature to try to avoid what is painful and to dislike bitter medicine. When one focuses only on the first step, it is only natural to feel aversion to it. But when one sees the second step of pleasure and the cure of one's illness, then the first step can be endured. Imbalance in power was also an unavoidable temporary measure to bolster the hearts of the people and attain proper order. It did not necessarily arise from evil intentions. It was the taking of the first step. However, even though this imbalance reached amazing heights of skill and perfection, when it finally came time to take the second step, the evil abuses of previous years came to light, to reveal the impossibility of drawing good from the first step. When you think of it, the more skillful absolute government is, the greater are the resultant evils; and the longer a reign of peace, the deeper society's ills. Eventually, a hereditary disease is handed on to future generations whose remedy is not easy to find.

The peaceful epoch of the Tokugawa reign is an example of this. At present we are trying to change conditions and progress to the second stage of human relationships, but we are finding it extremely difficult to get beyond the earlier stage. Why? Because Tokugawa absolutism was so skillful and its peace was so enduring. I once used a kind of folksy image to evaluate this situation. I said that dressing up absolutist government was like a retired old gent who had a cherished gourd that he polished all day long. The result of all his efforts was only to increase the shiny luster of the little, round gourd. Supposing you are trying to take a second step in order to adapt to changed conditions, if you cling to the old ways and refuse any alterations, if you seek the unattainable and paint fanciful dreams inside your head and then worry about whether these can be realized, you might just as well be polishing the gourd without noticing that it is already cracked. This is carrying stupidity to ever greater heights. Doesn't this analogy strike home? In any case, that person worries about the first step without any thought for the second, stopping at the first without proceeding to the second, impeding the second because of the first. Hence, rather than say order was brought into society by the first step of one-sided power, we should say that it really did not bring order, it brought death and decay to social relationships. Therefore we might have second thoughts about what San'yō called the pin-headed Ashikaga shogunate, as well as about the swollen-headed imbalance of the Tokugawa. People like San'yō look only at the first step and never get beyond polishing their gourds.

Let us look at Tokugawa rule to see how the people who lived under this state of imbalance of power viewed the affairs of society, and how they conducted themselves. The millions of Japanese at that time were closed up inside millions of individual boxes. They were separated from one another by walls with little room to move around. The four-level class structure of samurai, farmers, artisans, and merchants froze human relationships along prescribed lines. Even within the samurai there were distinctions in terms of stipends and offices. At one extreme, the occupations of Confucian teachers and doctors became hereditary too. Each of the other classes of society also had its own determining patterns of behavior. The walls separating them were as strong as iron and could not be broken by any amount of force. Having no motivation to employ their talents in order to progress forward, people simply retreated into the safety of their own shells. Over the course of several hundred years this routine became second nature to them. Their spirit of initiative, as it is called, was lost completely. For example, an impoverished samurai or commoner—ignorant, illiterate, inured to being despised by others, going from poverty to worse poverty, experiencing sufferings incomparable to anything known to most men in society—lacked the spirit to overcome his hardships; he lacked initiative. He could bear up under every unforeseen hardship that came his way, but he did not anticipate hardships or plan for future well-being. This same thing was true of scholars and merchants as well.

In general, we Japanese seem to lack the kind of motivation that ought to be standard equipment in human nature. We have sunk to the depths of stagnation. This is why there were so few people in this country who accomplished any great works during the 250 years of Tokugawa rule. The feudal *han* were abolished recently, but the Japanese people have not suddenly changed their character because of it. The ancient distinction between ruler and ruled has not changed one iota, even now. All of this is the result of the imbalance of power, an evil that has arisen from not paying attention to the second step of things. If we do not take cognizance of this evil and get rid of the disease of imbalance, whether the country is at peace or in turmoil no real progress will be made in the level of civilization of the country. But since the treatment of this disease is the task of present-day politicians, I do not intend to discuss it here. I am only diagnosing the situation.

Now, even in the West not everyone is equal in terms of wealth or prestige. The strong and wealthy often control the weak and poor in a cruel and arrogant manner. The weak and poor, in turn, may fawn on and deceive others. The ugly aspects of human life are certainly no different from what we find among Japanese. Sometimes they are even worse. But even with such social injustice there is still a pervading spirit of individuality and nothing hinders the expansion of the human spirit. Cruelty and arrogance are merely by-products of wealth and power and are not essential to them; flattery and deception are merely by-products of poverty and weakness and not to be feared. Neither might nor weakness is innate; they can be dealt with by means of human intelligence. If men have as their goal the handling of these problems by use of their intelligence, even if the solution actually lies beyond their control, they can still rely on their own powers and direct their own steps down the path of independent development, relying on their own efforts. If we question the poor, they might be unable to say what they want, but in their hearts they probably feel as follows: "Since we are poor we obey the rich, but only as long as we are poor must we submit to them. Our submission will disappear along with our poverty, while their control over us will vanish along with their riches." After all, the expansion of the human spirit points to this kind of attitude. We Japanese, however, have been controlled by one-sided regimes since the dawn of our history. When we deal with a person, be he rich or poor, strong or weak, wise or ignorant, capable or incompetent, we either fear him or look down upon him, entirely on the basis of his social position. A spirit of independence has never existed in even the slightest degree. If we compare the Western attitude of independence with that of us insulated Japanese, we can see how enormous the difference is.

The Economy Also Stagnates†

We cannot overlook the influence of this imbalance of power upon the economy of the whole country. Economic theory is very complex, extremely difficult to understand. And since conditions differ from country to country, we cannot, of course, directly apply Western economic theory to Japan. Nevertheless, there are two general principles which are universal for any country at any time. The first is that of accumulating wealth and dispersing it again. The relationship between accumulation and expenditure is close and inseparable, for accumulation of wealth is the art of expenditure, and expenditure is the means of accumulation. Thus, scattering seeds in the spring is the means to accumulate a harvest in the fall. Similarly, to spend money for daily necessities is to protect one's health and nourish one's strength and is a means of accumulating the things of daily life. It is also possible to have expenditure without a return. Fire or flood damage are examples of this. Wasting money on sensual appetites and luxurious tastes is to use up one's property with nothing to show for it; it is the same as loss by fire or flood. But the essence of economics does not lie in prohibiting expenditures. The merits or demerits of an expenditure and outlay of money can only be calculated by what comes back in return. If the gains outweigh the expenditures, it is said to be profitable; if they balance each other, it is said to be unprofitable. If gains are less than

---

† [This sub-heading has been added by the translators.]

expenditures, or completely non-existent, it is said to be a loss, or a total loss, respectively. The goal of economists is to make the gains outweigh the losses, and gradually to enhance the wealth of the entire nation by a steady process of accumulation and expenditure.

Therefore we should not think that either accumulation and expenditure is the means, while the other is the end. We should not prefer one over the other, give one greater priority or urgency, or try to decide which is more difficult or important. They are equal in value and must be treated as such. People who know how to accumulate but not how to spend will end up with little to accumulate, while those who know how to spend but not how to accumulate will end up with little to spend. The basis of national wealth lies in making both accumulation and expenditure prosper. A country which is a good illustration of this principle we call a rich country.

Accordingly, the accumulation and expenditure of national wealth must reflect the opinions of the people of the entire nation. National wealth is an index of a national mentality, for it is the product of the national temper. Since government income and expenditure is a part of national wealth, the fact that Western governments discuss their budgets with the people is traceable to such a national mentality.

The second principle is that, to accumulate and spend resources, there must be knowledge proportionate to the resources, and habits of handling them. These are the theory and practice of political economy. For example, neither the prodigal son who brings his house to ruin nor the addicted gambler can preserve his wealth for long. They do not have the knowledge or the habits suited to their wealth. To entrust very large sums of wealth to one who has neither qualification results not only in the wealth's being lost for nothing but also, like giving a small child a sharp knife, courts disastrous injury to the person himself or to others. There are many cases of this in ancient and modern times.

In the light of the above two principles, we can evaluate the results of economic policies carried out in earlier Japanese history. Passing over the imperial age, let us see what Katsuzan Hakuyū has to say in his *Treatise on Agricultural Development*[†]:

At the time of the Genpei wars, taxation was not dependent upon local government. The people had no idea to whom they owed allegiance. The same village unit or manor served the government, the Taira nobles, and the Minamoto warriors. Moreover, since their rice was taken away to feed the warring factions, the people, without a voice, were ground into the dust. Finally Shogun Minamoto no Yoritomo seized power and placed constables in the provinces and stewards in the manors, but since the old provincial and manorial officials still remained, the people had to pay allegiance to two overlords. . . . When the Ashikaga ruled the provinces, there were no conflicting sources of law; the provinces, their lesser units, and the manors were divided among the samurai and the taxes were determined by the individual lords, except for 2 per cent, which went to the Ashikaga. (For example, an area which produced 50 *koku* of rice tax sent one *koku* to Kyoto to fill the shogun's treasury.) There were years when this was increased to 5 per cent. Since the constables and stewards themselves controlled the management of the entire process, there were two taxes. . . . Besides that, three other taxes—*tansen, munabechi,* and *kurayaku*—were levied at unspecified times. *Tansen* was a tax paid for rice paddies, like the present-day *takagakari. Munabechi* was a tax paid upon the number of buildings owned, like today's *kagiyaku.* The *kurayaku* was levied only upon rich farmers and merchants, and it was equivalent to the present-day *bugenwari.* The *kurayaku* was levied in every quarter during Ashikaga Yoshimitsu's time; in Ashikaga Yoshinori's time it was every month. According to the *Ōnin-ki,*[‡] by Ashikaga Yoshimasa's time it had reached a point where it was levied nine times in the 11th month and eight times in the 12th, so that the farmers abandoned their fields and homes and fled, and the merchants closed their doors and stopped business. . . . After the unification by Hideyoshi, the laws established in the third year of Bunroku [1594] gave two-thirds of the taxes to the steward and one-third to the farmers. . . . It is also said that at the beginning of the Tokugawa the government lessened the severity in newly-won provinces and relaxed the taxes by one-third (i.e. 40 per cent for the lord, 60 per cent for the farmer). This relieved the extremity of the peasants.

---

† [A work completed in 1812 that related the development of the Japanese tax system in relation to changes in political rule. The author was a senior retainer of Takatō *han* in Shinano province.]

‡ [There is no known author or date for this.]

According to this account of the agricultural development of Japan, taxation in Japan was unquestionably severe. Even though the tax burden was lightened at the beginning of the Tokugawa, as time passed it reverted back to the severity of old. Again, according to the orthodox theories of earlier times, the farmers were considered the basis of the country, while the artisan and merchant classes were considered to be enjoying a life of ease, regardless of whether they paid taxes or not, and their very existence was considered unnatural. But if we really examine the facts, the artisans and merchants were not indolent at all. Occasionally there may have been rich and idle ones among the merchant class, but since they lived only on their own capital, they were no different from rich farmers who were able to live well because they owned a great number of fields. Although poorer merchants paid no direct public taxes, the difficulties involved in their livelihood were no less than those of the peasants.

From ancient times, artisans and merchants in Japan have not been taxed. Because there were no taxes, the number of people engaged in such pursuits naturally increased. Nevertheless, the extent of this increase reached a limit when agricultural profit equaled commercial profit. For example, in tilling a field under a system whereby 40 per cent went to the lord and 60 per cent to the peasant, in an average year a peasant could get by and provide for his family, but not luxuriously. It might seem that the artisans and merchants who lived in the cities and were not taxed had an advantage over the peasants, but many of them had a hard time fighting starvation and the sufferings of cold. What was the reason for this? It was competition among themselves. After all, there was a limit to the amount of work available for merchants and artisans in Japan. There would have been a stable situation if the job openings were more varied, but jobs were not increased. Instead, the number of workers was increased, so that a job which ought to have employed ten people employed twenty or thirty, and wages which should have been paid out to one hundred people were paid out to two or three hundred. Business which should have had 30 per cent profits had only 10 per cent. Wages which ought to have been 2,000 *mon* dropped to 500 *mon*. Thus the crush of competition lessened the possibilities of profit for the artisan and merchant classes. This created benefits of which even the peasants could avail themselves. Therefore, although merchants and artisans were untaxed, in actuality they were no different from the peasants who were taxed. When it did happen that artisans and merchants gained large profits, the reason was that the government, following the advice of experts, set up all manners of obstructions to discourage peasants from turning to commercial ventures. Since the number of people engaged in commercial ventures was thus limited, the authorities gave them, in effect, the advantages of a monopoly. From this it is clear that the peasants and the merchants shared the same advantages and disadvantages, and both performed useful functions within the feudal system. Although they differed in name, in so far as the former were taxed and the latter were not, neither one was really indolent. Both groups belonged to the class of citizens who accumulated national wealth.

Thus, whereas in social terms the division was between the rulers and the ruled, in economic terms, which is our concern here, it was a division between the productive and the non-productive. Those who were ruled, the farmers, artisans and merchants, produced the national wealth, while the samurai and above, the ruling class, produced nothing. Put another way, one was the group that accumulated the wealth, the other the group that spent it. The relationship between these two classes was such that their respective labors and profits were not equal, of course. But since people were forced to compete with one another for business because population exceeded the proportion of capital, the wealthier were able to be idle while the poor had to work.

This is true not only in Japan; it is a general imbalance found throughout the world. Since there is nothing that can be done about it, it is not my intention to find fault with it. Furthermore, although we call the ruling class of samurai and above the non-productive, spending class, their attention to civil and military affairs through the administration of government, and their maintenance of order, contributed to the solidity of the economic structure, and so we cannot say that the annual government upkeep was an unprofitable waste of money.

However, in the Japanese economy, what is particularly

undesirable—and also different from other civilized countries—is that we do not accord the accumulation and the expenditure of national wealth, each of which is equal in value, the equal esteem they deserve. According to the common law of Japan from ancient times, the people have always accumulated wealth. If, for example, we take the tax law whereby 40 per cent went to the lord and 60 per cent to the peasant, the peasant used the 60 per cent barely to support his family. Once the other 40 per cent left his hands, he had no idea where it went. He did not know to what use it was applied, or whether it was sufficient or insufficient. In general, then, he knew how to accumulate but not how to spend. The government, on the other hand, once it received this tax, forgot whence it came and gave no thought to the labor involved in producing it. It looked on it as something coming from Heaven. It spent and dispersed it as it pleased. In other words, it knew how to spend but not how to accumulate. The first rule of economics is that accumulation and expenditure are equal and should be dealt with in an equal way. But what actually is happening here is that two things which should be equal are being dealt with by two different frames of mind. To give a parallel, it is like letting one person write one half of a Chinese character and another person write the other half. No matter how good each person's writing ability, this will not result in good calligraphy.

Since the minds of ruler and ruled are different, their respective concepts of profit are different. There is no mutual understanding between them, and they are suspicious of each other's conduct. Is it any wonder that economic problems arise? Money that ought to be spent is not, and money that ought not to be spent, is. There is no reasonable proportion maintained. During a period of great warfare, Ashikaga Yoshimasa built the Ginkakuji; he indulged in luxuries to the extent of decorating the roof of his residence, so-called "Flower Palace," with 600,000 *bin* worth of gems, gold, and silver and spending as much as 20,000 *sen* on the papered sliding doors for one doorway of the Takakura Palace.[†] To pay for this he levied excessive taxes on land and buildings [*tansen* and *munabechi*], until the government had no money because everyone was poor. In the midst of a civil war Taikō Hideyoshi built Osaka Castle, and next he invaded Korea. He made unnecessary expenditures on armaments and indulged in sumptuous banquets. The reason he was able to accumulate such a huge surplus was that the lower classes of society were destitute while the ruling class was living in luxury.

Now the Hōjō lords Yasutoki, Tokiyori, and Sadatoki are considered to have been wise because they themselves followed a frugal policy. Later, in the early Edo period, there were a number of sage rulers and wise ministers whose government was above criticism. While this was completely different from the period of Yoshimasa's rule, one does not hear of anyone who promoted wealth among the populace or planned economic matters. The most outstanding legacies from the times of the Hōjō and Tokugawa are the Five Temples in Kamakura, the Edo and Nagoya castles, the Nikkō Tōshōgū, and the Kan'eiji and the Zōjōji temples in Edo. These are all magnificent works, but what is strange is that in Japan at that time people should have been able to afford such splendid works. I do not see how these works were compatible with the nation's economy. Throughout the land today there are, besides castles, numerous remains of temples and shrines, with huge statues of Buddha and great bells and massive temple buildings, but this does not prove that Buddhism and Shinto flourished. It is only proof that despotic rulers were flourishing. Only occasionally was some worthwhile public enterprise like waterworks undertaken, and then it did not originate among the general populace. It was only done at the whim of the ruler and his ministers, who sensed popular unrest and thought this would be the convenient solution.

Of course, in ancient times, when the people were ignorant, it was inevitable that the government had to do everything, and nobody thought this strange. Although we ought not be unduly critical of such actions from our present vantage point, neither wise rulers nor tyrants seem to have been able to avoid the mistake of treating accumulation and expenditure as two different things, thus causing severe economic problems. Therefore those in later generations who give this any

† [Yoshimasa was shogun at the outbreak of the Ōnin War (1467–77), which lead to the destruction of much of Kyoto. He was a great patron of the arts, particularly those associated with Zen Buddhism. The Ginkakuji, now a Zen temple, was built as his mountain retreat on the ruins of a temple destroyed in the war. He also spent money on rebuilding the official shogunal residence in Kyoto and the Takakura Palace, where his mother lived.]

thought at all should not make the same mistakes.

Although sage rulers and wise ministers should allot funds only for useful things, since what is considered useful is what the rulers and ministers decide is so, differences in men's inclinations will lead some to consider military things useful, others to consider civil things useful, some to consider really useful things useful, others to consider completely useless things useful. In the time of Ashikaga Yoshimasa laws were passed canceling all debts, and similar practices were followed during the Tokugawa period. This was called *tokusei*, "virtuous" or "beneficent" government, a benefit from the rulers. In both instances, because the country's accumulators had nothing at all to say about the spenders' handling of things, and the spenders were not regulating acquisitions, only outlays, there were no restrictions on either accumulation or spending. As long as the rulers looked out for the subsistence needs of the common people on the basis of previous levels, it was considered the highest degree of benevolent government. Year after year they continued the same type of policies, accumulating here and spending there—like two people writing one half each of the same Chinese character. This situation continued throughout the Tokugawa period. Thus a comparison of the economic situation then and now shows that Japan's progress has been strikingly slow.

For example, the 250 years of Tokugawa rule during which there was no warfare is unmatched in world history. Since the Japanese people had the opportunity to live in this incomparably peaceful society, as stupid as they were and as undeveloped as technology was, and even if accumulation was a slow process, still, during the space of 250 years there should have been a great deal of progress in the country's economy. Why was this not the case? The sole cause is not a lack of virtue on the part of the shogun and the various daimyos. Even supposing this underdevelopment were due to a lack of virtue and talent in these rulers, this lack was not the fault of any individuals. No one in those positions could help but lack virtue and talent; this was the way things were, and these rulers were swept along by their circumstances. Thus from the standpoint of economics the sage rulers and wise ministers were amazingly incompetent, and the peace in the land was amazingly profitless.

It has been said that while war is dreadful and evil, its effect on a nation's economy is like a clean sword cut: it may be a temporary shock, but as long as the wound is not in a vital part of the body it will heal quite quickly. What must be especially feared in regard to economics is not a sword wound but something like tuberculosis, in which health deteriorates month by month, day by day. According to this idea, then, while the Japanese economy has not shown a gradual deterioration, the reason why it has always been the same—or without ever becoming truly active in the past few hundred years—is that, because of the imbalance of power, the accumulators and spenders of the national wealth have been cleanly divided, with no communication with each other. The failure to advance economically during the 250 years of Tokugawa rule was a case of "economic tuberculosis."*

The second principle of economics is that the accumulation and expenditure of wealth require intelligence and habits equivalent to the task. Now, the prime requisite of finance is to strike a balance between lively initiative and thrifty industriousness: only by proper employment of these two factors, mutually checking and balancing each other, can you achieve a healthy growth in accumulation and expenditure. If you put all the emphasis on one of the two, say concentrating on thrift at the expense of initiative, then you wind up with miserliness. On the other hand, to forget about thrift to give free rein to initiative is to invite waste. Both ways go against the basic principles of finance.

As I said before, everyone in the nation can be divided into two distinct classes: the accumulators and the spenders. When the distinction between the two is clear-cut, the behavior of each class will be one-sided. One class will be the epitome of thrift and, losing all daring whatsoever, will fall victim to miserliness. The other will be bold and daring but will thus lose all notion of thrift and fall victim to

---

* Since long ago, scholars have claimed that taxation should have been divided between the central and local commissioners. The central commissioners' tendency toward heavy taxation could have been balanced out by the local commissioners in close contact with the people. Of course, dividing the task between two different kinds of officials within the same government would not have alleviated the situation. However, the existence of this debate shows that the people in ancient times were to some extent aware of the dangers of placing wealth entirely in the hands of the spenders.

extravagance. While we Japanese have not been widely schooled in these principles we are not innately stupid, so there is no reason why we should be particularly inept at finance. We are only inept because of the divisions in our social relations, which have resulted in habits in each group that produce divided behavior. Such behavior is not evil by nature. It is just that, suitably balanced, this division should give rise to the daring and thrift so necessary in financial matters, but instead it has resulted in waste and miserliness. The reason lies, as I said, not in any innate evil, but in a lack of balance. For example, if you mix oxygen with nitrogen, you have air, an indispensable compound for living things. But separate these two elements and they are no longer beneficial; on the contrary, they can be harmful to life.

A look at finance in Japan from ancient times shows that all those who spent money to accomplish some purpose have belonged to the ruling class—samurai and above. It was those in the government who built the buildings, planned all the civil and military developments, read all the books, discussed war, practiced the arts, and enjoyed refined pursuits. They decided everything, both useful and useless. All those who had any leisure time to devote to matters beyond their own immediate livelihood, people who could afford to concern themselves with the higher things in life, were, of course, only those of the samurai and above. These people were by nature vigorous and clever and possessed of a bold spirit. In truth, they formed the basis of Japanese civilization. And yet in the one area of finance they simply followed the ideas of the past. They knew how to spend but not how to accumulate, how to use what they had but not how to produce what they lacked. The inevitable result was waste. Not only that. Over time such precedents developed into a custom whereby the rulers were not supposed to discuss economic matters. It was not considered shameful to be ignorant about finance. Rather, it was shameful if one knew something about it. This resulted in a situation where the highest stratum of the ruling class was the least adept in financial matters. I might call it an extreme illogicality.

On the other hand, the farmers and merchants—the ruled—were totally separated from the rulers, forming an entirely different world. Their attitudes and customs differed. They were controlled by others, despised by others. How they were named and addressed was different, their seats were placed apart from those of others, their clothing was regulated, their legal status was unequal, and even their very lives were at the mercy of others. For it stated in Tokugawa law that, "If an *ashigaru* is insulted by, or meets with any insolent behavior from, a lowly townsman or peasant and is forced to cut him down, if upon examination it is found the *ashigaru* was in the right, his action shall be upheld."[†] Because of this law, peasants and townsmen were always in the presence of tens of millions of enemies, so to speak, and their very safety was hardly guaranteed. If they could not be certain of preserving their lives, how could they be free to contemplate other things? They had no spare time at all to devote to glory and honor or to cultivate literary and other cultural sensibilities. The only thing they did was follow orders from above and supply the expenses required by the government: both mind and body were completely fettered.

And yet the workings of the human mind are versatile and cannot be completely checked. At some point there will be an opening through which it will seek room to operate. Thus, while any advancement in their status was certainly circumscribed, there was little to prevent peasants and townsmen from developing their mental powers in the accumulation of private wealth and business ventures. And so there were those resourceful ones who, concentrating on amassing wealth, practiced thrifty industriousness in the face of countless hardships and ended up with a fortune.

Of course, these were people who accumulated wealth for its own sake rather than as a means to attain some other goal. The accumulation of wealth was the sole goal of their whole lives. Thus for them there was nothing in the world of man as important as wealth. There was nothing which could replace it. Things which were concerned with the elevation of mankind, such as learning, they had no time for. On the contrary they avoided such things, as being luxuries. When they saw how the ruling class conducted itself, they smiled in secret complacency at its extravagance. While there were grounds for their behavior in the

† [This is a quotation from Article 71 of the penal code section of *Kujikata osadamegaki*, a two-volume book of Tokugawa law dated 1742.]

situation they were in, the pettiness of their attitude and their lack of any initiative were certainly despicable. If we examine the origins and history of wealthy households in Japan, this is clearly borne out. The founders of rich merchant or farming families have not been learned gentlemen; ninety-nine out of a hundred have been unlettered and unskilled clods unashamed of the shameful and tolerant of the intolerable. They were people who accumulated wealth merely by miserliness.

Those who brought their houses to ruin, on the other hand, were the unresourceful who were lax in accumulating wealth or who squandered their money to satisfy their sensual appetites. Such people cannot be compared with those of the ruling class who disregarded production and devoted themselves completely to pursuing pleasure, with no concern about poverty. Though the ruination of a household is the same whether due to purposeful squandering of money on sensual pleasures or to carelessness, the upper class had the requisite leisure time to cultivate virtue and knowledge while the lower class seemed solely concerned with money and sensual pleasures. There is a great difference between these two kinds of behavior. In terms of what I discussed previously, the thrifty industriousness of the ruled turned into greed or miserliness while the lively initiative of the rulers changed into wasteful squandering. Neither was suitable for sound finance, and that is why we are in the situation we are in today.

Now, while it is said that Japan is a poor country, we are not deficient in natural resources. Actually, in the agricultural sphere there are many things we can boast of over other countries in the world. Nor are we a poor country by nature. Again, while taxation may be severe, we do not throw the collected taxes into the sea, but use them within the country; they are a portion of the country's finances. Why, then, is Japan relatively poor in today's world? It is not that we are poor in terms of wealth; we are poor in knowing how to deal with that wealth. Yet, it is not that we lack such knowledge, but that it is split in two, with the upper and lower classes each holding one part. Broadly speaking, from the beginning of history right up to the present, Japan's wealth has yet to be paired with the knowledge appropriate to it. Although it is of pressing economic necessity that we fuse these two parts of our knowledge into one for application to practical situations, the habits built up over thousands of years make such a fusion impossible to achieve overnight. It seems that we are now beginning to move in that direction, but still most people in both the upper and the lower classes learn the weak points of the other side without picking up its strong points. This, however, is something unavoidable, and no individual is to blame. Since the vast stream of history has been flowing down from the distant past, tumbling millions of humans in its path and sweeping them along in one direction, it is no wonder that we are unable to check its flow all at once.

Chapter TEN

A DISCUSSION OF OUR NATIONAL
INDEPENDENCE

THE PRECEDING two chapters dealt with the origins of Western and Japanese civilization; the overall evidence conclusively shows that the civilization of Japan is less advanced than that of the West. When some countries are more advanced than others it is natural for the advanced to control the less advanced and the less advanced to be controlled by the advanced. Although during the period of seclusion we Japanese did not even know that Western countries existed, now we know that they exist, we know what their civilization is like, we have compared theirs and ours and know which is more backward, that ours is behind theirs, and that a backward civilization is controlled by an advanced civilization. Armed with this knowledge, our prime concern cannot help but be our country's independence.

Civilization is a vast thing, and each and every endeavor of the human spirit lies within its domain. Therefore, the question of a country's independence from foreign countries is no more than one small part in a complete theory of civilization. However, as stated in the second chapter of this work, since there are levels of progress in civilization, there must be a proper means of proceeding on each level. The fact that our people are at present deeply alarmed about our country's independence is a sign that the level of civilization we have reached now is one of concern for independence; our spiritual energies being confined as it were to this one area, we have no time for the consideration of other matters. Hence, when in this last chapter of my theory of civilization I treat the question of national independence, I am only following in the direction our people have taken and presenting a discussion of the level the people have actually reached. As far as any detailed examination of civilization's finer points is concerned, that is a task I leave to a future generation of scholars.

Back in the feudal era, the primary relationships controlling society were between lord and retainers, master and servant. It was taken for granted that the samurai of the shogunate and the *han* would devote themselves totally to the service of their current lord; in addition, though, they had to keep in mind distant ancestral origins and devote themselves wholeheartedly to the interests of their lord's house. They believed that those fed by someone should die for him; they considered their very lives as belonging to their lord and never dreamed of acting on their own. The lord was called the father and mother of his domain and loved his retainers as children. Relationships between superior and inferior were strictly governed by an ethics of gratitude and duty, the beauty of which was indeed admirable. And even though a person may not have really been a loyal retainer, because of the fact that loyalty was held in high esteem in the popular mind, a person was forced to maintain a high code of conduct. When a samurai, for instance, admonished his children, he invariably appealed to his warrior status or the honor of his house, saying that base behavior was totally unbecoming a samurai, or that it would not be in keeping with the honor of the ancestors' house, or that it would be an inexcusable betrayal of his lord. The samurai's status, the honor of his house, and his lord were the great Way according to which the samurai lived and the basic bonds binding his conduct throughout life. In Western terminology, they were **moral ties.**†

This ethic was not observed only between the samurai and their regional lords; it permeated the entire nation—townsmen and farmers, even the suppressed class of *eta* and *hinin* observed it.‡ It prevailed

---

† [It is not clear exactly where Fukuzawa obtained this English phrase, but the concept of the tie is used by Guizot in *The History of Civilization* (volume III) to mean the interdependence of different parts of a society.]

wherever social intercourse existed, from the greatest to the lowest. With townsmen and farmers, for instance, there was an obligation between the main house and its branches, and *eta* and *hinin* had their distinction between the boss and the underlings. Duty was as exacting for them as it was in the lord-vassal relationship.

Whether this ethic was called loyalty between lord and retainers, or the tradition of one's ancestors, or moral obligation between superiors and inferiors, or the distinction between main trunk and branches, or whatever, it has ruled human society from the dawn of Japanese history to the present day. The achievements of Japan's present civilization are due to the strength of these ethical customs.

As a result of our recent ties with foreigners we have begun to contrast our civilization with theirs. Our inferiority to them on the external technological level is obvious, but our mentality also differs from theirs. Westerners are intellectually vital, are personally well-disciplined, and have patterned and orderly social relations. In our present state, from the economy of the nation down to the activities of single households or individuals, we are no match for them. On the whole, it has been only recently that we have realized Western countries are civilized while we as yet are not, and there is no one who in his heart does not admit this fact.

Perhaps this is why those intellectuals in the world attributed the prime cause of our being uncivilized to the fact that our ancient customs are unsuitable, and then embarked on wholesale reforms, by sweeping them away. Having begun with the abolition of the *han* and the establishment of the prefectures, they should have tried to do away with all the old abuses. Since daimyos now become peers, samurai become landed gentry, people can express their opinions to superiors, and men can get high-ranking positions on the basis of talent, it is also time for former ministers with salaries of 5,000 *koku* to become rank-and-file soldiers; for low-salaried *ashigaru* to become prefectural governors; for a wealthy merchant whose house goes back many generations to become

‡ [The *hinin* (literally "non-human") formed another outcast group. Like the *eta*, it was abolished in the Meiji period.]

bankrupt; for penniless gamblers to become government-backed merchants; for Buddhist temples to become Shinto shrines, and Buddhist monks to become Shinto priests.[†] It is time to make it possible for wealth, honor, and happiness to be entirely the fruit of a man's own efforts. The ideas of gratitude, loyalty, lineage, moral obligation, and class distinction which have permeated to the depths of our people's hearts from the dawn of Japanese history are finally disappearing and greater importance is now being attached to individual effort. If forced, I will have to admit that in our present society public sentiment has begun to awaken and civilization is making rapid strides forward.

And yet in this time of individual effort and rapid strides forward, Japanese intellectuals might wonder if we have attained our desired objective, whether we should consider these rapid strides in civilization as true progress and need not seek further. The answer is, No. We must not be content with the present level of civilization. For, if we look into the things that are relevant to our people's moral conduct, it looks as if they merely lifted from their shoulders the heavy burden of ancestral tradition and before shouldering the load that would replace it they were taking a little breather. The situation is strikingly clear. Since the abolition of the *han* there are no more lord-vassal obligations between a daimyo and his samurai. Any veiled attempt to exact such obligations, no matter how indirectly, is now inexcusable. When former *ashigaru* become squadron chiefs and direct their former chiefs, there can be no defying their orders. Although the laws appear stern in distinguishing superior and inferior status, former chiefs need only to pay money and they can avoid military conscription. Therefore, former *ashigaru* can be proud of becoming squadron heads, and their former chiefs can be equally proud of being men of leisure. If gamblers can swagger about as government-backed merchants, then bankrupt townsmen can find fault

---

† [There is certainly truth in the last two of these claims since in 1868 the new Meiji government issued orders for the separation of Buddhism and Shinto, which had up till then been closely linked, not only in terms of religious theory, but to the extent of sharing rituals and sacred space. Religious buildings and specialists had to become either Buddhist or Shinto. Since supporters of this move tended to be pro-Shinto and anti-Buddhist, the practical consequences of this separation were initially in favor of Shinto.]

with the times rather than with themselves and get through life comfortably. If Shinto priests can take this opportunity to live as they wish, then Buddhist monks also can openly lead married lives[†] and live as they wish. Generally speaking, the present age is one in which high and low, noble and base-born, are free to do as they please, and in which nothing (with the sole exception of poverty) exists to cause people suffering. Death on the battlefield and acts of revenge have lost their meaning,[‡] enlistment is dangerous, and committing *seppuku* painful. The goal of both scholar and civil servant is money alone. It is said that as long as one has money he need not work hard, and that money knows no enemy on the face of the earth; it is money which sets the prices on human conduct. When this state of affairs is compared to the restrictive era of old, one cannot help but call it an age of carefree living. This is why I say that people today are like men who have lowered a heavy burden and are taking a breather.

Still, the time for relaxing is when there is no work to be done. Finishing a job, getting a task out of the way, and then resting is all well and good, but in our present national situation we certainly are not without anything to do. Indeed these times present us with a task more difficult than in years past. The intellectuals among us are not unaware of this. They realize that this is not a time to sit back and relax, and are striving to guide the public mind forward. Scholars are founding schools and teaching, translators are translating original documents and publishing them. And yet, even though both government and people earnestly devote themselves to book learning and the arts, there is still no sign of noteworthy improvement in people's conduct. Although people do not seem to begrudge the time they spend cultivating book learning and the arts, when it comes to being alive to the importance of the times and having a willingness to sacrifice both property and life itself, people seem to be forgetful or, at least, are indifferent. No doubt about it: ours is an age of ease.

---

† [Buddhist priests were forbidden to marry during the Tokugawa period but this ban had been lifted by the Meiji government.]

‡ [It should be noted that Fukuzawa himself attacked the practice of taking revenge in *An Encouragement of Learning*.]

Certain people are concerned about the situation. They find much of present-day behavior frivolous, and attribute such conduct to disregard of tradition. They propose a return to the past through revival of the concept of "true relations of sovereign and subject." Advocating the cultivation of the doctrines of the past and seeking proof for their theory of national polity in Japan's ancient mythology, they think thereby to bolster men's hearts. This is known as Imperial Way Learning. The approach is not completely unjustified. It only stands to reason that, in a country with a sovereign, he should be revered and should hold the power of administration; since it is absolutely vital from the standpoint of government, no one can reject the idea of reverence for the emperor. However, the Imperial Way Learning scholars go a step further. Rather than deriving their reverence for the ruler from reasons of political desirability, they find it in people's natural nostalgia for the past. Worst of all, they do not abhor assigning the ruler an empty status, preferring sham to truth.

Now, the direction of men's feelings cannot easily be changed by a simple act. Therefore, in order to establish the teaching of reverence for the emperor by using people's natural sentiments today, the first thing to be done is to change men's sentiments and to do this by making them forget the old and pursue the new. For several centuries our people have had no personal experience of the emperor—the imperial institution was nothing more than a legend. It has been claimed that through the Restoration the government reverted in one stroke to its centuries-old form. However, there never was any really close bond of feeling between the Imperial Family and the people. Their relationship was only a political one. When it comes to close bonds of feeling, today's people have been on more intimate terms with their feudal lords than with the Imperial Family, and this has been true since the Kamakura period on. Loyalty to a single supreme sovereign under Heaven has been more of an abstract concept than a practical reality: I trust there are places in the world where such a concept of loyalty is not practiced.

According to present trends, it would seem the people are forgetting the past and their regard for their feudal lords is fading too. And yet it will be extremely difficult to make them loyal and devoted children of the Imperial Family, given our present level of civilization and people's present moods; in fact, it will be almost impossible to do this successfully. One theory has it that the Restoration was based on the people's attachment to the past, and that they yearned for the Imperial Family because they abhorred the government that was won by force of arms, but this interpretation is founded on ignorance. If, as this theory would have it, people are truly attached to the past, then why are they not attached to the shogunate government that ruled Japan for so many centuries? The appeal made by present-day ex-samurai and everyone else to ancestral tradition and so forth derives for the most part from the values of society from the Kamakura period on. The shogunate, too, can be said to have an old, extensive tradition. On the other hand, if public sentiment is supposed to forget the old and be attached to the new, since rule by imperial government predates shogunal rule and is much more ancient, it surely follows that the people should forget the older tradition rather than the more recent one.

Again, there is a theory that public sentiment toward the Imperial Family is not based on newness or oldness but is an effect of the concept of "true relations of sovereign and subject." Now, my answer to this view is that such "true relations" should be an immutable truth for all people of all ages. However, for nearly 700 years, from the Kamakura period on, the people had no personal experience of the Imperial Family. According to this theory, then, the people had gone astray for 700 long years; they endured a dark, barbaric age when even the concept of "true relations" had vanished from the land. Now, while it is true that one cannot judge the stability of human affairs just from the events of one year, or even several years, how could human beings put up with it for seven full centuries, knowing full well that they were straying from the right path! The historical facts bear this out, for in fact those seven centuries were not by any means filled only with turmoil and unrest. Trace the sources of present-day Japanese civilization, and you will find seventy to eighty percent of it is a legacy from this period.

In view of the above, then, the cause of the restoration of imperial rule was neither the people's dislike of the shogunate and attachment to the Imperial Family, nor their predilection for antiquity, nor again their suddenly recalling the idea of "true relations of sovereign and subject" that they had forgotten for hundreds of years. It stemmed entirely from people's desire to reform the shogunate government of their time. Now that the Restoration has been accomplished and political jurisdiction returned to the Imperial Family, as Japanese citizens we should give it proper respect, yet the relationship between the people and the Imperial Family is no more than a political one. Close ties between them cannot be created overnight. Any attempt to force such a relationship upon the people will have the reverse effect: the result would be subjects of the pseudo gentleman type, and it would lead people to an increasingly superficial brand of loyalism. That is why I say that the Imperial Way Learning scholars' appeal to national polity does not suffice as a means to bolster men's hearts and raise their conduct to a higher level.

Another sort of scholar laments the superficiality of present-day sentiment and, aware that even use of the national polity theory cannot avail to improve the situation, preaches a theory of spiritual renovation through Christianity so as to rectify men's errors, bestow spiritual peace and enlightenment, convert and thereby unify the masses, and establish a single great purpose at which mankind can aim. This view certainly does not stem from superficial sentiments. Let us consider the basis for this idea.

As these scholars see it, everybody in society today lives his own life and goes his own way. The masses not only have no uniform political opinion but even in religion they cannot choose between Shinto or Buddhism. There are also those who can be called completely irreligious, people who have no concern about even that most important of questions for the human race: the soul's final destiny. How, then, can they care about other human affairs? They know nothing of the Way of Heaven, or of the great ethical relationships between men. Our society is like a living hell in which there are no proper relationships between father and son, husband and wife, and so forth; those who lament the state of society must save the situation. Looking at it from another angle, they say that, once the hearts of men can be bolstered through religion, this will form a starting point on which the common people will be in agreement, which can then be broadened into the political sphere. Religion can in this way become the foundation for the independence of the nation as well.

Such is the general gist of this approach, and it cannot be dismissed as a silly theory. It does aim at educating the people, rectifying their errors, making them virtuous. Even if it does not lead to a perfect realization of the Way of Heaven, it can be the most effective means to highlight the relationships of father and son, husband and wife, and to encourage filial piety and marital fidelity. It does put a high priority on the education of children and repudiates licentious and immoral behavior. These things are of the highest value in regard to civilization, and so the basic idea cannot be faulted. However, when it comes to discussing the merits and demerits of things in our present society I find I cannot completely agree with this theory. For I have a slight difference of opinion regarding these scholars' view that the Christian religion should be spread about, extended to the political sphere, and be set up as the foundation for the nation's independence.

In essence the Christian religion takes eternity as its end, an eternity of everlasting bliss and comfort or of everlasting suffering and affliction. It fears punishment in the next world more than in this, considers future judgment more important than judgment in the present. In other words, it presupposes in its views a distinction between this world and the world to come. Christianity's doctrines are always vast and its general tenor completely different from those of other schools of thought. In so far as impartial and universal brotherhood are concerned, if the world is one family and all men on the face of the earth are like brothers, then love should be meted out equally to all. If the entire earth is as one and the same family, why is this family divided by national boundaries? Moreover, to divide the globe into sections, setting up national boundaries here and there, having the people form groups within those boundaries and call themselves nations, to set up governments whose purpose is to work for the benefits of only those groups, and worst of all, to take up weapons and murder one's brothers within other boundaries, to take their land from them, and to contend with them for business profit—this cannot by any means be the aim of religion. In view of these abuses it seems that we should set aside for a while consideration of eternal punishment in the afterlife and say that punishment in the present life is still inadequate. And the offenders are the Christians.

Be that as it may, there is no region in the world today that is not set up as a nation, and wherever there are nations there are also governments. When governments protect the people and the people work hard at commerce, when governments do the fighting and the people do the profit-making, then such countries are called *fukoku kyōhei* [rich country, strong army]. Why is it that these countries' citizens take pride in themselves, and that other countries' citizens envy them and strive so mightily to emulate their wealth and military power? Such things may run counter to the aims of religion, but power and wealth are essential in today's world. The people of one nation, in their private relationships, may be able to befriend people of other countries far away and treat them as old friends, but when it comes to relations between one country and another only two things count: in times of peace, exchange goods and compete with one another for profit; in times of war, take up arms and kill each other. To put it another way, the present world is a world of commerce and warfare. Of course, there are many types of war too—there are even wars for the sake of ending wars. Trade, too, being a reciprocal exchange based upon the principle of supplying each other's needs, was a most fair occupation originally. Thus neither can be called bad by nature. However, a closer look at the conditions of war and trade in all countries in the world shows that neither of them could ever be considered to be based on the lofty religious teaching of "love thine enemy."

If we judge the situation in the light of religion, therefore, trade and war may seem despicable, as being extremely brutal, but if we just take things as they are in reality, we shall see that trade and war are not that bad at all. For while trade is competitive, it is not engaged in solely on the basis of brute force but is an occupation that certainly requires intelligence. One must give credit for this to people today. Furthermore, if a nation attempts to trade with others, it must labor diligently to improve itself. Hence commercial prosperity can even be called a sign of national prosperity, for it makes people intellectually diligent within the nation, and their success in book learning and arts sheds a luster that reaches out to other nations. This is also true of war. If simply the art of killing people, it would be a hateful thing. However, if there were a nation that wanted suddenly to unleash its troops without a cause, even in the present imperfect state of civilization there are the express provisions of treaties, diplomatic negotiations, international law, and the criticism of scholars, so that such a nation could not easily get away with such lawless conduct. Moreover, alongside wars fought for the sake of profit are those fought for the honor of a nation and even those undertaken for the sake of justice. Therefore, while killing people and competing for profit are counter to religion's aims and are the enemy of religion, still it must be conceded that they are unavoidable in the present state of civilization. War is the art of extending the rights of independent governments, and trade is a sign that one country radiates its light to others.

Men who attempt to extend the rights of their own nation, to enrich the people of their own nation, to educate them morally and intellectually, and to make the glory of their country shine forth, are called patriots, and their spirit, patriotism. In their eyes there is a clear distinction between their own and other countries. They do not necessarily intend harm to other countries, but they do put their own country's interests first, and they aspire after its independence. Therefore, patriotism means trying to benefit one's country rather than oneself. It is, in other words, the biased, partisan spirit that divides the globe into smaller sections and establishes within each section political factions, then calculates what benefits these political factions. Therefore, it must be conceded that, though patriotism and partisanship differ in name, they are the same in their effects. Accordingly, it is clear the ethic of impartial and universal brotherhood is not compatible with the ethic of patriotism and establishment of national independence. Hence the theory that we can establish the basis of national independence by propagating a religion and extending it to the political realm should be branded a mistake. Religion pertains only to private virtue, and its goals differ from those of the spirit of national independence. Therefore, even if one were able to bolster people's hearts by means of religious teachings, as far as protecting the country and the people is concerned, religion cannot in actual fact be so very efficacious. Generally speaking, a comparison of present conditions in various countries in the world with the aims of religion would show religion to be too broad, too good and beautiful, too lofty, too impartial, while conditions in those countries would be seen as too narrow, bare, superficial, and partisan for the two to be reconciled.

Another sort of scholar, the specialist in Chinese Learning, takes a somewhat broader view. He does not, like the Imperial Way Learning scholar, merely rely on sentiments of nostalgia for the past. Yet, in the final analysis, his is the school of thought which would control the lower classes with the old Confucian ideas of ritual, music, and chastisement, and would attempt to bolster people's hearts by a combination of paternalism and law. It therefore cannot at all be made to suit present social conditions. If this theory were to be followed, the people would have personal knowledge only of the government but not of the people, of officialdom but not of personal endeavor—this would result in an ever-worsening situation, with elevation of general conduct eventually rendered impossible. Because both the seventh and the ninth chapters have already treated this matter, I shall not elaborate further here.

As I have pointed out, our nation is facing a critical period at the present time, but the people do not realize it. They seem to be happily relaxed after having, as it were, thrown off the yoke of the past. Hence it is that high-minded gentlemen grieve deeply, Imperial Way Learning scholars advocate theories of national polity, Western Learning scholars propose the introduction of Christianity, and Chinese Learning scholars espouse the Way of Yao and Shun. They all are trying, each in his own way, to bolster and unite people's hearts and thereby preserve Japan's independence. However, despite their efforts they have as yet not been a bit successful, nor are they likely to be successful in the future. How could we but breathe a deep sigh of grief for that!

However, if it is not amiss to do so at this point, I too feel impelled to air my own simple views. First of all, in discussing something we must first clarify its name and nature before ways to deal with it can be devised. For example, in order to prevent fires, first the nature of fire must be known, then the fact that it can be extinguished by water; after this it will be possible to devise ways of fire prevention. Men say that our country is in trouble, but exactly what trouble are they talking about? It is not that the laws are not being carried out, nor that taxes are not being collected, nor that the people have suddenly fallen into ignorance, nor that officials are stupid and dishonest. In these respects Japan is no different from the Japan of old, and so there appears to be no cause for further anxiety. In fact, when we compare Japan's conditions to what they used to be, we can even say our situation has greatly improved. If nevertheless some say that present-day Japan is in greater trouble and distress than in the past, then we must ask what, concretely, they are talking about, and what exactly we are supposed to be concerned about. It seems to me this "trouble" is not something that has come down to us from our ancestors but a sickness suddenly contracted in recent times, a sickness that is already affecting a vital part of Japanese life. Even if we tried to eliminate it we could not; if we tried to treat it we would lack sufficient medicines. Our old vital forces are unable to resist this sickness. The fact is that if Japan was the same as it has always been, we would have been completely calm. This proves that it is a new illness that is causing our anxiety. Even though the intellectuals among us must know that this is the illness that causes them such distress, what name do they give it? I name it "foreign relations."

Although these intellectuals do not label the illness clearly, their anxieties are identical to mine. Since their anxieties are caused by the problem of our present foreign relations, we have clarified the name. Next, its nature must be identified. Now, the only reason foreigners come to our country is trade. However, in the trade being carried on at present between Japan and other countries, the Western nations are manufacturer nations and Japan is a producer nation. Manufacturing adds human skill to natural resources; for example, cotton is spun into cloth, and iron is wrought into swords. To produce means to produce raw materials provided by the forces of nature. An example of this in Japan would be the production of raw-silk thread, or the mining of ore.

Therefore, for the time being let us call Western nations manufacturer nations and Japan a producer nation. Of course, it is difficult to draw a clear line of demarcation between manufactured goods and products; however, the former involves a significant contribution of human effort while the latter relies upon natural resources to a greater extent. Economically, there is surprisingly little relation between national wealth and the amount of natural resources produced. Actually, it depends solely on the quantity and quality of human effort involved. For example, India, which has fertile soil, is poor; Holland, which is deficient in natural resources, is rich. Therefore, in trade between manufacturer and producer nations, the former use the intangible, unlimited efforts of men, while the latter use the tangible, finite resources of nature; the exchange is one between human effort and natural resources. Upon further analysis, people of producer nations do not use their own minds and bodies, but hire the people of manufacturer nations overseas. They borrow these people's minds and bodies and set them to work, and give them the natural resources of their own country in exchange for their labor. To illustrate, a samurai with a stipend of 300 *koku* and ten dependents used to live in leisure, producing nothing; his daily food and drink were delivered by caterers, his summer and winter wardrobes were bought from dry-goods stores, each and every one of his household necessities were produced in town—in exchange for all this he annually paid out 300 *koku* of rice. Three hundred *koku* of rice were equivalent to natural resources, as it were, yet because he used them up year after year, he had no prospect of accumulating wealth. This is roughly what happens in our present state of trade with the West. We are clearly making a loss.

Again, the Western nations have grown rich through manufacture. Their populations increase year by year because of the ever new achievements of civilization; England, for instance, is outstanding in this regard. The people of the United States of America are descendants of the English, and the Caucasians in Australia emigrated there from England; there are English in both the East and West Indies—it is almost impossible to reckon the number of Englishmen. If, for argument's sake, the English who are now scattered throughout the world, as well as the descendants of those who migrated from England centuries ago, were repatriated to their motherland (present Great Britain and Ireland) and housed in the same space as the thirty million Englishmen already there, then it is certain that their present natural products would not suffice to provide them all with food and clothing, and the greater portion of level land would surely be used for residential sites. This shows that, when civilization progressively moves forward and human affairs go well, population increases. In fact, as far as producing offspring is concerned, there is no difference between men and mice. Mice cannot protect themselves, and so they sometimes die of cold or starvation or are caught by cats, as a result of which their number does not increase greatly. However, when human affairs are going well, when the afflictions of starvation, cold, wars, and epidemics are few, human fertility increases at the same rate as that of mice. Hence it is that in the old countries in Europe population problems are already becoming acute. According to their economic theorists, one stratagem for putting an end to such afflictions is to export goods manufactured domestically and to import foodstuffs and clothing from more naturally blessed nations. A second would be to have citizens emigrate overseas and colonize. The first stratagem has its limitations and would still not be enough to relieve the afflictions; the second would be costly and perhaps ineffectual anyway. Therefore, a third plan would be to make profits by lending capital abroad and putting the interest into domestic circulation. Now, so far as overseas emigration is concerned, places already developed are best; however, there already are nations and governments in such places, and, since they have their own fixed ways and customs, it is not easy to step in from an alien land, mingle with them, and hope to gain some benefit. The one and only practical hope is if the overseas countries are poor and still ignorant of how to stimulate industry, have a shortage of capital but an abundance of manpower; in this case a country could loan surplus domestic capital to these poor nations with a high rate of interest. In this way it could gain profit without labor. In other words, the method is one of penetrating a country by money rather than by men.

Because of customs and traditions it is difficult to send men into another country. However, gold looks the same all over, whatever the country of origin. Thus it is that men who make use of such gold are only concerned about interest fluctuations, unsuspectingly they put into circulation other countries' money, and before they know it are paying interest to people from those countries. And the gold owners chalk up another gain!

Japan has already acquired some foreign debts, and the merits and demerits of such a course ought to be weighed. In the first place, when a civilized nation and an uncivilized nation are compared, their standards of living are completely different. The cost of living rises in proportion to the degree of progress of civilization. Therefore, even aside from the problem of population increase, part of the expenses involved in everyday living must be sought elsewhere. Where? In the underdeveloped countries, where the poverty of the whole world tends to become concentrated. To borrow the capital of civilized countries and pay them interest makes the rich richer and the poor poorer. Therefore, while lending and borrowing capital are not connected merely with population growth, I have raised this question here in order to help scholars understand one obvious reason why Japan should compete with the Westerners for profit.

The above is a discussion of the advantages and disadvantages of relations with foreigners from the financial standpoint. Now let me point out the influence of these relations on the behavior of our people. Recently we Japanese have undergone a great transformation. The theory of equal rights has flooded the land and has been universally accepted. However, equal rights does not merely mean that all men within a single country are equal. It means equality between a man from one nation and a man from any other nation, as well as between one nation and another nation; it means that, regardless of power or wealth, everyone's rights are exactly equal. However, while there have been, ever since the foreigners came to our country and began trading, clear provisions in their treaty documents for equality between them and us, in actual practice things have been different. This problem has been described in an article by my colleague Mr. Obata. He argues that at the time we first let Commodore Perry bring his squadron of warships into our waters, the gist of the argument given to persuade us into trade relations was that all men on this earth are brothers, sharing the same sky above and the same earth beneath, that if we turn a man away and refuse to deal with him we are sinners against Heaven, and so, even if it means fighting, trade relations must be opened. How beautiful Perry's words, and how unseemly his deeds! His speech and conduct were diametrically opposed. To put it bluntly, he was saying, "If you don't do business with me, you'll be doing business with the undertaker."[†]

A little later in the same paper Mr. Obata points to the present state of affairs in Tokyo. Those who haughtily ride about on horses or in carriages, scattering everyone in their way, are almost all Westerners. When they get into an argument with anyone, be he a patrolman, a passerby, or a carriage-bearer, the Westerners behave insolently; they punch and kick at will, and the cowardly, weak common people lack the courage to pay them back in kind because, they say, "They are foreigners." Many simply swallow their anger and do not report such incidents. And even when there are grounds for litigation over some business dealing, to press charges one must go to one of the five ports, where one's case will be decided by their judges. Since in these circumstances it is impossible to obtain justice, people say to one another that, rather than press charges, it is better to swallow one's anger and be submissive. They act like a young bride before her old mother-in-law. Since the foreigners already are so imposing, when they come from their rich countries to our poor country and make heavy purchases, those who are eager for profit stumble over one another to fawn on them, hoping to fill their own pockets. Therefore wherever the foreigners go—hot springs, posting stations, tea houses, or sake shops—a kind of coarseness in sensibilities follows them about. Caring nothing about right or wrong, people care only about money, thereby just encouraging the already insolent foreigners to become even more impudent. It is disgusting just to look at this.

The above is the statement of Mr. Obata, and I feel the same way. Other areas of relations with foreigners include foreign settlements, inland travel, the employment of foreigners, and taxes on the use of the

† [Reference here is to Obata Tokujirō's article, "Naichi ryokō no bakugi (On travel by foreigners outside treaty limits)" published in the eighth issue (1875) of *Minkan zasshi*, a periodical issued by Keio-gijuku 1874–75.]

ports. In all these areas too, though lip service is paid to equality of rights between nations, in reality the idea of equality and equal rights is unrealized. Because we have already lost our equal rights with foreign countries, and yet nobody pays any attention to this, the conduct of our citizens cannot help but deteriorate day by day.

As I said before, many people in society have lately been advocating the theory of equal rights. There are also some who proclaim the necessity of realizing equal rights throughout the country even if it means abolishing the titles of the aristocracy and ex-samurai, and who maintain that this is the way we must refine the conduct of the people and make a clean sweep of all the demeaning old customs. Why is it that, despite the appealing vigor of this argument, there are so few who invoke the theory of equal rights in regard to dealings with foreign nations? Whether aristocrat and ex-samurai or commoner, all alike are citizens of the Japanese nation. And yet, because of the imbalance of rights and privileges between them, certain people find it harmful and strive for equality. Why is it, however, that no one laments the imbalance of rights between Japanese and foreigners, whose interests, feelings, languages, customs, and even physical characteristics are so different from ours? It is a shameful state of affairs. Although there are several different causes, of course, as I see it two stand out most clearly. The first is that those who advocate the theory of equal rights in society have as yet not attained a deeply personal experience of the doctrine. The second is that relations with foreigners are a recent phenomenon and we have yet to experience much trouble from them. I shall take up each of these points below.

Firstly, although there are not a few Japanese thinkers who advocate the theory of human rights in present society, those who do are for the most part people of learning: they are men of samurai background, men of the upper stratum of society, and men who have enjoyed special privileges—not the powerless with experience of oppression by others, but the powerful, the oppressors of others. So whenever they start talking about equal rights it is hard to listen to them without some impatience. If one does not eat of a certain dish, he cannot appreciate its true taste. If one has never been a prisoner himself, he cannot speak of the real sufferings of imprisonment. If the peasants and townsmen could be educated to a point where they could recount to us the anger they felt when they were oppressed by the powerful, and if we could hear details of what happened to them, then we might arrive at a true understanding of the meaning of equal rights. But when an ignorant and timid people experience something that should infuriate them, they either do not know why they should be infuriated or, if they do get infuriated, they do not know how to express their feelings, and it is very rarely that anyone else can learn exactly how they feel. There must be many men in society today who are angered and enraged by inequalities in rights, but there is no way of knowing exactly how many. I can only infer their secret feelings from my own. This is why I say the present theory of equal rights is entirely the product of men's speculations. If scholars want to search for the true meaning of equal rights and produce solid arguments, they cannot seek elsewhere but must turn in on themselves and reflect on and intellectualize their own relevant experiences from their youth down to the present day. No matter what class of people they were, whether aristocrat or former samurai, if they reflect upon their own lives, they will certainly find that at some time they experienced, personally, resentment against an imbalance of power. Therefore they must search within themselves, not in others, for true feelings of resentment and rage against inequality.

I will give an example based upon a personal recollection. I was born into a family of minor retainers in the service of a weak *fudai* daimyo[†] during the time of the Tokugawa shogunate. When within the *han* I met some illustrious high retainer or vassal, I was always treated with contempt; even as a child I could not help but feel resentment. However, unless one also were of the same status one could not understand how I felt. The high retainers and vassals would, even today, be unable to imagine how I felt. Again, when I traveled outside the *han* confines I would run into Court nobles, officials of the Bakufu, or retainers of the collateral houses of the Tokugawa house. At post towns they would monopolize the palanquins, at river crossings they would be ferried over first; since high and low were not permitted to stay at the

---

† [*fudai* daimyo: a hereditary retainer of the Tokugawa house.]

same time in the same lodging house, there were times when I was suddenly turned out in the middle of the night. The circumstances of those days seem ridiculous today, but it is still possible to imagine the rage I felt at the time those things happened. This rage is no more than my own personal experience as a retainer of a *fudai* daimyo. The Court nobles, officials of the Bakufu, and retainers of the three Tokugawa collateral houses who caused it were hardly aware of it; even if they had been completely conscious of it they probably would do no more than treat another's anger as a speculative problem. Be that as it may, I belonged to the samurai ranks, to the middle class and above of society, and though my status caused me to feel resentment against those above me, I in turn must certainly have caused the farmers and merchants below me to feel resentment. However, I was unaware of doing so. Things of this sort are extremely common in society; no one can know the actuality of a situation without personal experience of it himself.

Thus the current arguments for equal rights, while they may appear to be accurate, are not elaborate enough, for they are not arguments based on personal experience but speculative arguments set down for the benefit of other people. Hence when people discuss the harm of an imbalance of power, their arguments cannot avoid being superficial. Even when they discuss the matter as a purely domestic problem, their arguments are imperfect and do not touch upon all the problems. How much more inadequate are they when extended to cover the area of foreign relations and the struggle for power with foreigners! They still have not had the time to think about this. Perhaps some day these people will come into more frequent contact with Westerners and struggle for power with them. When they receive the kind of humiliations that our peasants and townspeople received at the hands of the samurai, or that a minor retainer received at the hands of Court nobles, Bakufu officials, or retainers of Tokugawa collateral houses, only then will they finally understand the irrelevance of their present doctrine of equal rights. They will then understand how evil, how hateful, how infuriating, and how painful an imbalance of power is.

And yet the Court nobles, Bakufu officials, and samurai vassals, even when they were discourteous and mean, were still Japanese. When any of them were less than clever, the commoners did not hesitate to placate them with outward forms of deference while secretly stealing their money. Though this was of course evil trickery, it was a means of allaying some of the discontent. But the cunning of the foreigners we are dealing with today is in a different category altogether. The foreigners are able to trick people with their cleverness and deceive people with their smooth talk. They are fearless in war and strong in battle; we can even call them a special kind of aristocratic class that combines cleverness, persuasiveness, courage, and strength. Since we live under their control and are subject to their restraints in so many ways, we Japanese are figuratively suffocating, as though the density of their abuses does not allow us a breath of air. When one imagines what might happen in the future, one's hair stands on end!

Let me take the example of India as a mirror which can reflect the situation of Japan. It is truly appalling how heartless and cruel the British are in their administration of the East Indian provinces. Allow me to cite one or two examples. As regards employment of men of talent in the Indian government, both Englishmen and natives have equal rights, and there are laws providing for examinations that test both ability and learning. However, the testing of native Indians is confined to those under eighteen years of age; the examination material is, of course, in English, and if one is not conversant with things in England he is unable to answer the questions. As a result, by the age of eighteen the native Indians have to finish both native subjects and in addition English subjects, then compete with Englishmen on the basis of English studies. If they are not better than the Englishmen, they cannot pass the examinations. If one completes his studies at the age of nineteen, because of the age limit he is disqualified, regardless of his talent, learning, or personal qualities, and is not permitted to take part in any local government affairs. The English are not content with these heartlessly severe laws; they even enact laws by which the examinations are always to be held in London, so that the native Indians are forced to make the long journey to London. Therefore, even if the natives had the scholastic aptitude to take and pass the examinations by the time they were eighteen, they are limited by the fact that without a great deal of money and the long trip overseas, they cannot enter government service. Regardless of their learning ability, if they are not from rich families they cannot become officials. It sometimes happened that a boy studies hard, spends a great deal of money for the trip to London, and takes the examinations, only to fail; in this way family fortunes are merely dissipated for nothing. Such a disadvantageous position defies comparison. The English tyranny is truly clever. In legal trials in the Indian government, the law excludes Indians from participating and limited the membership to Englishmen.* Once when an Englishman was brought to court for having shot an Indian dead in an outlying district in India, his defense was that he had caught sight of something moving and, thinking it a monkey, had shot at it, but it turned out to be a man. The story goes that the jury unanimously acquitted the defendant.

Recently several scholars in London have been busily engaged in forming a private association aimed at reforming conditions in India. My old friend Mr. Baba Tatsui—who was in London at the time—reports that the incident I related above was recorded in a letter sent by an Indian to the association in the spring of 1874.† Mr. Baba actually attended meetings of that association and personally observed what went on there. He said there were countless similar incidents.

Secondly, it has been less than twenty years since commercial relations were begun between Japan and the West and the five ports were opened, but imports and exports have been limited. The major focus of foreigner activity has been Yokohama, followed by Kobe; contacts at the other three ports have been relatively insignificant. According to the formal provisions in the treaties, settlements were created in each of the ports and boundaries were set up between the foreign and Japanese areas of residence. Foreigners were given

---

* Here I [Fukuzawa] am talking about **juries**. See the section on Britain in the third volume of *Seiyō jijō* [Conditions in the West].

† [Baba Tatsui (1850–88) was a disciple of Fukuzawa. He spent most of the period from 1870 to 1878 studying law in London, where he came into contact with students from India. The organization to which Fukuzawa refers is the National Indian Association which had been founded by Mary Carpenter in 1870. On his return to Japan, Baba became a prominent activist in the People's Rights Movement.]

permission to travel within a radius of twenty-five miles from each port, beyond which limits they could not pass without special authorization. In addition there were many laws made and distinctions set up between nationals and foreigners in regard to the buying and selling of real estate and the lending and borrowing of money, as a result of which even today, when dealings between both sides are inclined to be quite numerous, there has been very little contact between nationals and foreigners. While there are some Japanese who have suffered injustice as a result of these relations, they generally are people in the immediate neighborhoods of the open ports, so that the general populace rarely gets wind of these things. Moreover, since the opening of the ports, all relations of a political nature have been the doing solely of the government. The people know nothing of what goes on—such as the 100,000 British pounds paid out for the Namamugi incident,[†] the 3,000,000 dollars for the Shimonoseki indemnity,[‡] the ordering of warships from America by the Bakufu, the opening of a shipyard in Yokosuka by contract with the French, the purchase of warships after the Restoration as well, the construction of lighthouses, building of railroads, hanging of telegraph lines, floating of foreign loans, hiring of foreigners, and so forth. There have been many troublesome negotiations involved in all of this, and though we may not have suffered a total loss, you can be sure we were compelled to take some losses at the negotiating tables. The Westerners were clearly not losing anything, while it is extremely doubtful that we have reaped proportionate profit and prestige. However, since it was the doing of the government alone, the people are as yet ignorant of it. It is not simply the low-born masses who are unaware of it; the intelligentsia, too, and even government officials who have had no direct part in the matter, are in no position to know about it. Therefore, in regard to

---

† [In the Namamugi Incident (1862), four English people riding in the Yokohama area were assaulted by retainers of Shimazu Hisamitsu, father of the daimyo of Satsuma *han*, because they had not dismounted to wait while his procession passed by. With one person killed and two injured, the British Minister strongly protested to the Bakufu, which paid an indemnity.]

‡ [As a result of the bombarding by Chōshū *han* of Western ships passing through the Shimonoseki straits in 1863, in 1864 the allied squadron of Great Britain, France, the United States, and the Netherlands attacked Chōshū and captured the battery. Again, the Bakufu had to pay an indemnity.]

foreign relations we Japanese do not know whether or not there is a true balance of power between ourselves and the foreigners; we do not know whether or not we are being subjected to injustice; we do not know what benefits have accrued to us; we do not know what our losses have been. And so we look on in indifference at matters connected with foreign countries. This is one reason we Japanese people have not contended for power with foreign countries. Those who know nothing of a situation cannot be expected to be concerned about it.

Now, it was only in the recent past that foreigners came to our land. As yet they have not inflicted on us any notably great harm nor robbed us of our national honor, and so people's feelings on the subject are mild. However, those who have any concern for their country at all must carefully consider some facts of world history, both past and present. Whose country was present-day America originally? Is it not true that the Indians who owned the land were driven away by the white men and now the roles of master and guest are switched around? Hence the civilization of present-day America is really the civilization of the white man and cannot be called the civilization of America. What about in countries of the East and the islands in Oceania? In all places touched by the Europeans are there any which have developed their power, attained benefits, and preserved their independence? What has been the outcome in Persia, India, Siam, Luzon, and Java? The Sandwich Islands were discovered by the Englishman Captain Cook in 1778 and their development is reputed to have been more rapid than the various islands nearby. However, at the time of its discovery, the native population was three or four hundred thousand; by 1823, it has been said, barely 140,000 people were left. The decrease in population in the span of fifty years was approximately eight percent per year. Since there surely are various factors involved in population fluctuation I shall not go into that question now, but what does this so-called "development" mean? All it means is that the rustic islanders were made to stop their cannibalism and were converted into suitable slaves for the white man! In China, for instance, the land is so vast that the interior has as yet to be penetrated by the white man, and he has left his traces only along the coast. However, if future developments can be conjectured, China too will certainly become nothing but a garden for Europeans.

Wherever the Europeans touch, the land withers up, as it were; the plants and the trees stop growing. Sometimes even whole populations have been wiped out. As soon as one learns such things and realizes that Japan is also a country in the East, then though we have as yet not been seriously harmed by foreign relations we might well fear the worst is to come.

If what has been said above is true, then foreign relations in our country are a critical problem, from the standpoint both of finance and of rights; it is a deep-seated disease afflicting vital areas of the nation's life. Since this affliction is a matter of concern to all the people in the nation, its remedy must be personally sought by all the people alike. The spread of the disease is the concern of everyone, as should be its confinement. Since it is of vital importance to each and every one of us, we must not rely on others in the slightest degree. Shortsighted men foolishly rejoice, seeing that social conditions have changed in recent times, and call this civilization. They think that, since our civilization is a gift bestowed on us by foreign relations, the more foreign relations flourish the more our civilization can advance apace. But what they call civilization is merely its outward appearance, in which I have no interest. Even if such civilization were refined to a very high degree, if our people had not even a shred of independent spirit, civilization would be of no use to us. We could not call that Japanese civilization. In geography, a country can be described in terms of land, mountains, and rivers, but in what I am discussing "country" refers to both land and citizens together, and "a country's independence" and "a country's civilization" refer to a citizenry taking concerted action to defend its country, fully exercise its rights, and achieve full status. If this were not the case and the independence and civilization of a country have to do only with land and not with men, we ought to congratulate the Indians when we see the civilization of present-day America. Similarly, in the case of Japan, shall we leave political institutions, learning, and so forth, entirely up to the civilized Europeans, become their slaves and puppets, and then, as long as the land itself is unaffected, become an independent civilization a hundred times better than we are now? How ridiculous can one get?

Again, certain scholars hold that, since foreign relations are based on universal justice and men are not necessarily intent on exploiting others, nations should trade freely, ply back and forth freely, and merely let nature take its course. If we were to lose our rights and our benefits, we would have only ourselves to blame. It is a poor principle not to cultivate oneself and yet seek much from others. Since we already have peaceful relations with other countries, by showing every sign of good faith we should strengthen our friendship with them and harbor no suspicions at all. This is what they claim. And there is truth in what they say. Yet, though in private relationships between individuals there must indeed be this kind of trust, relations between countries and private relationships between individuals are completely different things. Have people forgotten how relations were between the *han* in feudal times? Nobody can accuse the people in any one *han* of being dishonest, but in dealings between *han*, each *han* necessarily put its own interests above that of the others. In regard to those outside the *han* it was a private good, but within the *han* itself it was a public good, certainly. In other words, every *han* had strictly private affairs. These private considerations could not be done away with by an appeal to universal justice, for as long as there were *han* there would necessarily be such private interests. These interests were first eliminated some years ago with the abolition of the *han*, and today it appears that the people of the former feudal domains have finally done away with the old *han* spirit; yet as long as the *han* were in existence, people were not allowed to find any fault with the system. If this was the situation with regard to the various *han* within Japan itself, what is the likelihood that we can rely on universal justice when it comes to relations with foreigners who have come from different areas from opposite directions of the globe? This is unbelievably loose thinking. Crudely speaking, it is thinking worthy of a naïve simpleton. It proclaims that universal justice should of course be the ideal. Have the Western nations not made contacts with Japan in accord with universal justice? Therefore we must be willing to respond to them and by no means turn them down. I say that if that is really the case, then we ought to abolish national governments throughout the world the same way we abolished the old *han*. Scholars should set this as their goal. As long as there are countries which set up national governments, there can be no way to eliminate their self-interests. If there is no way to eliminate their self-interests, then we too must have our self-interests in any contacts with them. This is why partisanship and patriotism differ in name but mean the same thing.

As stated above, foreign relations have become the great affliction of Japan. If we cannot find the remedy ourselves we shall have nowhere to turn. Our responsibility is great, and our liability heavy. As I stated at the beginning of this chapter, this is a time of crisis for our country. Moreover, this crisis is more troublesome than in years past—foreign relations are truly the most troublesome affliction there is. It is in this area of foreign relations that we should be willing to sacrifice everything, even our lives. If so, how can we Japanese of today fritter away our days in ease, how can we enjoy idle leisure? What since our early history has been termed the loyalty between lord and retainers, ancestral tradition, moral obligation between superiors and inferiors, and the distinction between main trunk and branch have today become loyalty toward Japan, the traditions of Japan, moral obligation between Japan and foreign countries, and a distinction between Japanese and foreign. Have they not all increased a hundredfold in importance? The story is told of how, in the old feudal days, there was a standing feud between the Shimazu house of Satsuma and the Itō house of Hyūga. The retainers of the Itō house bore such a deep-seated grudge against the Satsuma clan that every New Year's Day, when the entire body of retainers assembled at the castle, their first words to one another were a reminder not to forget vengeance against Satsuma—and only after this did they celebrate the New Year. In Europe, too, during the reign of Napoleon I of France, Prussia was subjected to unprecedented disgrace after her defeat at the hands of the French; thereafter, the Prussians harbored a deep resentment and the thought of revenge never died. Not only was the desire for revenge kept alive in people's hearts in churches and other public places where citizens gathered; pictures were also hung that reproduced the lamentable results of their humiliating defeat and disgrace by the French. Through these and other means people's hearts were stirred up and directed toward the single goal of revenge, till finally, in the year 1870, they paid the French back.

Both sets of behavior stemmed from a wicked spirit of revenge, so they cannot be termed praiseworthy. However, from them it is possible to know how people suffer when they cannot defend their nation. Although in our relationship with foreigners we have not as yet undergone sufferings comparable to those of the Itō house or of Prussia, in view of what happened to India and other countries our vigilance must be like that of the Itō and the Prussian people. Rather than once a year on New Year's Day, the Japanese people should admonish each other every morning before breakfast not to let their guard down in foreign relations, and only afterwards proceed to eat.

Considered in this light, it is not true that we Japanese put down the heavy burden passed on to us from our ancestors and have no other burden in its stead. Rather, a burden is upon our heads; what is more, it is a hundred times heavier than the former one. The responsibility to shoulder that load requires that we exert a hundred times more energy than people did in the old days. Our past charge was to endure with restrait, but today's charge requires energetic activity as well as restraint. The elevation of people's conduct depends, indeed, on both this kind of restrained morality and timely activity. However, those who now take up this burden and yet inwardly are still carefree are simply ignorant and unaware of its nature and relative importance. Perhaps even though they may be aware of its nature, they are mistaken as to the methods of dealing with it. For instance, there is no lack of men in society who hate foreigners, but their hatred of them is misplaced. They do not hate what should be hated, and hate what should not be hated. Harboring jealousy and envy, they are angered by trivial matters they see in front of their noses. They bring harm to Japan by their assassinations and their advocacy of the expulsion of foreigners [jōi]. They are a variety of lunatics, who can only be described as the sick victims, as it were, of a plague-stricken nation.

Another group of patriots, somewhat more far-seeing than the jōi advocates, has no wish indiscriminately to expel all foreigners, but sees the problem of our relations with foreign powers as basically a matter of simple military weakness. They feel that we could have sufficient power to oppose the Western powers if we simply increased our military preparedness; hence they call for larger funds for the army and navy, the purchase of large warships and cannons, and the construction of forts and armories. The idea seems to be that, if England has one thousand warships, and we too have one thousand warships, then we can stand against them. Now, this is the thinking of men who are ignorant of the proportions of things. The fact that England has one thousand warships does not mean that she has one thousand warships only. If there are one thousand warships, there have to be at least ten thousand merchant ships, which in turn require at least one hundred thousand navigators; and to create navigators there must be naval science. Only when there are many professors and many merchants, when laws are in order and trade prospers, when social conditions are ripe—when, that is, you have all the prerequisites for a thousand warships—only then can there be a thousand warships. In like manner armories and forts also have to be proportionate to every other element in society. If things are not in proportion, then even the best instruments are useless. For instance, placing a twenty-inch cannon in front of the gate of a disorganized household where the people lock neither the back nor the front door cannot provide appropriate protection against burglars. In countries where there is an imbalanced emphasis on military strength there is apt to be no sense of proportion—indiscriminate military expenditures drain the national treasury and thus undermine the country. Now, while warships and cannon can be a match for an enemy with warships and cannon, they cannot be a match for the enemy of debt. Even in present-day Japan our military needs for everything from warships to rifles and even uniforms are met almost entirely by foreign-made products. Maybe it is true that our manufacturing techniques are not yet highly developed, but the fact that these manufacturing techniques are undeveloped is proof that the country's civilization is not yet ripe. When conditions are so unripe it would be to lose all sense of proportion and render things useless if Japan today were to attempt to build up only military armament. Hence our present foreign relations should not be supported by means of greater military power.

As I stated above, proposals to assassinate and expel the foreigners are not worth discussing; going further, even efforts to expand military preparedness are of no practical avail. Moreover, the arguments for national polity, for Christianity, and for Confucianism referred to earlier are also insufficient to bolster people's hearts. What, then, will? I say, there is only one thing: namely, to establish our goal and advance toward civilization. What is that goal? It is to be clear about the distinction between domestic and foreign, and thereby to preserve the independence of our country. However, the way in which to preserve this independence cannot be sought anywhere except in civilization. The only reason for making the people in our country today advance toward civilization is to preserve our country's independence. Therefore, our country's independence is the goal, and our people's civilization is the way to that goal. In all human affairs, if proper attention is given to the end and the means to the end, there is no limit to the number of steps one can take. For instance, spinning cotton is the means to make thread, and making thread is the means to weave cotton cloth; cotton cloth is the means to make clothes, which are the means of keeping people warm. In this way, each of several steps is the goal of the preceding one and the means to the next, the final goal being the preservation of bodily temperature and the body's health.

In this chapter I have set up as the ultimate goal our country's independence. At this point you may recall my argument at the outset of Chapter One that the merits and demerits of things cannot be decided unless one discusses their purposes. I hope you readers will recall my previous discussion. Someone may say that mankind's conditions do not allow us to make national independence our only goal; we must in addition set our sights on more lasting, more noble values. This is true. The summit of human knowledge and virtue naturally aspired after is what is lofty, and we must not confine ourselves to such small matters as one nation's independence. Just barely evading the contempt of other countries cannot be called being civilized, this much is obvious. However, as things are in the world today, there is still no place in international relations for talking about lofty things, and anyone who would talk about them would be branded a stupid and fanciful dreamer. When we consider the situation Japan is faced with right now, we realize more and more the urgent crisis before us and have no time to look at other things. The first order of the day is to have the country of Japan and the people of Japan exist, and then and only then speak about civilization! There is no use talking about Japanese civilization if there is no country and no people. This is why I have narrowed my parameters and proposed the argument that the goal of civilization is simply our country's independence. Therefore, since my argument takes into account present world conditions, aims at the good of Japan as it is today, and seeks to respond to the crisis Japan faces today, it is obviously not some far-off and subtle mystery. You scholars, do not jump to any wrong conclusions about the purpose of civilization as soon as you see this; treat not my argument with scorn, nor do violence to the true meaning of my words!

Moreover, although I make independence the goal, I am not trying to turn all men in society into political debaters, nor do I wish people to be engaged in such debates from morning to night. Every man fulfils a different function, and must fulfill a different function. On the one hand, there are those who in pursuit of lofty scholarship are addicted to their learning and their lengthy discourses so much that they forget to eat. On the other hand, there are also men who are actively involved in business affairs and have not a moment's peace day or night, who run hither and yon so much that they neglect their household affairs. Not only would it be wrong to find fault with them; we must even praise their efforts as great contributions to civilization. I only wish that their intense preoccupation with their own endeavors would increase their sensitivity to what bears on the country's independence, so they would react as rapidly to its problems as they would to the sting of a bee.

Some people say that if national independence is our exclusive goal, then the best means would be to cut off foreign relations. They argue that before the foreigners came to Japan, Japan was, albeit uncivilized, a completely independent nation. Therefore, if independence is our aim, a return to our former national isolation would be the best policy. They argue that the present anxiety over independence was never felt before the 1850s. To open the country and then worry about the country's independence is no different from deliberately catching some disease and then worrying about it afterward. Once one realizes he has made a mistake, the best thing to do is to turn back the clock to the time when one was healthy. I deny this; I say that "independence" refers to a dynamic power which enables us to be independent. It does not refer to any semblance of independence accidentally come by. Japan's independence prior to the coming of the foreigners was an independence truly devoid of such a dynamic power. We were just assuming a semblance of independence by accident, because we had not yet come into contact with foreigners. To use a simile, it is impossible to know if a house is solid enough to withstand the elements if it has not experienced the buffets of a storm. Wind and rain are external circumstances, the solidity of the house an internal one. Until a storm blows there is no way to prove the solidity of the house. Of course a house will stand if there is no wind or rain, but we can only call a house solid if it will stand up under any gale and any downpour. What I mean by national independence is putting our people into contact with foreign countries, making them maintain their dynamic spirit through a thousand trials, and turning them into a house that can withstand gales and downpours. Why should we shrink into our shells, return to the past, and act so proud of the accidental independence that once fell to our lot? Besides, the proper execution of present foreign relations will arouse our people's spirits; such dealings can serve as a stimulus that will hit them between the eyes, as it were. They should, therefore, instead be a great benefit to Japanese civilization. My objective is to attain the fruit of independence by going forward, rather than to go backward and preserve an independence in empty name only.

Therefore let me return once more to the argument I have developed above. National independence is the goal, and Japan's present civilization is the means of attaining that goal. Since I wish to give the word *present* special emphasis, let scholars not pass over it casually. In the third chapter of the present work I stated that there is nothing greater or more vast than civilization, so that all aspects of human life have it as their goal; there I argued that the true aim of mankind was the attainment of the essence of civilization. However, here at least my position is limited to Japan of the present day, so the range of my argument has naturally been narrowed, and I have tentatively used the term *civilization* with reference to what produces our nation's independence. Hence what I have just called "Japan's present civilization" does not mean the essence of civilization; I have only considered our national independence as the first necessary step in the process, with everything else only secondary, to be left for some later day.

Now, when the argument is restricted in this way, then a country's independence equals civilization. Without civilization independence cannot be maintained. Whether one speaks of independence or of civilization makes no difference, then; however, the term *independence* has the advantage of presenting a clearer picture to the imagination and of making for easier understanding. When one uses only the term *civilization* by itself, without reference to national independence and civilization, then it means civilization. Something can even do harm to both national independence and civilization and still appear to be civilization. Let me give an example of this. Today there are ships from Western countries anchored in various harbors of Japan; on shore they have built huge, sprawling trading houses, so that they do almost as thriving a business as in their harbors in the West. However, fools unaware of realities take one glimpse at these flourishing conditions and proclaim with pride that a visit to the ports is enough to show how the peoples of the five continents cherish the liberality of Japan's laws and are vying with one another to flock to the empire, and that our trade is increasing by the day, and our civilization progressing by the month. What a great mistake! The foreigners are not flocking to the empire; they are flocking to the empire's tea and raw silk. The flourishing activity of the ports is certainly a sign of civilization, but the ships in the harbors are foreign ships, the trading houses on shore are foreign owned, and none of them have any connection whatsoever with our independence and civilization. Again, some speculators have used foreign capital to expand their businesses in the country, but all their income has gone back into the pockets of their backers and they only seem to be doing a thriving business. Some have borrowed money from foreign countries and with that money bought goods from them, then disposed of these products domestically, thus creating the appearance of civilization. I am referring to such things as stone houses, steel bridges, ships, and cannons. Japan cannot be called the birthplace of civilization, but only its place of temporary residence. In the end this commercial prosperity and this appearance of civilization are bound to invite national poverty and, in the passage of time, eventually harm our national independence. The reason that I here use the word *independence* instead of *civilization* is solely to avoid such misunderstandings.

In this way, when the ultimate goal is set down to be national independence and all aspects of life are made to converge on this single goal, then the means leading to that end are unlimited in number. Whether institutions, learning, business, or industry, they are all means to this end. Besides such things as institutions, learning, etc., even vulgar and popular aspects of life, even pleasures and amusements fully understood for what they are and what they can do—they can all come under the category of civilization. Therefore when people discuss the merits and demerits of various things in human life, it is not easy to come to a decision if they do not see the whole picture. Thus, from of old there have been countless arguments among scholars. Some have put the stress on frugality and simplicity; others have preferred taste and refinement; there have been those who thought autocracy and despotism expedient, while still others advocated open-heartedness and freedom. Such opinions are too varied to count them all. Mention "West" and someone will shout "East"; take a position on the left and someone will oppose from the right; and so on almost endlessly. In the extreme, there are no definite opinions at all, people simply take a position that conforms with their own status, and their positions change as their status changes. Even worse than that are the types who make use of the government to hide behind, taking advantage of political power to spread their private views, without the least regard for the merits or demerits of their views. How low can people stoop? Their actions may be likened to shooting arrows without a target or bringing lawsuits where there are no courts. Can we determine right and wrong in their cases? They are only children playing games.

Consider for a moment what happens when one discusses things out of their full context: there is nothing that is not right, nothing that is not wrong. Thus, frugality and simplicity may resemble crude rusticity, yet in the life of the individual they ought to be cultivated. Taste and refinement may resemble luxury and extravagance, yet if the living standard of the people throughout the nation is kept in mind, daily progress in good taste is definitely to be desired. Although it may seem that the inflexibility of the theory of national polity is very detrimental to the cause of popular rights, it is most expedient for determining the key policies of the present government and for maintaining administrative order. It may seem that the violence of a theory calling for more popular rights is very harmful to a monarchical government; but if used as a means to sweep away the old evil custom of servility in the common people, then it is extremely expedient. The ethic of the faithful and loyal retainers, or the theories of Christianity, of Confucianism, and of Buddhism, can only be called wise or foolish depending on how they are practiced. Moreover, even when it comes to those who support the assassination and expulsion of foreigners, only their acts ought to be censured; analyze their motivations and you will be sure to discover traces of patriotism. Therefore, as I said at the beginning of this chapter, such values as loyalty between lord and subject, ancestral tradition, moral obligation between superiors and inferiors, and the distinction between the main trunk and the branches are aspects of human conduct to be esteemed; in other words, because they are means of civilization there are no grounds for condemning them. However, whether they benefit or harm social affairs depends entirely on how they are used.

Generally speaking, people do not harbor the evil intention of selling out their country, and therefore there are none who do not wish to contribute to their country's welfare. In cases where people do harm to their country, their crime is usually due to ignorance of the proper goal, and committed accidentally. Every achievement in society involves a concentration of various means leading to its execution; these means require much effort and cannot help but be many. However, it is absolutely necessary, when there are many means to be used, to make no mistake about how and where to use them. Does this means have any connection with the end? If it does, how does it lead to the end? Directly? Or is some other means to be interposed? If there are two means to the end, which should be preferred, which deferred till later? A great deal of deliberation is needed. Ultimately, one has to keep clearly in mind the final, the most important end one is aiming at. This is exactly as in chess, where each player has thousands of possible moves, but his one end is to protect his own king and checkmate the opponent's king. Anyone who sets more store on his rook, for instance, would be called a poor chess player. Hence, if by limiting my attention in this chapter to the question of Japan's independence, I have clarified the distinction between domestic and foreign and thereby shown the way the people in general should take, then for the first time the relative importance of things can be considered properly, as well as their relative urgency. If what is important and what is urgent are clarified here, then things that yesterday aroused indignation can today become sources of joy, and what was pleasant last year will now be cause for concern. Sources of confidence can become the cause of worry, pleasure can turn into pain, but on the other hand enmity into friendliness, strangers into brothers; sharing the same joys and sorrows, the same anxieties and pleasures, we can direct them all towards the same goal. As I see it, this is the only way to bolster the spirits of our Japanese people today.

Appendix
Chronology of Japanese history, with special reference to Fukuzawa Yukichi and *An Outline of a Theory of Civilization*

Adapted from the chronology in John W. Hall's *Japan: Prehistory to Modern Times* (New York: Delacorte Press, 1970)

660 B.C.	Mythical date of the succession of Jinmu, the first Emperor
ca.A.D. 300–645	**Yamato period**
538(or 552?)	Introduction of Buddhism and Confucianism from Korea
607	First embassy to the Sui Court in China
645	Taika reform
710–784	**Nara Period**
752	Dedication of the Great Buddha (Daibutsu) of Tōdaiji in Nara
781–806	Reign of Kanmu; revival of Taihō Code; capital moves to Nagaoka in 784 and then to Heian (Kyoto) in 794
794–1185	**Heian Period**
805	Introduction of Tendai sect of Buddhism by Saichō (Dengyō Daishi)
806	Introduction of Shingon sect of Buddhism by Kūkai (Kōbō Daishi)
838	Last embassy to the Tang Court in China
995–1027	Influence of the Fujiwara family on Imperial rule reaches its peak with Fujiwara no Michinaga
ca.1002–1019	Writing of *Genji monogatari* (The Tale of Genji)
1086	Shirakawa resigns in favor of his son and takes Buddhist orders. However, he uses his influence over his son to rule indirectly and obtain the subsequent accession of his grandson and great grandson. This pattern of rule is known as *insei* (cloistered rule).
1159–1160	Heiji War; military supremacy gained by Taira no Kiyomori
1175	Founding of the Jōdo (Pure Land) sect of Buddhism by Hōnen
1180–1185	Genpei War between the Taira and the Minamoto, led by Minamoto no Yoritomo
1185–1333	**Kamakura Period**
1185	Title of shogun granted to Minamoto no Yoritomo
1203	Hōjō Tokimasa appointed *shikken* (shogunal regent)
1221	Jōkyū War between the court at Kyoto and the Bakufu at Kamakura, ending in victory for the Hōjō

1274, 1281	Mongol invasions
1333	Kenmu Restoration under Emperor Go-Daigo leads to a temporary return of power to the court and the end of the Kamakura Bakufu
1336–1573	**Ashikaga (or Muromachi) Period**
1336–92	Period of the Northern and Southern Courts, when Japan had two rival Emperors, in Kyoto and Yoshino respectively
1338	Title of shogun granted to Ashikaga Takauji
1368–94	Yoshimitsu (1368–1408), third shogun
1449–73	Yoshimasa (1435–1490), eighth shogun
1467–1568	Sengoku (or Civil War) Period
1467–77	Ōnin War starts a period in which Japan has no stable central government
1542 (or 1543)	Portuguese traveling in a Chinese junk are shipwrecked at Tanegashima, leading to the introduction of Western firearms
1549	St. Francis Xavier begins missionary work in Japan
1568–1600	**Azuchi-Momoyama Period**
1568	Occupation of Kyoto by Oda Nobunaga, who is now in a position to dominate all other military leaders
1582	Nobunaga assassinated by Akechi Mitsuhide
1586	Osaka Castle built by Toyotomi Hideyoshi
1590	Hideyoshi unifies Japan
1592	Hideyoshi's first invasion of Korea
1598	Death of Hideyoshi and withdrawal of troops from Korea
1600	Victory of Tokugawa Ieyasu at the Battle of Sekigahara
1600–1868	**Tokugawa (or Edo) Period**
1603	Title of shogun acquired by Ieyasu
1614	An edict expels all missionaries from Japan. Most of them leave; some remain in hiding.
1614–15	Capture of Osaka Castle, the stronghold of Hideyoshi's son
1622–23	Period of the greatest Christian persecutions
1623–51	Institutional foundations of the Tokugawa shogunate by Iemitsu, third shogun
1637–38	Shimabara Rebellion: a peasant uprising in Western Kyushu in which many Christians participated
1639	The last in a series of edicts designed to control contacts between Japan and the outside world is passed. Japanese cannot travel abroad; foreign contacts are limited primarily to trade with Dutch and Chinese ships at Nagasaki, trade with Korea via Tsushima *han*, and smuggling.
1641	Dutch factory moved to Deshima at Nagasaki

1787–93	Supremacy of Senior Councillor Matsudaira Sadanobu; Kansei Reforms
1804–29	Bunka-Bunsei Era
1804	Arrival of Nicholai Rezanov at Nagasaki
1835	Fukuzawa Yukichi born in Osaka
1837	Rice riot in Osaka led by the Confucian scholar Ōshio Heihachirō
1841–43	Tenpō reforms undertaken by Mizuno Tadakuni; *Kabunakama* (merchant guilds) abolished
1853	Arrival of Commodore Perry at Uraga
1854	Treaty of Kanagawa with the United States
1858	Treaty of Amity and Commerce with the United States Fukuzawa opens school of Dutch Learning in Edo (later Tokyo)
1859	Ports of Yokohama, Nagasaki, and Hakodate opened to foreign trade
1860	Fukuzawa joins Japan's first mission to America
1862	*Sankin kōtai* (alternate attendance) relaxed. Namamugi Incident (Richardson Incident) Ordered to go to Europe as an official translator for the government, Fukuzawa visits France, England, Holland, Prussia, Russia, and then Portugal.
1863	Bombardment of Shimonoseki
1865	Imperial ratification of treaties with foreign powers
1866–67	Yoshinobu (d. 1913), fifteenth and last shogun
1867	Enthronement of Mutsuhito (later Emperor Meiji) Fukuzawa's second visit to America as attendant to an official delegation to receive delivery of a warship
1868–1912	**Meiji Period**
1868	January 3, Restoration of Imperial Rule; the separation of Shinto and Buddhism
1868	ca. May: Fukuzawa names his school Keio-gijuku (later Keio University)
1869	Return of *han* to the Emperor
1871	The abolition of the *han* and the establishment of prefectures
1872	Fukuzawa begins the publication of *An Encouragement of Learning*
1873	New national military conscription law; new land tax system; establishment of the Home Ministry
1874	Public Party of Patriots led by Itagaki Taisuke presents their demand for an elected national assembly
1875	April: the establishment of the Senate, Supreme Court, and the Assembly of Provincial Governors. June: Japan exchanges with Russia Sakhalin for the Kuriles. October: the publication of *An Outline of a Theory of Civilization*

Fukuzawa Yukichi: Some Representative Writings

a) Pre-Restoration Writings, 1860–69:

   1865   *Tōjin ōrai* (Comings and Goings of the Foreigners)
   1866   *Seiyō jijō* (Conditions in the West; second part, 1867)
   1867   *Seiyō tabi annai* (Guide to Travel in the Western Countries)
   1868   *Kinmō kyūri zukai* (Illustrated Book of the Natural Sciences)
   1869   *Sekai kunizukushi* (All the Countries of the World)

b) Post-Restoration Writings, 1870–1901:

   1872–76   *Gakumon no susume* (An Encouragement of Learning, originally
               published as seventeen pamphlets)
   1875   *Bunmeiron no gairyaku* (An Outline of a Theory of Civilization)
   1878   *Tsūzoku minken ron* (Popular Discourse on People's Rights)
               Tsūzoku kokken ron (Popular Discourse on the Rights of Nations)
   1879   *Kokkai ron* (On a National Diet)
   1881   *Jiji shōgen* (A Critique of the Trend of the Times)
   1882   Founded a daily newspaper, the *Jiji shinpō*, in which many of his
               writings after 1882 appeared in serial form.
   1885   *Nihon fujinron* (On Japanese Women). Also *Onna daigaku hyōron* (A
               Critique of "The Great Learning for Women") and *Shin onna
               daigaku* (The New Great Learning for Women), 1899.
   1897   *Fukuō hyakuwa*, *Fukuō hyakuyowa* (Miscellaneous Essays)
   1898   *Fukuō jiden* (Autobiography, as dictated to a secretary)

Further Reading

I. On Fukuzawa Yukichi

Blacker, Carmen. *The Japanese Enlightenment: A Study of the Writings of Fukuzawa Yukichi*. Cambridge: Cambridge University Press, 1964.

Craig, Albert. "Fukuzawa Yukichi: The Philosophical Foundations of Meiji Nationalism." Reprinted in *The Autobiography of Yukichi Fukuzawa*. New York: Columbia University Press, 2007. 373–429. First published in *Political Development in Modern Japan*. Edited by Robert Ward. Princeton: Princeton University Press, 1968.

———. *Civilization and Enlightenment: The Early Thought of Fukuzawa Yukichi*. Cambridge, MA: Harvard University Press, forthcoming.

Dilworth, David A. "Was Fukuzawa a Philosopher?" In *Kindai Nihon Kenkyū* (Bulletin of Modern Japanese Studies) 25 (October 2008): 1–26.

Macfarlane, Alan. *The Making of the Modern World: Visions from the West and East.* New York: Palgrave, 2002.

Meiroku zasshi: Journal of the Japanese Enlightenment. Translated by William Reynolds. Tokyo: Tokyo University Press, 1976.

Nishikawa Shunsaku. "Fukuzawa Yukichi." *Prospects: the Quarterly Review of Comparative Education* 23 (1994): 493–506. http://www.ibe.unesco.org/fileadmin/user_upload/archive/publications/ThinkersPdf/fukuzawe.pdf (accessed August 4, 2008).

Tamaki Norio. *Yukichi Fukuzawa, 1835–1901: The Spirit of Enterprise in Modern Japan.* Houndmills, Basingstoke: Palgrave, 2001.

II. Background Reading on *An Outline of a Theory of Civilization*

1. Sources mentioned by Fukuzawa that are available in English

Analects of Confucius. Translated and with an introduction by Chichung Huang. New York: Oxford University Press, 1997.

Arai Hakuseki. *Lessons from History: The Tokushi Yoron.* Translated by Joyce Ackroyd. St. Lucia: University of Queensland Press, 1982.

Buckle, Henry Thomas. *History of Civilization in England.* 2vols. New York: D. Appleton and Company, 1872–73.

Guizot, François. *General History of Civilization in Europe.* 1828. New York: D. Appleton and Company, 1870.

Kojiki. Translated and with an Introduction by Donald L. Philippi. Princeton: Princeton University Press, 1969.

Man'yōshū: A Translation of Japan's Premier Anthology of Classical Poetry. By Ian Hideo Levy. Tokyo: University of Tokyo Press, 1981.

Mencius. Translated and with an introduction by D. C. Lau. Harmondsworth, Middlesex: Penguin Books, 1970.

Mill, John Stuart. *On Liberty.* 1869. Edited by David Bromwich and George Kateb. New Haven: Yale University Press, 2003.

———. *Principles of Political Economy.* 1848. Oxford: Oxford University Press, 1998.

———. *Considerations on Representative Government.* 1861. New York: Harper, 1862.

Nihongi; Chronicles of Japan from the Earliest Times to A.D. 697. Translated by W. G. Aston. Rutland: C. E. Tuttle, 1972.

Sources of Japanese Tradition. Compiled by Wm. Theodore de Bary, et al. 2nd ed. 2 vols. New York: Columbia University Press, 2001–06.

2. Secondary Works

Brownlee, John S. *Japanese Historians and the National Myths, 1600–1945: The Age of Gods and the Emperor Jinmu*. Vancouver: UBC Press, 1997.

Gong, Gerrit W. *The Standard of "Civilization" in International Society*. Oxford: Clarendon Press, 1984.

Gordon, Andrew. *A Modern History of Japan from Tokugawa Times to the Present*. Oxford: Oxford University Press, 2003.

Howland, Douglas R. *Translating the West: Language and Political Reason in Nineteenth-Century Japan*. Honolulu: University of Hawai'i Press, 2002.

Mazlish, Bruce. *Civilization and its Contents*. Stanford: Stanford University Press, 2004.

Schad-Seifert, Annette. "Constructing National Identities: Asia, Japan and Europe in Fukuzawa Yukichi's Theory of Civilization." *Nationalism and Internationalism in Imperial Japan: Autonomy, Asian Brotherhood, or World Citizenship?* Edited by Dick Stegewerns. London: Routledge, 2003. 45–67.

Totman, Conrad. *Early Modern Japan*. Berkeley: University of California Press, 1993.

INDEX

903), 68
Su Qin 蘇秦, 71
Sweden, 132

Tang 唐, 39, 112*n*. *See also* China,
Chinese
Tang 湯, 9, 53, 198
Taiheiki 『太平記』 (Chronicle of Medieval Japan), 152
Taikō 太閤, 61*n*, 62, 63*n*, 117, 188
Taira clan 平, 73, 74
Taira no Atsumori 平敦盛 (1164–84),
116, 116*n*
Takatō *han* 高遠, 213*n*
Takakura Palace 高倉御所, 216, 217*n*
Takizawa Bakin 滝沢馬琴 (1767–
1848), 85*n*
Tales of the Heike 『平家物語』, 116*n*
taxation: *tansen* 段銭, 213; *munabechi*
棟別, 213; *kurayaku* 倉役, 213;
takagakari 高掛り, 213; *kagiyaku* 鎰役,
213; *bugenwari* 分限割, 213
technology, xvii, 111–12, 218; steam
engine, 69, 107–08, 113, 117–18,
128, 137 telegraph, 110, 118, 137,
247; warship, xv
Ten Commandments. *See* Christianity
Tendai sect 天台宗, 132, 191n. *See also*
Buddha, Buddhism
Tenmei, and Bunka, eras, 天明文化
(1781–1818), 84, 85*n*, 86
Terutora 輝虎 (Ashikaga Yoshinobu),
205
theocracy, 26, 28, 29, 39, 161
to 斗. *See* units
Tōeizan 東叡山, 191
Tokugawa house 徳川家, 83, 184, 187,
194, 203, 203*n*, 205–09, 213–14,
243, 243*n*; feudal system of lineage,
xiii
Tokugawa Bakufu (shogunate) 徳川幕
府, xix, 85*n*, 86, 184, 207, 208, 213,

214, 243; imbalance of power, 209;
foreign relations 86
Tokugawa period (Edo period), 12, 85,
192, 194, 205, 208, 218, 229*n*
Tokugawa Ieyasu 徳川家康 (1542–
1616), 73, 134, 203*n*
tokusei 徳政 (virtuous or beneficent
government), 218
Tokyo 東京, 65, 115, 139, 140, 141
Tōshōji 東勝寺, 153
Toyotomi clan 豊臣, 135, 135*n*, 205
Toyotomi Hideyori 豊臣秀頼 (1593–
1615), 134, 205*n*
Toyotomi Hideyoshi 豊臣秀吉 (1536?–
98), xxiv, 61*n*, 62, 63*n*, 73, 134,
205*n*. *See also* Hashiba Hideyoshi and
Kinoshita Tōkichi
tranquility, 149, 154, 158; and peace,
134; of the barbarians, 144, 150; of
civilization, 150. *See also* peace
trend of the times, 72–78, 83, 100, 143,
166, 181, 188. *See also* right time
Turkey, 17

U.S.-Japan Treaty of Amity and
Commerce 日米通商修好条約, xiv
Ueno 上野, 191
Uesugi Kenshin 上杉謙信 (1530–78),
186*n*, 240
Uesugi Norizane 上杉憲実 (1410–66),
205
uncivilized, ages, the, 114, 157, 197;
countries, 32, 124, 132, 240; people,
149, 227, 255
uneducated, and illiterate, the, 11
United States, xv, 33, 54–55, 57, 139,
247*n*; civilization in, 17; as
descendents of European people,
238, independence of, 76; U.S.-
Japan Treaty of Amity, xiv. *See also*
America, Americans
units: *gō* 合, 82, 82*n*; *kan* 貫, 82, 82*n*;

TRANSLATORS

David A. Dilworth (1934–) is Professor of Philosophy at the State University of New York, Stony Brook. He earned his Ph.D.s from Fordham University and Columbia University. His publication includes *Philosophy in World Perspective: A Comparative Hermeneutic of the Major Theories* (Yale University Press, 1989), *Sourcebook for Modern Japanese Philosophy: Selected Documents* (editor; Greenwood, 1998), translations of Fukuzawa's *An Encouragement of Learning* (with Hirano Umeyo; Sophia University Press, 1969) and Nishida Kitaro's *Last Writings: Nothingness and the Religious Worldview* (University of Hawaii Press, 1987).

G. Cameron Hurst, III (1941–) is Professor of Japanese and Korean Studies at the University of Pennsylvania and Director of its Center for East Asian Studies. He holds a Ph.D. from Columbia University, and has extensively contributed to collected volumes, periodicals and newspapers, including *Cambridge History of Japan, volume two* (Cambridge University Press, 1999). He is the author of *Insei: Abdicated Sovereigns in the Politics of Late Heian Japan, 1086–1185* (Columbia University Press, 1976) and *Armed Martial Arts of Japan: Swordsmanship and Archery* (Yale University Press, 1998).

CONTRIBUTOR

Inoki Takenori (猪木武徳 1945–) is Director-General of the International Research Center for Japanese Studies, Kyoto. He earned his Ph. D. in Economics from Massachusetts Institute of Technology, and has (co-)authored and edited over 20 books both in Japanese and English, including the award-winning *Keizai shisō* (Economic Thought) (Iwanami, 1987) and *Jiyū to Chitsujo: Kyōsō shakai no futatsu no kao* (Liberty and Order: Two Faces of the Competitive Society) (Chūō kōron, 2001). Among his English publications are *Aspects of German Peasant Emigration to the United States, 1815–1914: A Reexamination of Some Behavioral Hypotheses in Migration Theory* (Arno, 1981) and *Skill Formation in Japan and Southeast Asia* (co-authored with Koike Kazuo; University of Tokyo Press, 1990).